PURSUING THE GLORY OF GOD

December 2005

To Scott & Tricia

with great appreciation
for your friendship and
your many kindnesses
especially during Dee's
illness and her journey
to health.
        Gratefully
            Tom & Dee Burton

This will help you better
understand the Burtons

The Personality and Passion
of Paul F. Bubna

Pursuing
the Glory
of God

**Ronald D. Jones
and David E. Schroeder**

CHRISTIAN PUBLICATIONS, INC.
CAMP HILL, PENNSYLVANIA

✠CHRISTIAN PUBLICATIONS, INC.

3825 Hartzdale Drive, Camp Hill, PA 17011
www.christianpublications.com

Faithful, biblical publishing since 1883

Pursuing the Glory of God
ISBN: 0-87509-914-9
LOC Catalog Card Number: 2004102518
© 2004 by Ronald D. Jones and David E. Schroeder
All rights reserved
Printed in the United States of America

Contents

Foreword vii

Preface xi

Acknowledgments xv

1   Entering His Gates 3

2   A House Divided 11

3   Seeds of the Ministry 23

4   Youthful Zeal 45

5   Crossing Over 59

6   Becoming a Kingdom Person 75

7   Becoming a Kingdom Pastor 95

8   The Great Commission Gets Personal 121

9   Life—One Day at a Time 143

10   Pastor Paul at Long Hill Chapel 163

11   The ATS Years 179

12   President Bubna 195

Appendix 1:
Message for the Memorial of Dr. Paul F. Bubna.............213

Appendix 2:
Grief: God Is My Portion 223

Appendix 3:
Candidate Questionnaire for
The C&MA Presidency (excerpted) 229

Appendix 4:
"And It All Happened in Africa"! 237

Foreword

His life was more about being than doing. As a boy, he was quiet. Through adulthood he described himself as an introvert. He was bright and insightful. He was a good athlete and usually on the honor roll with his studies. He became an exceptional preacher.

Like A.W. Tozer, who was his mentor during his ordination process, Paul Bubna believed that the most important thoughts he had each day were those about God. The things about God that are true gave stability to his life. He was not always that way, however.

Throughout his youth he struggled with anger. He was an exceptional softball pitcher and a clever basketball player—and he didn't like to lose. It was hard on his ego. When we played on intramural teams in college and we got behind, he wanted to argue most calls that went against us. When we lost, he wanted to fight the referees or the other team. His anger was evident to all.

This led to a crisis during his college years at John Brown University. At the end of his sophomore year, a girl he really liked jilted him. Things were closing in on him. While working in California in a summer camp program, Paul experienced a "nervous breakdown" that became a breakthrough in terms of his walk with God. Coming to the end of his own sufficiency, he surrendered his anger, his ego and his all to Christ. From that brokenness came a new man. The fullness of the Holy Spirit had become a reality in his life. The tendency to anger could still sometimes arise inside him, but he learned to exercise the fruit of the Spirit in self-control. He once told a group of missionaries that he was an expert on the subject of anger because he had dealt with it so much in his life.

Through the indwelling of the living Christ and choosing to walk in the Spirit, Paul Bubna became a man who sought for the glory of God.

He was my brother. Except for my wife, he was my closest confidante. Through he has been gone for several years, my daily thoughts of him continue to be a blend of gratitude and grief. I greatly miss his wise and understanding counsel. We all knew him to be a great listener. He could ask extremely thought-provoking questions. The two of us loved to talk about how God was at work in our lives.

He placed a high value on truth, openness, integrity, having a clean heart before God and being quiet and reflective. His family was his first priority after his relationship with God. He was a sensitive and loving husband and a very caring father.

He once told me that the highest thing on his daily agenda was "to get my heart warm before God each morning so I can start the day." While he was a disciplined man in terms of his inner life, his life was not about having devotions but about living devotionally. He took long walks every morning and often at night and talked with God. His writings from *Alliance Life* reflect his heart and passion. They are very pastoral. When he became president of the Alliance, he said, "Pastoring is not something I do, but it is who I am."

He was a strong biblical preacher. He loved preaching through the Bible a book at a time. He even enjoyed preaching from the more difficult books like Job and Ecclesiastes. He always lifted people to the God he loved and served, refusing to beat up on or talk down to people. Invitations to speak frequently came to him from many places. He taught me more about preaching than anyone else in my life.

Much of his pastoring was within the context of being a teacher and mentor. Hundreds of us have been deeply affected by his personal touch in our lives. His tools were listening and asking good questions. He didn't enjoy a lot of surface talk. The real issues about life and godliness always beckoned him. An Alliance leader and mentoree said, "Paul Bubna asked me the hardest questions I've ever been asked in my life."

Though we lived thousands of miles apart as adults, we were close emotionally and saw one another often. When he went to Vietnam for thirty months in 1970, we began to exchange conversational cassette tapes every other week. We maintained this practice for over twenty-five years. My last tape from him arrived just after he died.

Paul's continuing influence on my life is mostly in two areas: First, his constant pursuit of God. His life verse was Matthew 6:33. Life to him became "seek[ing] first the kingdom of God, and his righteousness" (KJV). He rested wholly on the truth that everything else would be added as needed. Second, investing his life in the Church, the people of God, by mentoring formally and informally whoever came across his pathway in life.

I am grateful that two of Paul's mentorees, Ron Jones and Dave Schroeder, have brought together their wealth of memories and research to document God's work in a choice servant. I have had the joy of previewing each chapter because Ron and Dave wanted to ensure the book's accuracy. They got it right, and I am glad to commend the book to you.

Some time back my brother gave me a small volume of daily Bible readings and biblical prayers. Inside the cover he wrote, "To brother Don—fellow pilgrim in the pursuit of God. Love, Paul."

It is my prayer and hope that his writings in this volume will also aid you, the reader, in your pursuit of God.

—Donald L. Bubna
Pastor at Large
The Christian and
Missionary Alliance, USA

Preface

Paul F. Bubna was on a journey—an extraordinary journey, a unique journey. Yet Paul's journey was one that many people—professional, blue-collar, sophisticated, simple, city-bred or country-born—can identify with. We can identify with it because he lived through poverty and prosperity, self-doubt and affirmation, loneliness and limelight, frailty and empowerment, restlessness and consolation. Experiencing and comprehending all these things, however, did not define his life. Paul Bubna was striving to see a bigger picture of life, one that would punctuate his perspective with the goodness and glory of God, who alone could give significance to all the seemingly disjointed pieces. But amid all these pieces, two ideas were steadfast, like the horns on the altar of sacrifice: Paul was pursuing the glory of God, and he would best apprehend it through his own suffering.

One story Paul related with great passion illustrates the redemptive impact of suffering, which was such a part of his journey:

> I was touched by the account of a young man who sensed God's call to missionary medicine. When he completed his training, he went to a North African nation where there was a dismal lack of medical care. He was offered a position on the hospital staff in the capital city where there was some semblance of the comforts of home. His vision, however, was to go to a primitive place where there was no medical help.
>
> He hired porters to carry their supplies and he and his pregnant wife walked behind and headed into the jungle. Finally they reached a village on a little stream that seemed to him the proper place for a mission that would heal bodies and communicate God's grace. In a clearing outside the village he built a little home and a clinic where he began to treat the diseases of the villagers. They came eagerly. He invited them to a church service each Sunday but even though he

clanged the bell (a tire iron on an old rim), no one came. He and his wife worshiped alone, that is, until their little son was born.

The little boy was a delight to them. They watched with pride as he toddled around the clearing and explored the environment. One day the doctor noticed that his son seemed to be falling frequently. He tried to ignore it but realized that it fit the symptoms of a fatal jungle fever. He tried desperately to save his son but in short order the little boy succumbed to the tropical disease.

The doctor constructed a wooden box with his own hands and laid his son in it. He and his wife held a simple memorial service, expressed their awful grief and then he placed the box on his shoulder, took a shovel in hand and started toward the burial ground on the other side of the village.

The villagers stared as he walked through the village with the box on his shoulder. One villager followed him from a distance and watched as he dug the grave, tenderly placed the box in it and covered it with the dirt. Suddenly overwhelmed with his loss, the doctor fell headlong onto the grave and began to convulse in tears.

He had no idea how long he lay in the mud but his next remembrance was a hand grabbing him by his hair and lifting up his head. There he stared into the face of a wide- eyed villager. As his head dropped abruptly back into the mud he heard footsteps running rapidly toward town and a man yelling at the top of his lungs, "The white man cries just like we cry, the white man weeps just like we weep." When the doctor banged the tire rim on Sunday morning most of the village gathered to worship with him and his wife.

God is writing a message across the life of every believer. This message has to do with the way that the mighty power of God is meeting human frailty in the suffering that characterizes the fallen creation.[1]

In many ways Paul's own journey through human frailty became the message God was writing across his life. He allowed others to witness his journey, and many identified with his pilgrimage because he was forced to come to grips with his frailty or to forfeit the message God was writing through his life. Rather than protesting that his formal training was inadequate, his managerial style imprecise or his physical constitution extremely vulnerable, Paul simply gave God permission to display His glory all along the way God had ordained for him to travel.

This book attempts to reflect the wisdom and glory of God that were unveiled and unleashed for and in Paul Bubna. We write not for Paul or for those who miss him intensely and still grapple with the untimeliness of his death. Nor do we write for those who for many years called him "Pastor Bubna" and were nourished week after week by healthy, thoroughly biblical teaching. This book is for those who wrestle with their own frailty and finitude. We write for those who yearn to serve God and yet feel inadequacy and weakness that all too easily can define their existence. This book is for those who would gladly grant God the right to interpret their circumstances and transform them into a "good" that surpasses human comprehension—if only they could see how it turned out for someone who has taken that risk with God.

Paul Bubna took those risks. So we offer to you a picture of a journey that we believe was walked well. The journey from unpromising beginnings to the triumph of casting a vision for an entire Christian movement was not a heroic adventure. It was rather a simple determination to take the next step and then the next step, until a discipline of "pressing on" framed an invitation to the rest of us: "Come walk with me." His journey was not a level path, but an upward, winding and rocky trail, perhaps not unlike the one you may find yourself traveling at this moment.

The two of us were privileged to walk parts of his journey with him, as we were two of the many Paul Bubna disciples (although he would disapprove of the notion of disciples because of his reluctance to be seen that way). We write as self-confessed admirers of Paul, but hopefully ones close enough to him and secure enough of his legacy to write with objectivity.

Ron has pulled the lead oar of this writing vessel, having penned chapters two through nine. He served as Paul's associate at Long Hill Chapel from 1983 to 1989. Far beyond being colleagues, however, Paul and Ron became close friends, and Paul's guiding influence in the Jones family has been huge.

Dave's walk with Paul began in 1968 at Northbrook for one year, continued in 1978 at Long Hill Chapel for nine years (as associate and then elder) and resumed at Nyack in 1993.

Occasionally, because of Paul's impact on our lives, we refer to and identify ourselves in the narrative. Many others have had a hand in this story, as will be seen in the Acknowledgments.

Notes

1. Paul F. Bubna, *Second Corinthians* in *The Deeper Life Pulpit Commentary* (Camp Hill, PA: Christian Publications, Inc., 1993), pp. 96-7.

Acknowledgments

This book is an account of Paul Bubna's journey. Tracing that journey has connected us to many who traveled with him, some for a brief time, others for many years. Because of his personality and passion, no one he knew was merely a professional contact. He affected people personally and deeply. By God's design and enabling, Bubna's influence effected radical transformations in many. Their motivations and ambitions were altered because they were privileged to share a part of his life. Likewise, writing about him engaged the authors on a far deeper level than merely doing the mechanics of research. We were impacted first by knowing him and then again by his life's impact on those whose accounts are woven through this story. Because Paul Bubna was this kind of man, we wish first to thank God for the privilege we had of knowing Paul intimately.

We wish to thank the Bubna children: Laurie, Steve, Tim, Joel and Grace. They reviewed every chapter for accuracy and contributed personal recollections that by their own admission reawakened emotions of private sorrow over their father's untimely passing. We thank Patti, Paul's bride and wife of only eight months, for her endorsement of this biography and helpful insights. We are especially grateful to Rev. Don Bubna, Paul's brother, cherished colleague and friend his entire life. Paul's story reflects, in part, Don's story. Don's affirmation and utter transparency during the writing process have made the book a most satisfying endeavor for the authors.

Others who have contributed substantially to this work are the authors of the brief vignettes that precede each chapter, as well as the people whom we have quoted extensively in the narrative.

We want to thank former Christian Publications, Inc., publisher K. Neill Foster for supporting the publication of this book from the very beginning. Finally, we wish to thank those whose letters and interviews were not included in the material but whose insights were invaluable contributions to the project, for illuminating more fully different stretches of Paul's journey. We thank you and trust that this account will extend God's glorifying work in your lives to the benefit of many others.

—Ron Jones
—Dave Schroeder
November 2001

The Personality and Passion
of Paul F. Bubna

*Of all the people who would likely have made the most profound
impact on my life, Paul Bubna would not have made my list. Here
was a guy who 1) was a pastor (I didn't look to pastors as my role
models—athletes and business leaders, yes; pastors, definitely
not); 2) had nary an ounce of external charisma (in my shallow-
ness, I respected the superficial); and 3) was a country boy (I had
rejected my midwestern roots and adopted a more urbane per-
sona). By all accounts, Paul Bubna and I were incompatible.*

*One thing drew me to him. Like no one else I had known, here
was a man who had so fully given himself to God that a divine
magnet within him compelled me to enter the deepest, closest relationship he would allow. All the incompatibilities were swept aside
as the pearl of our relationship surfaced. Paul found a young man
eager to know and to grow. I found a mentor whose walk with God
I fully trusted.*

*For three decades Paul Bubna was a force in my life. WWJD
(What Would Jesus Do?) had not yet surfaced as a cultural theme,
but WWPS (What Would Paul Say?) functioned powerfully in my
life. Sometimes the question was posed directly to him. For thirteen
of those thirty years we worked together closely, so I could and did
frequently ask for guidance. Of course, he rarely gave it directly,
but I had come to accept and even interpret his silences—a good
grammar school for my walk with God!*

*During his time at Long Hill Chapel, after his second heart at-
tack and while he was recovering from heart surgery, I was thrust
into pastoral leadership of the church. Preaching every week to a
thousand people was heady stuff for a young man, and I so longed
for Paul's affirmation as a preacher. Instead, Paul consistently revealed his pastoral heart and my glaring weakness by asking questions like, "Dave, have you visited Lou (or Jean or Richard or Elsie
or a score of other names) lately?" It amazed me that this introverted man, who could barely hold a conversation at a church fel-*

lowship dinner, could so genuinely and deeply care for individual people and could so powerfully pastor them from the pulpit. I am glad I was one of them.

—David Schroeder,
colleague, friend

Chapter One

Entering His Gates

The glory of God is best displayed in mud pots. God is not looking for superstars, just mud pots.[1]

—Paul F. Bubna

One of the vivid memories in my life is January 1979 when Jeanie and I were flying back from Myrtle Beach, South Carolina, to Washington, DC. Our two-engine, propeller-driven airliner had about an hour-and-a-half flight bound for Washington's national airport. When the allotted time was up, I noted the lights of the city on the right. A few moments went by, however, and I noticed them on the left, then on the right again and then on the left. It occurred to me that something was wrong with the plane, and as I watched the actions of the stewardesses and then one of the men who came from the cabin, it confirmed to me that we were in trouble. Finally, the captain came on the intercom and told us that the front landing gear apparently had not lowered and that we were preparing for a crash landing at Dulles Airport.

A similar incident had happened on the West Coast just a couple of weeks before and six people had been killed as the plane had burned. We had about twenty more minutes before our fuel would be properly used up and the landing attempted. During those moments Jeanie and I talked about what might be the case if both of us were killed in this plane crash. We prayed together and then decided to write a letter to our children. Jeanie used the comfort bag that is found in the seat pocket in front of you on the plane and tucked the letter in her Bible, figuring that if there were a fire, it would likely not burn inside of a book.

We wanted to convey our deep love and affection to our children, but we also wanted to make a statement about our faith. It was a very interesting and moving experience.

—Paul Bubna[2]

Paul Bubna did not have such a reflective moment before his death on March 31, 1998. But he didn't need one. He was doing one of the things he loved most, perhaps one of the things that had lengthened his life far beyond expectancy. Paul was playing tennis. Doubles. He loved the game. For him, tennis was a parody of life. It was played within bounds, but offered a lot of freedom. You experienced victory, you experienced defeat, but either way you always won, because it was the playing that was the goal. But Paul would never admit that.

In fact, that afternoon as he was leaving home for his tennis game, Paul's wife Patti said, "Good-bye. Have fun!" Paul wryly replied, "It's not about having fun; it's about winning."

Joining Paul on the court that afternoon were three colleagues from the National Office of The Christian and Missionary Alliance: Duane Wheeland, Bob Sanford and Phil Skellie. They had played one set and were having a great time, as usual. And, yes, Paul's team was winning. One reason Paul enjoyed tennis so much was that it took his mind off everything else. Certainly, as president of the denomination he had a lot of work waiting for him at the office. On Sunday he had returned from a few weeks of ministry with the Alliance missionaries in West Africa—but the work could wait. Basically, Paul was feeling well. A bit concerned about the swelling in his feet, he had talked with his doctor on Monday. The swelling was due, he was told, to the lengthy travel, and his heart was in great shape.

For Paul Bubna, that meant something quite different than it would for others. You see, Paul had survived two serious heart attacks and a quadruple bypass surgery which had not been fully successful. But that was in 1979, and since then he had vigorously pursued a life of extreme discipline in diet and exercise. Because only one of his four replaced arteries remained useful, Paul's exercise program had enabled him to develop a huge network of capillaries that fed his heart with the blood supply he needed. In fact, he reported that one doctor told him that he would certainly not die of a heart attack because of that network.

Paul was ready. He was ready for the next serve, and he was ready for another court. And on that March 31 afternoon in 1998, even though a whole worldwide denomination was not ready for it, Paul "entered his courts with praise" (see Psalm 100:4). Sensing some travel fatigue in Paul after the second set, Duane Wheeland asked Paul if he wanted to continue. The answer was predictable: "Of course!" Soon, just before Paul was to return a serve, Duane looked across the net and saw Paul slowly slump over and lie down on the floor. Duane and the others thought Paul was just teasing about being tired. But he didn't get up. He had already entered the heavenly court.

A Timeline of Life

Paul Bubna sort of expected to die in 1983. He indicated this during a staff meeting that took place early in 1980 at Long Hill Chapel. Paul's second major heart attack had occurred in the summer of 1978; in February of 1979 he underwent the somewhat successful quadruple bypass surgery. He was on the mend and beginning to enjoy new health and energy, working a full schedule by the time of that particular meeting. All the staff was feeling good about working together in the roles they had expected to fill now that Pastor Bubna was back.

Steve Armstrong, who was pastor of counseling, led the staff meeting and gave these instructions: "Draw a dot on the left side of your paper, then draw a line across the paper, and then

another dot. Now put the year of your birth above the first dot
and the year you expect to die above the second dot."

Most of the staff, being in their twenties or thirties, wrote anticipated years of death well into the twenty-first century. As they
went around the circle, it was a time of some levity until Paul
spoke. He said, "Well, I was born in 1932, and I will probably die
in 1983." Neither Steve nor any of the others were prepared for
that kind of answer. 1983! That was only a few years away. Paul
was still in his prime. Why would he answer that way? Someone
dared to ask him why he put down that date. He answered,
"When you've had the kind of surgery I just had last year, the sta-
tistics say you will probably live only another four or five years."

What amazed the staff was not only the answer itself, but
also Paul's calmness and objectivity. His expression would have
been no different had he been talking about forty years rather
than four. He was not a fatalist or a pessimist, nor was he easily
going to settle for being an average statistic, as his life of vigor-
ous physical exercise would demonstrate, but he realistically
understood his fragility and mortality.

People who did not know Paul prior to his 1968 heart attack
never saw him seriously overweight. Nor could they imagine
his weighing 230 pounds! But that was the man who had that
first serious heart attack. After recovering from that episode,
Paul became extremely disciplined with his weight. His exercise regimen was amazing. Riding his exercise bicycle, playing
aggressive tennis and long, early-morning prayer walks were
some of the ways he stayed in shape. And every morning before
getting out of bed he would do 100 leg risers. Few young men
would find that to be an easy task.

Paul's competitive fire, such a spiritual albatross and even a
besetting sin in his youth, never left him. By God's grace, he
learned to harness his competitive nature and channel it into
things that mattered, but everyone who played tennis with him
or against him learned that Paul Bubna hated to lose.

Few things brought as much joy to Paul as playing tennis. In his
earlier years he was an avid softball player, and folks from his first
few churches still have memories of their chubby, left-handed-

batting pastor walloping the ball a mile into right field and chugging around the bases. But in his latter years Paul limited his competitive sports to tennis and an occasional round of golf.

As a tennis player, he especially loved doubles because he was smart enough to figure out how to complement the playing style of his partners. He was a sneaky, quick-reflexed net player and enjoyed nothing more than a quick volley. Rarely did he travel without his tennis racquet.

When news of his death came, after recovering from the shock, many of his friends said he went exactly as he would have wanted to go—on the tennis court.

Even though most people who knew Paul Bubna knew that he had suffered two serious heart attacks and quadruple bypass surgery, the news of his death came as a shock. He seemed to be the picture of health. More important, the vision and mission God had given him as president of The Christian and Missionary Alliance seemed to be, in Patti Bubna's words, "like an insurance policy that he would not die soon."

While sixty-five is a few years short of life expectancy, many people die that young, so the shock was not that the Lord would take someone of that age. The shock was more that the death seemed so untimely. President Bubna's fresh vision and leadership had captivated the denomination. Alliance people sensed a growing momentum to move from the malaise that grips all century-old institutions to a new day of spiritual and organizational life. The question *Why?* seemed to be on the lips of everyone.

So it was a sad, confused group that gathered on April 4, 1998, to say farewell to their departed father, pastor and president. The family had asked one of Paul's first interns and colleagues to bring the memorial address, which is printed as an addendum to enable you to enter into the atmosphere of that day (see Appendix 1).

No Ordinary Mud Pot

Several years before his death, Paul's only book, a commentary on Second Corinthians, was published. Significantly, Second Corinthians focuses on suffering, a theme the Apostle Paul understood experientially and biblically far better than almost any other Christian. That book expresses both the nobility and the fragility of human beings. One of the images of humans that the Apostle Paul used is translated "earthen vessels" or "clay jars." Paul Bubna gave his own translation to the concept in commenting on Second Corinthians 4:7: "The glory of God is best displayed in mud pots. God is not looking for superstars, just mud pots."

Paul Bubna was no ordinary mud pot. His life and legacy continue, not only in his family, who have contributed generously and insightfully to this biography, but also through hundreds of ministers of God whose lives Paul deeply impacted. Few of them, however, know the humble beginnings, stressful childhood, uncertain future or physical challenges which all might have undermined what God wanted to do with this mud pot.

Notes

1. Paul F. Bubna, *Second Corinthians* in *The Deeper Life Pulpit Commentary* (Camp Hill, PA: Christian Publications, Inc., 1993), p. 58.
2. Paul F. Bubna, "Finish the Race, Keep the Faith" (sermon preached June 12, 1983, from 2 Timothy 1:8-14). The letter was found after Paul's death. It read: "Dearest Kids—We're prepared for a crash landing. We love you with ALL OUR HEARTS. Love and care for each other and walk with God until we meet you in glory. We have great peace. I've just finished reading the book *Home Before Dark*."

The Personality and Passion
of Paul F. Bubna

My dad and mom's marriage was a living monument to the power of God's redemptive grace in the life of a family. Dad had grown up in a home with parents who loved the Lord but couldn't live at peace with each other. The frequent parental conflict in their home caused a lot of pain, fear and insecurity in Dad's life as he developed. In the natural scheme of things, you would expect that a child raised in that type of environment would be destined to repeat that same cycle in his own marriage. But just the opposite was true in my dad's life. He made a conscious commitment that, by God's grace, his marriage would be different than the one that had been modeled in his home. And the five of us children grew up to reap the benefits of that commitment.

In contrast to what he had known in his childhood home, Dad's marriage to Mom was characterized by love, admiration and peace. In the cedar chest at my house are literally hundreds of cards that Dad gave me before he died. Both he and my mom saved all the cards they had sent to each other for birthdays, anniversaries and other holidays over forty years. Reading the messages in those cards is like getting a peek into a beautiful love story that grew better through the years.

But you wouldn't have had to read the cards to sense the love between Mom and Dad. It was readily apparent for all to see and resulted in a home that was full of love, affirmation, security and peace. We had normal amounts of bickering and fighting that come with five children in one house. But there was so little conflict between Mom and Dad that we kids have joked that we were shocked when we got married and had our first fight! We assumed that Mom and Dad never had disagreements and figured that the absence of conflict was a necessity for a healthy marriage. It wasn't until we were older that we understood the folks had had normal conflicts just like we all do. But they had chosen to work them out privately and peacefully in order to maintain harmony and security *in our home. How blessed I feel to have grown up with such a legacy!*

—Laurie (Mrs. Marty) Berglund,
daughter and oldest child of Paul and Jeanie Bubna

Chapter Two

A House Divided

The secret to spiritual living is the building of an altar at the very center of our being. An altar where relationship to God is an ongoing fellowship. An altar where sacrifice has been made that covers our guilt and sin and is the basis for an ongoing peace and fellowship with God.[1]

—Paul F. Bubna

Recollection

One may find it curious that Paul Bubna seldom told stories about his childhood. He would entertain others telling about places he had visited and people he'd met and stories about recent journeys, but regarding his own early years he was mostly quiet. His son Joel relates, "As I have pondered the stories I remember Dad telling about his growing-up years, I have realized there were not very many." His mind and temperament were not altogether suited to rehearsing personal historical details. He was much more at home sharing ideas and perceptions of the larger world. But there were enough exceptions to capture at least some personal reflection about his early years.

He could and did vividly recall moments in his early years when relationships provided stability and warmth. He often reflected on the spiritual values that his parents had emphasized when he was young. And he had fond memories of individuals who had significantly influenced his family or him, especially at critical junctures in his development. From these reflections, along with insights by members of his family and childhood friends, emerge a somewhat clear picture of his early years and the influences that shaped his life.

When asked what he would want his children to understand about his childhood, Paul responded,

> I had lots of joys and moments of happiness. I'm glad for them. I had much pain and loss. I see now that the suffering is what in the long run has helped me grow and opened the door for joys I could not have known otherwise. And no doubt [this is what] prepared me for my ministry—and for the glory that lies ahead.[2]

These honest observations introduce us to a childhood that was a puzzling amalgam of "joys and moments of happiness" mingled with "pain and loss." The Depression years account for some of the unpleasant aspects of Bubna's early years, but to a degree everyone in those days tasted the pain of unemployment and even hunger. And one doesn't feel pain and loss in a unique sense when a whole generation endures it together.

In Paul's case, what made his childhood perplexing and difficult was that his parents' rock-solid Christian convictions were not complemented by sufficient wisdom or will to overcome a destructive pattern of continuous friction in their relationship. The unsettling effects their strife had upon the Bubna home could have mortally wounded the spirit of a boy whose serious and sensitive temperament longed for tranquility and positive reinforcement from his Christian family. Yet miraculously God mysteriously compacted these incompatible elements into fertile soil that would not only welcome the seed of the gospel, but also produce a rich harvest of compassion and wisdom in Paul Bubna's character, to the benefit of others and for the glory of God.

In order for us to understand the lay of the land, the pitches and steep upgrades in Paul Bubna's pilgrimage, we must trace the paths of his parents, George and Georgia, and comprehend how their paths converged, only to diverge again later in life. Their story surely braids the sovereign goodness of God with the stark reality of the Fall and its plunder of human nature.

Friendship Evangelism

Paul's father, George Bubna, was the oldest of ten children in a family with roots in Springboro, Pennsylvania. In 1927 he boarded a train in Pittsburgh and headed for St. Louis with a promise of work. The St. Louis area had just experienced a tornado. Such a disaster to local folks spelled havoc and destruction, but to a young man in search of steady employment, it was an invitation to move west.

Actually, the move was prompted as a result of his new acquaintance with a contractor whom he had met in a hospital in Pittsburgh, Pennsylvania. His sister Ruth, who was seriously ill, shared a room with a woman whose family were members of the Northside Alliance Church (what would become Allegheny Center Alliance Church). The contractor, a member of that family, befriended George and informed him that he was heading out to St. Louis to do some bricklaying. He offered George an apprenticeship in the bricklaying trade, an offer George decided to accept.

When George arrived at the train depot in St. Louis, he was startled to be welcomed by members of that kind family who had aligned themselves with the St. Louis Christian and Missionary Alliance (Affiliated) Church. They offered him a few nights' lodging and eagerly assisted him in getting settled into a place of his own. With his heart warmed by their welcome, George began as apprentice for that Christian contractor, who in turn sensed that God was at work in their relationship. He began to plant seeds of the gospel in George's unenlightened heart. Before long, he invited George to accompany him to special meetings being held at the Alliance church, featuring guest speaker Dr. R.R. Brown.

R.R. Brown, a Nyack College graduate, had been personally inspired by Dr. A.B. Simpson, the founder of The Christian and Missionary Alliance. Early in his ministry he burned with a desire to reach the people of St. Louis with the good news. Dr. Brown was one of the first ministers to use radio for preaching the gospel. A man of unusual giftedness, Brown was the founding pastor of the Omaha Gospel Tabernacle and led that church for forty-one years. Moreover, his missionary vision "helped inspire the first missionary rallies at General Council," highlighted by the Preachers' Chorus, which he organized and led. In 1922 he was invited to broadcast a religious message on St. Louis radio station WOW when it first went on the air. The response was so positive that he continued to broadcast weekly gospel messages on a program entitled "World Radio Chapel" for more than forty years on the same station. And, to the credit of his witness in that city, after his death in 1964 the station continued to air Brown's messages![3]

During these special meetings at the St. Louis Alliance Church, and under the preaching of the man who would someday inspire and guide his own son Paul into the ministry, George Bubna was convicted of his unbelief and trusted savingly in Christ. That decision he never regretted, nor was it one that he ever veered from—he followed it with dogged perseverance throughout what would be a difficult life.

His conversion might have gone unnoticed in the annals of Alliance history—he was a hard-working, blue-collar transient from back East who was just one of thousands who were impacted by Dr. R.R. Brown—but something else occurred during those evangelistic meetings at the Alliance church. George noticed a young lady wearing a red hat, singing with gusto in the church choir. Soon he was introduced to Georgia Irene Matthews, whose home was in the neighborhood of the church.

Georgia, like George, had grown up in a nonreligious home with no church affiliation. Her father had died when she was very young, and her mother, with five children clutching her skirts, emigrated from Ohio to St. Louis in search of a better life.

Georgia's spiritual journey resembled her future husband's in that her conversion was the fruit of friendship evangelism. In her situation, the witness of a faithful laywoman from the St. Louis Alliance Church prepared the ground. That elderly woman felt a burden for the neighborhood where Georgia lived, and she began to walk door-to-door passing out children's evangelistic leaflets and sharing the gospel whenever she was permitted. Georgia was still a young girl when that woman knocked at their door and invited the Matthews children to attend Sunday school with her. Being the youngest in a family without the presence of a father, Georgia welcomed the attention and thoughtfulness behind the kind invitation and eagerly responded by accompanying the woman to church. She was the only one in her family to do so.

That was Georgia's first taste of church life. She absorbed all she could of the message that a heavenly Father loved her enough to send his only Son to die for her sins. Her heart ached for the love and attention of a father. The Alliance church quickly became her family of choice, and in her teen years she professed personal faith in Christ and immersed herself in the activities of her newly adopted family. She particularly enjoyed singing in the church choir.

Spiritually Matched

When George met Georgia during those special meetings with R.R. Brown, neither had the slightest inkling what a Christian courtship or marriage should look like. But a spiritual life was budding in their hearts, and they trusted that life to enfold a romantic relationship for which neither was quite prepared. Not long after they met, George proposed marriage, and Georgia accepted. Years afterward Georgia would hint to her friends that she had had misgivings about the courtship and marriage from the beginning. Perhaps greatly affecting their life together was her sincere belief that she had let the Lord down because she dropped out of Bible school and did not go to the mission field, but married George instead. Be that as it may, in June of 1928 they were married, both new believers with no Christian legacy in their immediate families from which they could summon wisdom to build a Christian marriage and raise a family of their own. Nevertheless, they were full of zeal, and both desperately wanted to please and serve the Lord.

Spirit of the Times

The Great Depression was a time filled with ironies, when people were jobless because machines had replaced them. Yet these same workers were often blamed by society for their unemployment and routinely portrayed as lazy and unmotivated. The Depression left American families traumatized by upheaval and role deprivation. However, for the Bubnas there was never a shortage of the essential things, nor any foreboding about the future. George Bubna was now a skilled bricklayer and a conscientious worker. He was a hard-working man and, in his son Don's words, "was proud of his craft." Driving around town, he would routinely point out to his sons the projects he had "laid brick on."

Yet there came a time when the market for his skills dried up, and he joined the swelling ranks of the unemployed. He was very aware of his solemn responsibility as a husband and new father of baby Don. The changing dynamics in work and industry never quite meshed with George Bubna's spiritual stirrings and traditional hankerings. For instance, after being laid off and while looking for another job, he discovered a good work opportunity and was elated about it—until he learned that he would have to work on Sundays. He instantly turned down the job offer, choosing unemployment before he would violate his beliefs about the Lord's Day. Eventually he was forced to take a job working in maintenance for the J.C. Penney Company at their warehouse in St. Louis. But here again his spiritual convictions would clash with the spirit of the times. Some years into the Depression, the area in which he worked at J.C. Penney became unionized. George reluctantly joined their ranks, but when they took a stand on an issue that violated his personal beliefs, he quit his job, choosing again to be unemployed rather than compromise himself.

A Lonely Journey

In addition to espousing ideological views that were not in sync with the times, George suffered from other liabilities—a weak heart and subsequently (though unrelated) epileptic seizures. In the late 1940s he began having attacks of epilepsy, which signaled a visible deterioration in his health. Unfortunately, it also signaled accompanying trouble in his marriage. One can only imagine that George, a tireless worker, must have comprehended at some point that his battle for his health and for his marriage were becoming insurmountable struggles that he might not win. He walked a lonely journey during those troubling years.

George, however, was not a complainer. Actually, he was a man of few words. Notwithstanding this disposition, he was very intentional and possessed strength of conviction and moral resolve that belied his unassuming and soft-spoken demeanor. Those who knew him personally perceived the steel-hard spiritual nerves that disciplined his responses to life's challenges. It was clear to them that when George Bubna made decisions, his convictions would not be compromised. That enduring trait in George left its mark on his sons, and especially on Paul, whose temperament was often compared to his father's.

Georgia, by comparison, was the antithesis to George in almost every respect. She was outspoken and opinionated, always ready with a word—in or out of season. Unlike George's restrained manner, she was forceful and blunt (though when pushed George could also be brusque). However, like her husband, she was a committed and uncompromising Christian. A disciplined church member, she was dutifully present every time the doors were open, always arriving early (sometimes by thirty minutes) as if to punctuate the principle of being faithful.

She loved the church hymns and sang them wholeheartedly, though what others particularly remember is how *loudly* she sang. She was never shy and certainly not ashamed to give a witness about her Lord. The Christian lifestyle of Middle America had offered her a niche that she fit perfectly. And she gave her energies wholeheartedly to the Alliance church and its programs.

Divine Custody

There was a profound mystery to George and Georgia's marriage that had the markings of divine custody. These two personalities, so opposite each other, were yet somehow attracted to each other. It's very tenable indeed that besides the red hat and loud voice projecting from the front of the church, it was Georgia's commitment to the Lord and to the gospel that riveted George's attention that evening of special meetings when he first sighted her in the choir loft. And it's equally tenable that besides the profile of independent and self-sufficient masculinity, it was George kneeling at the altar and professing his allegiance to Jesus Christ that focused Georgia's attention when she first sighted him in the church.

In the divine equation God had ordained a redemptive aspect of what would become a painfully unhappy marriage, namely that godly character and Christian values would be consistently taught and reiterated by *both* parents—two people completely devoted to their children. George and Georgia's parental and often sacrificial love would lay a foundation for the spiritual formation of three remarkable sons.

In their best moments they both were enabled to trace God's hand in their lives, particularly when their sons followed the call to become ministers of the gospel. But sadly, as the years passed, their marriage became a wound that couldn't be healed. Georgia construed her husband's reserved and laid-back temperament as a symptom of his lack of affection. And George couldn't surmount the obstacles of his own temperament to answer the felt needs of his wife. In contrast to his ability to oppose ideologies at work, George did not have a counterpoint to his wife's perception of him.

A psychologist might have blamed the fracturing of their marriage on the Great Depression and its assault upon the spirit of the man, pounding into him and many American workers feelings of inadequacy and inferiority. George might have taken refuge in the fact that his quiet and reserved demeanor made him especially vulnerable, and Georgia in the thought that her unmet emotional needs compelled her to become judgmental. But neither George nor Georgia shirked their personal accountability for the choices they had made, nor did they pin the blame on others any more than on themselves for the disintegration of their relationship.

However, as the years went by, they made hurtful choices in respect to their marriage, and in the aftermath of those years the bread they had cast upon the waters returned to them (see Ecclesiastes 11:1), moldy and decayed. George became increasingly withdrawn from the marriage, while Georgia became increasingly irritable and impatient. The pattern of withdrawal and impatience—alternating with confrontation and exchanges of many unkind words—frustrated attempts over a long period to close the widening breach in their relationship.

They would remain together until their youngest son, George, Jr., was old enough to leave home. When their nest was finally empty, they quietly separated. They remained separated, without divorcing, for the rest of their lives. And they both continued faithfully serving the Lord, only in different locations and spheres of ministry, carrying a lingering regret that the grace they had so faithfully attested to others could not be applied to healing the wound in their own relationship.

Notes

1. Paul F. Bubna, "The Promises and the Promised Land" (sermon preached April 28, 1985, from Deuteronomy 27:1-10).
2. Paul's responses to questions in a memory book filled out for his daughter Laurie.
3. Robert L. Niklaus, John S. Sawin, Samuel J. Stoesz, *All for Jesus: God at Work in The Christian and Missionary Alliance over One Hundred Years* (Camp Hill, PA: Christian Publications, Inc., 1986), p. 259.

The Personality and Passion of Paul F. Bubna

Paul Bubna was "driven" even when he was a teenager. He was a fighter. I remember attending a high school football game with him in St. Louis in which he chose to fight rather than run or give in. We were walking around the stadium on one of the benches when suddenly there appeared another youth in front of him, daring him to continue on walking forward on the same bench.

Paul kept on walking, brushing the fellow off the bench. Immediately, about six guys showed up and began pummeling Paul. I tried to pull them off and was prevented from interfering while they gave Paul a good beating. Afterward, Paul just said, as he brushed off his clothes, "I wasn't going to give in to anyone." He was ready to pay whatever price there was to see his goal accomplished. And he continued walking around the stadium on the bench!

That kind of determination characterized Paul in most everything he did. He was a fighter in college as well and got into a few scuffs with some of the students who didn't share his view of things (or were in competitive clubs or associations). And he was determined to know God, to serve Him and to be His representative in whatever sphere God called him to. He was willing to be a fighter for His Lord too .

Paul was a good player in almost any sport he put his mind and body to. He played baseball, football and basketball in college and excelled in each, even though he did not have an athletic build or have a bent to be a real sportsman. But he played hard in every sport and always wanted to win. Later Paul loved to play tennis. He seemed to like competition and played hard to win.

Paul was more of a musician than most people knew. He sang well, could carry a tune and sing tenor or bass, and often we would sing together in a trio or play our musical instruments together. Paul was a lover of good music but didn't feel it was something he wanted to give his life to. He led singing in the church youth group and in the citywide youth club we belonged to, and he played a mean saxophone.

Many who knew him probably never heard him play. He was influenced to play the sax by Merv Rosell, a former musician/preacher who used to travel much and speak at Youth for Christ meetings around the country. Since I played the marimba, Paul and I would often get together and play duets at young people's meetings or at church.

And Paul learned to play well. He had a natural talent on the saxophone and he could really make it sing. He told me that he loved music, and he loved the saxophone, but he was sure that wasn't to be his calling. But he did want to glorify God with his instrument, and through his high school and college years he brought pleasure to a number of folks and praise to His God through his playing. I don't know if he played it much after college, but his goal to glorify God probably had something to do with his curtailing of the saxophone ministry (it took quite a bit of practice to keep his lip in shape). Paul always had that underlying desire to please God. He believed that the way to do that was to concentrate on preaching the Word. It was on that that he would finally concentrate.

—David P. Harvey,
boyhood friend

Chapter Three

Seeds of the Ministry

I have told you about the man who was my pastor when I was a boy, and who still has input into my life. I asked him several years ago what he would do differently if he were starting over. The first thing he said was, "I wish I had taken more risks for God." I was taken back because I do not know anyone who has been so foolhardy for God.[1]

—Paul F. Bubna

When their first son Don was still a toddler, George and Georgia Bubna located an apartment at 1909 Arlington Avenue, St. Louis, in close proximity to Georgia's mother and siblings. The house was nestled in a lower-middle-class neighborhood comprised mostly of immigrant and Jewish families. A small home, it consisted initially of only "three straight rooms" that were heated by a wood/coal-burning stove in the kitchen and living room. In spite of the modest surroundings, for the next fifteen years these sometimes cramped quarters would be home to the Bubna family. There they would brighten the lives of many as they opened their home to hundreds of guests, most notably during the war years when servicemen passing through St. Louis on their way overseas would often be invited to stay in the Bubna home. In these environs the Bubnas would experience more happiness than at any other time that the family was together.

Their second son, Paul, was born on September 13, 1932, three and a half years after his brother Don. As youngsters, Don and Paul slept in the living room on a studio couch that folded out into a bed. During the day their bedroom became the living area where family and guests congregated. When Paul turned ten, his parents acquired the additional three rooms directly above them, at which time Paul inherited a bedroom, which he shared with his younger brother George. Even then, Paul and his brothers often had to sleep on the floor because visitors were given their beds. Don reflects on the impact of their parents' hospitality during the Depression and war years:

> Mom and Dad's deep commitment to hospitality was probably one of their greatest gifts to their three sons. Although poor by many standards, they enthusiastically offered food and a bed to those they felt needed it. Many Saturdays during World War II I remember Mom and Dad going downtown to bring home as many as four servicemen who were on leave in a strange city. Whenever our church had a visiting pastor or missionary, he came to our house for dinner. We boys relished the flavor these folks brought, and got the impression early that serving Christ was the most exciting activity in the world. Had it not brought all these different people to our home? Hospitality, more than any other single influence in our youth, probably directed each of us brothers toward our future calling as pastors.[2]

Quiet Child in a Noisy Home

Paul may have happily assimilated the busy and noisy activity that was taking place around him in their little home, but he exhibited none of it himself. He was a quiet child with a very solemn comportment. His family observed that as a toddler he was noticeably slow in learning to talk. So reluctant was he to verbalize that his parents feared that he had a learning disability. Their fears proved unfounded when eventually he did begin to speak, and did very well at that. But, like his father, he remained somewhat aloof in temperament; he never wasted words. Even as a boy, he seemed more interested in pondering ideas than engaging in frivolous conversation. Quite possibly he took longer than most in learning to speak because even as a child he wanted to be sure that he had something to say!

Perhaps other noises in the Bubna home were enough to suppress any inclination he may have had to express himself. Grandmother Barnes, Georgia's mother, lived within walking distance of the Bubnas and shopped at the market across the street from their house. She habitually found a reason to "drop in" and did so many times each week. Being a domineering person, she could quickly fan into flame any residual tension between George and Georgia, and the noise in the home during her calls was not altogether pleasant.

Another regular guest was Georgia's brother Everett, Paul's favorite uncle. He used profanity and he smoked, which were big taboos in the Christian culture. But often he stopped by to visit, savoring the hospitality of the Bubna home. And he always enjoyed teasing the boys, sometimes unmercifully. In Paul's memory, even though Uncle Everett was not a believer, he made room in his life for his nephews. Paul perceived that underneath that rough exterior was a generous and kind man who died at a very old age with no certainty in anyone's mind that he had become a believer. His conduct represented many gestures of kindness and attention that were offered by individuals who were not "in the fold." Many Christians might dismiss such kindnesses as insignificant, but they were never lost on Paul. Already during his formative years he was exercising powers of discernment, grasping a bigger picture of the sovereign grace of God and comprehending God's truths that lay buried beneath the stereotypes.

In a home that was at times tempestuous, Paul Bubna longed for spiritual affirmation. One brief moment in particular made a lasting impression on him. The family was attending a church function in the home of their pastor, Rev. Frierson. Paul was still too small to be noticed by most adults, and Rev. Frierson was a very tall and big man—gargantuan in comparison to little boys like Paul. Yet Frierson was also very gentle, and at one point in the evening while he was seated next to other adults, he invited the small Bubna boy to climb up onto his lap. Then Pastor Frierson looked into Paul's somber eyes and told him how very *special* he was! That look and those words—coming from such a big man—created a remarkable sensation in Paul's sensitive spirit. It was a moment that he would remember for the rest of his life.

Some might get the impression that Paul's quiet demeanor implied that he was mostly inactive. On the contrary, he was completely absorbed with things that captured his attention. He was an avid reader with an engaging mind and good grades in school. He devoured spiritual classics like Bunyan's *Pilgrim's Progress*. He also liked homespun tales like the Sugar Creek Gang series by Paul Hutchens, who wrote stories for and about Christian boys who refused to be labeled soft or weak because they were Christians. Throughout his life Paul defied the stereotype of Christians as weak and helpless creatures. He liked to take the part of the underdog who wins through sheer endurance and willpower. He was undaunted by activities that were rugged and challenging and possessed a single-mindedness that characterized his approach to everything. His brother Don relates a childhood incident that humorously shows Paul's dogged determination:

> I remember that as a boy on Arlington Avenue in St. Louis I belonged to a very exclusive club with my best friend, Billy. Our club met in his basement, and my brother Paul, who was three-and-a-half years younger, always tried to join us. To him we were the in-group, because we were older. He would endure all sorts of things to be counted one of us. When Billy's dog Bing spent the night in the basement and did things dogs shouldn't do indoors, we let Paul earn his way into the club by cleaning up after Bing. On those days my little brother looked as though he felt ten feet tall.[3] (It should be noted that when his services in Don's exclusive club were no longer needed, Paul's membership was suspended!)

With a determined temperament and natural athletic ability, Paul developed into a fine young competitor, spending countless hours playing pitch and catch with a softball in an alley a couple of lots from their home. It wasn't long before he was chosen ahead of his older brother Don in pickup sandlot games in the neighborhood (much to Don's chagrin!). His childhood companion David Harvey recalls:

> Whatever Paul did, he did with all his might, and usually quite well. Basketball, baseball, football, tennis, the saxophone, singing—whatever; Paul wanted to do what he did with excellence and even as a boy understood that all should be done for God's glory.

His boyhood wasn't devoid of lighter moments. For instance, he liked all kinds of mind games. Harvey shares this memory:

> As young boys, we formed a club (just the two of us) called YPS. We talked about it a lot. And especially in the summertimes we liked to play YPS (that's spy, spelled backwards). We would go back and forth behind cars, telephone poles and light posts, zigzagging here and there spying on people. Of course they didn't know we were spying on them and couldn't have cared less, but we were great pretenders!
>
> And Paul played hard at the YPS game. He would run and hide, puff and grunt like it meant his life if he got "caught." He played hard. One time he ran so hard back to where I was crouching behind a car that he slipped on the curb, ran into the bumper of the car and cut his lip. And then he looked up at me and said, "Dave, I don't think he saw me!" Paul's intensity as a child carried on through high school, college and into adulthood where he "played hard" in his quest to know the will of God and to do it.

These glimpses into his childhood portray Paul as a sensitive, somewhat aloof boy with an engaging mind and a hotly competitive spirit, striving always to give everything he had to everything he did. And at the core of his being, the light of the gospel was already making an impression.

Spiritual Stirrings

When Laurie asked her father what, as a child, he dreamed of becoming later in life, he responded, "At various points, a pilot, a truck driver, a man rich enough to buy all the candy I would want! But early on I knew I would be a pastor or missionary." Early in his life he encountered Christ as his personal Savior. Paul actually regarded his spiritual birthday as December 13, 1942. He was sitting in the front row during a Sunday evening service. The pastor was giving an object lesson about the heart with its many rooms. Paul was deeply convicted, but instead of going forward, he went all the way to the back of the church and found his mother. He later testified, "I believed savingly upon Jesus Christ. That was a memorable event in my life, a pivotal event. I became spiritually alive in Christ, and I began to grow."[4]

What were influences in his childhood years that turned his heart toward Christ and his calling to ministry so early in life? We can trace several significant influences that positively shaped his view of God and ministry.

His Parents' Earnestness

The first influence was undoubtedly his parents' spiritual earnestness and candor. It was no revelation to family and friends that George and Georgia had a troubled marriage. There were moments when their bickering made it unpleasant for the boys to be in the home. Don recalls one very poignant moment:

> Late one night my younger brother Paul and I awoke suddenly in the hide-a-bed sofa where we slept in the living room. From the kitchen came the sounds of yelling. Between the accusations, dishes flew and shattered against the wall. Finally my father left, slamming the kitchen door after him. Mother dressed Paul and me, and we walked to a nearby fire station to call a taxi to take us to a friend's house for a few days. As a six-year-old, I wondered if I would ever see my father again.[5]

That was very traumatic for Paul, who grew up with a latent fear that his parents would get a divorce. In answer to Laurie's question, "Did you ever experience homesickness?" Paul admitted, "Because of the tensions between my parents, getting away from home for a while was always welcomed." Don adds, "A lot of our childhood was about fearing the breakup of our parents' marriage and everything that goes with that." Observers of that dysfunctional union might have expected Paul and his brothers to draw the conclusion that the open sore in their parents' marriage invalidated their profession of faith, making it a façade that barely covered the disharmony beneath. But somehow the robust faith of both parents and sons withstood the cracks in the domestic foundation.

George and Georgia's marriage certainly was an enigma that— from a distance and much later—their grandchildren strained to comprehend. Of course, they viewed it from the security, warmth and tranquility that Paul and Jeanie's marriage and home provided them. Joel recalls one occasion when he happened to be sitting at the top of the stairs, eavesdropping on a conversation his father was having with Grandpa Bubna. Paul was trying to mediate a dispute that had erupted between George and Georgia, and little Joel finally mustered the courage to ask his dad the inevitable question: "Why are Grandpa and Grandma separated?" Paul answered his son's searching question in this manner: "Grandpa and Grandma are both wonderful people who *really love* the Lord. But they have just had trouble working out some of their differences."

That gracious perspective was warranted because, in the midst of deep personal pain, George and Georgia remained unswerving in their commitment to Christ and just as unswerving in their commitment to guiding their sons spiritually. Paul's own reflection conceded that his parents were not able to bring their faith to bear on their relationship. The need to live out the faith in relationships would become a cornerstone emphasis in both Don's and Paul's ministries. Yet despite their inability to get along, both parents were determined to encourage their sons in their relationships to Christ. That resolve helps us to comprehend how his parents' spiritual sincerity could make such a powerful impression on Paul in those early years.

For instance, there was the time when as a small boy Paul was sitting in church next to his father. The pastor was preaching about grace. Paul remembered looking at his dad and noticed that his cheeks were wet with tears. George had been quietly weeping. Paul asked his father why he was crying, and the answer he received was, "I am just a sinner who doesn't deserve God's grace." Surely the most beautiful worship in the world is the prayer of a broken heart. Paul witnessed his own father engaged in the most genuine worship a man can ever offer to God. He was deeply moved by his father's confession. Later he shared the importance of that event for his own understanding of grace—realizing that his very own father was a sinner, saved by grace. Far too often, this profound truth is the last thing fathers wish to divulge to their sons.

His mother Georgia was a strict disciplinarian and not afraid to confront her sons, or for that matter, the teens in her youth group at the church. But her "kids" never forgot how much she loved them and how diligently she prayed for them. Paul recalled how she would "pray for us boys as we went out the door to school each day. I felt like the power of heaven had been placed upon me. It was a powerful protection!" His mother also helped Paul at about age ten to find a "life verse" in his new leather-bound, zippered New Testament. Paul recounted:

> My mother suggested one day that I might want to ask God to give me a portion of Scripture as a life verse, a "truth" which God might build into my life. We agreed that each of us would pray and ask God to reveal that verse or portion of Scripture to us separately. When, after a week or two, we talked again together, both of us had been impressed with the same text. The text was Matthew 6:33, "But seek first his kingdom and his righteousness, and all these things will be added unto you."[6]

Paul's son Steve asserts, "This is extremely profound, because that verse defines his life as well as anything else that could be said."

Other memories that Paul told his own children were largely a recollection of stories that touched on his parents' values and their example of genuine piety. George and Georgia were very strict in enforcing respect for the Lord's Day. Paul chafed under the rule that prohibited him from playing ball on Sunday. Yet in later years he was grateful for his parents' commitment to honoring God in the very practical, visible routines of life. Paul shared this reflection on the uniqueness of the Lord's Day in their home:

> One of the blessed gifts our parents gave us is the gift of *Shabbat*. While they had stricter rules about the way we lived on Sunday than most people would, and perhaps I enjoyed, it was still the happiest day of the week. The main task of Saturday was getting ready for Sunday. The big family meal remains as one of my happiest memories. The joy of being together with our friends at church. The quiet Sunday afternoon of reading, simply being together as a family. The worship at the end of the day, the finishing of Sunday with a sense of rest and renewing for another week. What a gracious gift![7]

The Bubnas were committed to giving a tithe of their income to the Lord in addition to their personal investment in the ministry of hospitality. That practice was all the more remarkable because they surely must have initiated that sacrifice in the middle of the Depression. Paul reflected, "I was a small boy when my parents started me on the discipline of bringing the first ten percent of what came into my hands to give to God. Since that time this has been part of our day-by-day lifestyle."[8]

Regarding the issue of stewardship, Paul once overheard a conversation between his father and Uncle Murphy. The topic was money and savings. Uncle Murphy was critical of George for not putting away money for his sons' education (no doubt he was equally proud of the fact that he had done so). George, without hesitating, answered that after giving their regular tithe there wasn't enough left to save for the future. However, he added, "If God wants my boys to go to school, He will take care of that." As it turned out, neither of Uncle Murphy's children went on to school, while all three of the Bubna boys attended college. That forward-looking confidence in God's care regarding all the exigencies that clouded the future of families during the Depression years profoundly strengthened Paul's faith.

The Redemptive Role of a Church

The second powerful spiritual influence in Paul's life was the Church. The Bubna family played an active role in their church throughout his childhood. Marital friction, rather than precipitating a withdrawal from church life, compelled the Bubnas to depend more heavily on relationships in the Body of Christ. George and Georgia seemed to accept the limited potential in their family environment for mentoring their sons, and they compensated for that by encouraging outside contacts with mature Christians. Undoubtedly the Bubnas initiated that "spiritual networking," perhaps in desperation, and certainly at the risk of exposing their own unresolved marital troubles. Perhaps, due to being relatively young in the faith, they were still naïve enough to think that when couples are struggling, the best medicine is the Church and God's people (which it is by design!).

Paul understood the redemptive role of the Church in his life. When asked to share a memory of going to church when he was growing up he said,

> Church was very important. We went to every service, but it was not a problem. My parents' marriage was in trouble, and the church was a place where our family functioned well. My friends were at church, not school, so I loved going there. Our youth group was alive and active. It was somewhat like an extended family.

The hospitality of church people was a healing antidote for the Bubna clan. Paul explained it this way: "It was always a blessing to us kids because Mom and Dad seemed to do better when other people were around. In some respects, I was raised by the modeling of other families and by seeing my parents in community. [This is] a good picture of what a loving church can do."

Sometimes that hospitality evolved into a boarding-house ministry at the Bubnas'. On more than one occasion people in transition referred to the Bubna residence as their home away from home. For instance, Harold Segard, who served in the military and was stationed near St. Louis, often stayed with the Bubnas on weekends. And after the war he lived with the Bubna family while attending a college in St. Louis. Paul remembered Harold this way: "His discipline and diligence touched me deeply. He later started a Boys' Brigade club and trained me to be a leader. He believed in me and trusted me."

Then there was Olga, who rented a room during a time while she worked as secretary for Pastor Harvey and with Youth for Christ. She was a gracious person and literally became like part of the family. Individuals like Harold and Olga were godsends to the Bubna family. The Bubna boys eagerly assimilated them into the family and relished the attention and kindness they received from these guests.

Happy Holidays

Another highlight of church life for the Bubnas were seasonal celebrations. Tim Bubna, Paul's son, recalls that while there was not a lot of talk about birthday celebrations, Christmas, Easter and the annual Sunday school picnics aroused many wonderful memories. Paul's daughter Gracie adds, "I always got great joy in seeing Dad shine on Christmas and Easter. He just was caught up in praising and worshiping God. He was also this way on church picnic days. It was like the little kid in him was jumping out in excitement. It was neat to see him that way and to know that it was that way since he was a child . . . and why."

The "why" that explained Paul's spontaneous enthusiasm on these occasions can be found in the role that the church in St. Louis played during the holiday season, which was a time when the stresses at the Bubna home appeared to be magnified. Paul recounted, "It seemed that our family did more things together [at Christmas] and there were fewer tensions expressed. . . . The programs at school and church gave a fresh touch to life."

Christmas and Easter holidays seemed to charge the Bubnas spiritually. And through them God channeled the energy of His redemptive grace to others who experienced similar or even more distressing circumstances at home. God used the family to be a healing balm to others despite their unhealed wound at home. They intuitively modeled the ministry of the Apostle Paul who wrote in Second Corinthians 1:6-7:

> If we experience trouble we can pass on to you comfort and spiritual help; for if we ourselves have been comforted we know how to encourage you to endure patiently the same sort of troubles that we have ourselves endured. We are quite confident that if you have to suffer troubles as we have done, then, like us, you will find the comfort and encouragement of God. (Phillips)

In a message preached during the Christmas season, Paul shared why Christmas hymns became so precious to him:

> The carols are special to me because I have known them by heart since I was a small child; the singing of them often evokes fresh and pungent memories out of childhood.
>
> One of the carols that does that most for me is "It Came upon a Midnight Clear." It is an unusual carol in that it speaks of the future glory of Christ's return as the object of hope; but it also identifies the painful experience of human suffering into which the angels came to sing.
>
> I can recall singing this as a small boy. The third stanza was something that deeply impressed me because of the experiences of our family. One of the memories is from when I was about six or seven years of age—the late 1930s, the winding down of the Great Depression years, the heating up of the war in Europe as Hitler began to annex one country after another. It was about then that the persecution of the Jews began. It occurred to me the other day, when I saw some of our children exchanging baseball cards, that the big thing in my day was war cards: on one side the pictures of bombed out

cities in Europe, with the story of the bombing and attacks on the other side. In the third stanza [of the carol] we are told of the troubles that touched the heart of this little boy:

> And ye beneath life's crushing load,
> Whose forms are bending low;
> Who toil along the climbing way
> With painful steps and slow;
> Look now for glad and golden hours,
> Come swiftly on the wing;
> O rest beside the weary road,
> And hear the angels sing.

It was not so much the rumble of war in Europe that made the words of the carol so poignant to me, but rather the pain in our family. My mother's sister was married to a man who drank a lot and, for whatever reason, he seemed to drink more at Christmas. Those late Depression years were difficult financial ones for all families. Apparently, my uncle would drink up what little money might have been left over to provide Christmas for the family. It would result in raucous domestic battles. I can recall Mother bundling up my brother and me, walking the long blocks over the hill to where my aunt lived and there, try to plead for peace. I remember sitting there as a little boy and watching the painful encounters.

Then there was the long walk home, sometimes with tears running down my mother's face. We would get back home to our house where the Christmas tree was up. Our home was not without its difficulties, but there was a sense of joy at Christmas because we could hear the angels sing.[9]

However outmoded the traditional Sunday school picnic has become to us, in the 1930s and '40s that annual event elevated the spirits of the Bubna family like no other. Tim recalls his father's mouth-watering descriptions of the fried chicken, potato salad, apple pie and lemonade all spread to overflowing on tables in the park. The annual picnic was such a luminous occasion that the St. Louis Alliance Church usually planned it around the Independence Day holiday! Paul shared this vignette:

We would decorate our cars, meet at the church and go in a parade to a private picnic grounds about twenty-five miles south of St. Louis. Free lemonade and ice cream, lots of games and good food. One day I pitched over twenty innings of fast-pitch softball. July 4th was among my happiest childhood memories.

Don adds this comment:

The yearly Sunday school picnics were such a joy. We no longer had time for picnics as a family in those years. And the wonderful food—and all you could eat!—was especially great for Paul, who was a large eater and a big guy. . . . Our home not being a happy one, it was special being with people who *were* happy.

We have only to leaf through the hundreds of sermons that have been left in manuscript form to grasp the importance of the Church in Paul's thinking. As a pastor he was always convinced, even in the midst of the most unsavory aspects of church politics, that the Church is God's idea and ultimately His means of redeeming and restoring people to wholeness. He preached:

In the biblical view the Church is not an organization; it is a living organism of people who are organically joined spiritually in Christ. It is not an organization that needs to enlist people to serve the organization. It is an organism whose intent is to enable every member to experience the sheer delight of ministry, of knowing that their life is positively affecting the lives of other people in a way that will make an eternal difference.[10]

Perhaps the reason for the strength of his conviction about the redemptive role of the Church is that a small struggling church in St. Louis in the 1930s and '40s made an eternal difference in his life, and its effects are still rippling through the Alliance movement today.

Godly Mentors

A third and very significant influence in Paul's life was the mentoring that he received from godly men. At the top of that list was Dr. Richard Harvey. The Harvey family came to the St. Louis church in late 1941. They brought a fresh spirit to the church. Dr. Harvey's preaching was uplifting, and soon after his arrival Paul trusted in Christ. Paul's memory of Dr. Harvey reveals that Harvey's example and personal attention inspired Paul throughout his life. In an article entitled "The Story of a Mentor and Protégé," Paul wrote:

> Dick Harvey assumed the pastorate of our congregation in St. Louis when I was about eight years of age. I remember it well because I came to saving faith through his ministry just about a year later. The Harveys had three sons and a daughter, and the boys were approximately the same age as the three Bubna boys. David, the middle son, became one of my closest friends and remains a significant person in my life. We frequently stayed overnight in each other's homes or would be guests for Sunday dinner. So I was exposed to life in the parsonage almost as if I had grown up in one. The times of prayer about their table and the conversations about life in the local church began a training process for ministry that I did not understand until years later. . . . It occurs to me that at eighteen years of age I probably had a better feel for what ministry is about than many seminary graduates. It was not so much a cognitive knowledge but a subconscious understanding—like fire in my bones.
>
> The congregation I grew up in was not exactly a model church. It split twice while I was growing up, had frequent times of severe tension and never grew beyond a couple hundred. Yet during those years there were about twenty men and women who entered vocational ministry from that congregation. It was a conundrum to me and others that such a troubled congregation would produce so many ministry candidates.
>
> How then was he [Richard Harvey] a model? Though his preaching style was not something that I wanted to emulate, he preached about a *great God*. He lived in obedience and fellowship with the *great God* that he preached, and as a result he inspired faith and response. While at times he was less than kind to the King's English, I have seen few preachers who could move an audience to such deep and

profound response to God. It was those inward responses that shaped my walk with God as I sat under his ministry.

His personal qualities shaped my view of ministry. Dick Harvey cared about people, and he did so in costly ways. His loving concern for my family during times of distress was like a light in a gloomy place. My pastoral instincts were shaped by the model of a shepherd who cared deeply and gave of himself freely.

There were two attitudes easily discernable. One was that there was an open door. Not just an open door to his study, but an open door to his life. Hospitality is not simply opening one's home, it is also the attitude and lifestyle of making room in one's schedule for people. I understood that my pastor carried heavy responsibilities and lived with a packed schedule, but it was always clear that he was available. . . . Another awareness I had was that Dick would take initiative to interject himself into my circumstances, if necessary, to rescue me in my journey. He never interfered or tried to run my life but I always knew that I was not alone in the battle.

Dick Harvey's home going was a sizable loss. I was with him just a couple of months before he died. It was good to be able to tell him again of his profound influence in my life. His prayer for me that day was a keen reminder that who I am now was mostly determined by the investments other people have made in me. My commitment to being a mentor grows out of that experience.[11]

Paul would be continually amazed through the years at the intervention of God in his life through godly men who were grooming him for ministry before he was even aware of their contribution. Not surprisingly, a man God powerfully used to mentor him and others in his generation was Paul's own father, George. Paul related this account of his father's influence in young people's lives:

The commitment that I have to feeding God's people comes from models that have touched my life. One of those was my dad. My dad died in heart surgery just a year after I had my first heart surgery. My brother and I were there for the surgery and stayed over for the funeral. It was held at the little Alliance church were my brother had been the pastor. My dad was a faithful, committed worker there. After the funeral, we gathered back at the church for lunch, and I was visiting with different people. I noticed a fellow standing off to the side by himself, and I went over and spoke to him. He was waiting to talk to me.

He was from the community, not really a part of the church. He wanted to show me the baptistry that had been built out on the lawn. It's a warm climate there, and they had built the baptistry outside. He said, "Your dad built that." I told him I knew that. He said, "I was here to help a little bit the day they started. We had to dig the hole. Your dad shouldn't have been digging. He had to stop and rest every couple moments because he was having congestive heart failure." Then he said, "After we did the heavy work of mixing the cement and all, your dad laid up the blocks and the bricks."

"But," he said, "that's not the important thing I wanted to tell you. My thirteen-year-old boy was baptized there about a month ago. He came to know Christ in your father's Sunday school class." I was doubly touched, on the one hand, because my dad was in his sixties—very quiet and reserved, not the kind of man you would think would be teaching young boys. But I was also touched because my dad was suffering from congestive heart failure. And you wouldn't think he'd spend his energies that way. But he did. He took them deep sea fishing. My mother and dad, though both were believers, were separated at that time. It was a painful time in their marriage. Dad was living alone. He had all the kinds of excuses that would be normal for him not to teach a boy's Sunday school class. But he did. And this father was not yet himself a Christian. But he said, "I had to come today because I'm so grateful for your dad's interest in my son."[12]

George Bubna wasn't given to communicating verbal affirmation to his son Paul. But he was dedicated to living out a purpose that was unmistakably clear, one that transferred rich values to his son. Paul's son Joel relates a story his father told in a message to the African Alliance leaders on his last trip overseas the week before he died in 1998. He

> talked about the fact that although he knew his father loved him, he rarely expressed those kinds of things. The day that grandpa [George] went into heart surgery, he called his sons to his side. He took their hands and said, "Today I am going to win. . . . If God gives me more time to serve Him here, I win! However, if I die, I will be with Him. And if I die, I want you to know that I will die a very rich man. I am leaving behind sons that love the Lord and who preach the gospel!"[13]

Those were the last words that George spoke to his sons. For Paul they were life-giving, for they encapsulated the purpose for which his dad lived, a purpose that amidst great odds was actualized in Paul's life beyond anything his father could fathom.

Simplicity of Life

A final factor that influenced young Paul Bubna toward the ministry was being nurtured in a climate with few distractions. Television did not intrude into family to steal precious time from relationships. Money did not wield the power it has today to seduce many young people to the pursuit of empty possessions or pleasures. The pressure of merely putting food on the table was so real that it was not uncommon for young people to quit school in order to find work to help support the family at home. Yet that environment assisted the Bubna family in nurturing a clear and singular purpose that took root in the fertile soil of Paul's heart very early on. He recounted this in a message on living simply:

> I grew up in a home where life was fairly simple. My parents were new believers. They were not highly educated, but that is not what I mean when I say "simple." By simple I mean uncomplicated. At the center of our personal lives, at the center of our family value system, things were clearly defined. My parents had made a commitment to one solitary Master. Pleasing Jesus Christ was the singular purpose

of their lives. That purpose for them involved the cause of world missions and the planting of the Church.[14]

Paul lived in a home where his parents' convictions reinforced that purpose. On one occasion that simple conviction resulted in his father being unemployed because he refused to violate the Lord's Day. On another it was Paul being unable to play on sports teams that practiced or played on Sunday. Continually their single-minded Great Commission lifestyle tested their faith in God to care for all their needs while they dedicated themselves to tithing all their resources to the Lord. God never let them down, nor did they ever go without the basics of life. The stream of godly servants—missionaries, soldiers, Bible school students who received a warm welcome and often a bed for the night in the Bubna home buttressed their understanding of what it means to be connected in the Body of Christ.

And regularly the family attended various gatherings held at their church, offering their energies wholeheartedly to the Lord and underscoring the centrality of the church in their lives. Someone once asked Paul if he felt deprived by all that. He answered, "Deprived, no. I was greatly enriched!" He added,

> I grew up in a home where life was simplified by clear choices. I wonder how many children growing up in Christian homes have the opportunity to see the commitments and purposes spelled out in clear choices. That was a gift for which I shall be eternally grateful.[15]

Notes

1. Paul F. Bubna, "Living under the Son" (sermon preached June 28, 1987, from Ecclesiastes 5:1-7).
2. Donald L. Bubna, *Building People* (Wheaton, IL: Tyndale House Publishers, 1978), pp. 47-8.
3. Ibid., p. 18.
4. Paul Bubna, "Self Image and Divine Revelation" (sermon preached April 9, 1989, from Ephesians 1:3-4).
5. Donald L. Bubna, *Encouraging People* (Wheaton, IL: Tyndale House Publishers, 1988), pp. 20-1.
6. Paul F. Bubna, "The Witness of God's Grace" (farewell message at Long Hill Chapel preached April 7, 1991, from Matthew 6:33).

7. Paul F. Bubna, "Holiness and Wholeness" (sermon preached September 20, 1987, from Proverbs 3:1-10).

8. Paul F. Bubna, "Acknowledge Him in All Your Ways" (sermon preached September 27, 1987, from Proverbs 23:1-12).

9. Paul F. Bubna, "In Christ We Can Know God" (sermon preached December 11, 1988, from Jeremiah 9:17-24).

10. Paul F. Bubna, "Every Member a Minister" (sermon preached January 3, 1988, from 2 Corinthians 1:1-11).

11. Paul F. Bubna, "Story of a Mentor and Protégé" (chapter from an unpublished manuscript, 1992).

12. Paul F. Bubna, "MBHO, or Management By Heavenly Objective" (sermon preached September 18, 1988, from Luke 12:35-48).

13. Joel Bubna, "And It All Happened in Africa," newsletter, Spring 1998.

14. Paul F. Bubna, "Living Simply in a Complex Age" (sermon preached July 31, 1988, from Philippians 3:7-14).

15. Ibid.

The
Personality and Passion
of Paul F. Bubna

Early in Paul's ministry he pastored a small congregation that could afford to pay him very little. He never demanded, or even requested, that they do more. He willingly accepted the work that was available. The area around Colony, Kansas, in the 1950s was known as the prairie hay capital of the world. Many of the local young men grew up hauling baled hay and took great pride in the number of bales they could "stick a hook in" in a day. There was an art to baling that made it look easy.

Paul decided to haul hay since he really needed the money—there could be no other reason for a St. Louis city kid to resort to buckin' bales. Paul was a competitive guy and figured he could get his hook in as many bales as anyone else. Besides, they paid by the bale and Paul had four mouths to feed. Unfortunately, however, he never mastered the art of lifting with the knee and tossing with the hands. He comically "wrestled" the hay, lifting each bale up in his arms and then trying desperately to get rid of it. It must have felt like wrapping your arms and legs around a potbellied stove and having someone throw dirt in your face!

But he never complained. Each day, within thirty minutes, he would be filthy dirty with his clothes full of hay and his light complexion a bright and sweaty beet red from the sheer effort of wrestling hay bales in 100-degree heat. He persevered and he gained our respect by his tenacious, uncomplaining attitude. Paul moved lots of bales, and even though it was not a pretty sight, I always suspected that the Lord noticed . . . we did.

—Dan Neuenswander,
brother-in-law

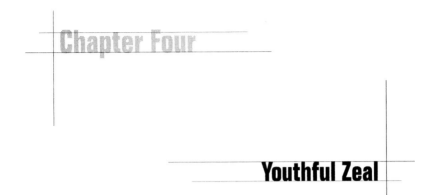

Chapter Four

Youthful Zeal

I will never forget what a remarkable revelation it was a number of years ago when it finally dawned on me that the crucial issue in my spiritual life was the giving of my mind to Christ. My idea had always been as long as I don't think hateful thoughts or lustful thoughts, what I do with my mind is my own business. It dawned on me one day that my mind was terribly flabby and totally undisciplined.[1]

—Paul F. Bubna

A Shepherd's Eye

Richard Harvey assumed the role of pastor of the St. Louis Alliance Church when Paul was still a young boy. Paul's pastor exuded a sincere and unclouded love for God and for the flock under his care. And he had an eye trained for young people with acumen and calling to ministry. At some point Harvey, whose spiritual instincts gave him an intuitive knack of picking out and motivating the next generation of spiritual leaders, set his sights on Paul and his godly childhood aspirations. Paul was a thoughtful and observant boy, and Harvey's preaching was uplifting. The chemistry of their friendship had all the markings of a divine appointment. About a year after Harvey's arrival,

Paul made a public profession of faith, and the tremor of God's call upon Paul Bubna to be a minister of the gospel settled into a purposeful conviction.

During the critical years of early adolescence, the tensions in his own home became more personally unsettling, and Paul, unconsciously perhaps, counterbalanced that by soaking up generous portions of affirmation and tranquility in the Harvey home. Because the Harveys also had three sons of their own, their door was always open to the Bubna boys.

Pastor Harvey's ministry kindled a flame in Paul's heart to pursue a calling to full-time Christian work, not because of Harvey's style or outward success, but because of his heart for God and spiritual integrity. Soon Paul was emboldened to look for opportunities to serve in the expanding youth program at the St. Louis Alliance Church. Don remembers the first time Paul spoke publicly. It was at an Alliance Youth Fellowship meeting. Paul was junior high age and addressed his peers on a subject that even most adults find hard to grasp—prayer. Don was struck by how much wisdom and discernment Paul had, even in early adolescence!

The Needle of Conscience

His promising gift of discernment was accompanied by the lively functioning of that "needle" in his heart that we call conscience. In a sermon about drawing near to God, Paul drew upon an illustration from that period in his life:

> I recall when I was a teenager and my parents left me to run the household for a while, and left me some money. I used some of it for my own entertainment. I felt justified in doing so, but still knew that I was violating the agreement. And my conscience bothered me. For several months this hindered my fellowship with my parents. One night as I lay down to sleep and sought to have fellowship with God, I knew I could no longer do so without making this right. And I slipped into my parents' room and confessed to them that I was wrong. To my amazement, they were not surprised. They knew that I had done it. They had forgiven

me. But my confession restored both my fellowship with them and with God.[2]

Paul related another story that illustrates his parents' role in keeping the "needle" of his conscience lubricated and working:

Engraved indelibly upon my mind is a moment in my teenage years. My parents were called away for a week because of an emergency in my father's family. They took my younger brother, but my older brother and I, though we were both teenagers, were for the first time charged with staying home alone and being responsible. The instructions were clear: Keep the house clean, do the dishes every day, be home on time in the evening and be responsible. We did fairly well, though we decided that because we had a lot of social life in the evening after we worked all day, that we would stack the dishes and do them all on one night.

The night before our parents were expected home, we began our tasks. We began to do the dishes, we set the furniture out so that we could clean the floors, and we straightened up the house so that things would be in order when our parents got home the next evening. The phone rang and friends invited us to come over and play Rook for the evening. It sounded like a great party was going on, and we decided that if we went and came home at a decent hour, we could still get all this done. And things would be fine when Mom and Dad got home the next evening. So we went.

We stayed longer than we planned. It was a dark moment when the phone rang at our friend's home. Our parents had come home a day early and found the furniture in disarray, the rugs rolled up, the sink full of dirty dishes. At first they thought the house had been robbed and we had been carried off. Then they began to call our friends and traced us to the party. It was a long ride home that evening. When we got there, the storm was worse than we expected.[3]

Youth Awakening

The St. Louis Alliance Church relocated to Lindell Avenue in 1943 and occupied what previously had been a lavish three-story mansion with a full basement and many rooms. The Bubna boys had never seen such a lovely place. Jean Helker, a friend and peer of the Bubna and Harvey boys, recalls,

> The parsonage/church was a mansion on a prestigious street in St. Louis. It had twenty-two rooms and at least eight or nine bathrooms! The first floor was designated for the church, the second assigned as a residence for the Harveys, while the third was reserved for visiting missionaries.

The Bubna boys had a standing invitation to visit the Harveys in the lovely mansion. They often did so, and on many occasions extended their stays to sleepovers.

The upheaval of the war years sowed seeds for a rich spiritual harvest and opened doors for evangelism, especially among young people. Richard Harvey perceived that the "fields were truly overripe for harvest" and seized that potentially fleeting opportunity. He aggressively targeted young people by combining the resources of his local church with the zeal of the budding Youth for Christ (YFC) movement that he helped to found. In this respect he possessed a rare sensitivity to God's perspective on a world beyond the walls of the local church and exhibited an extraordinary willingness to take risks. These were qualities that became deeply embedded in Paul's own frame of reference, and they deserve illustrating from Richard Harvey's account of the birth of Youth for Christ, as written in *Seventy Years of Miracles*.

> One day in the fall of 1943, I stood on the corner of Eighth and Olive Streets in downtown St. Louis. The high school nearby had just let out. As hundreds of young people crossed the street in front of me, God spoke to my heart: "I'm going to hold you accountable for these young people."
>
> I argued with God. "They won't come to my church, nor will they listen to my radio program."
>
> But from that moment, the responsibility for the souls of the youth of that city came down upon me. I cried out for them at night and was so troubled during the day that I could think of nothing but those young people on their way to hell.[4]

Training

In the youth programs that were fed by the YFC movement, Paul played an increasingly active role. The emphasis on outreach was challenging to an introverted kid like Paul Bubna, particularly in view of the weakness he felt about his own gifts in that area. By his own admission, "I did well as a student and was a leader in Youth for Christ and in our church youth group. I wanted to be a better witness at school but didn't really get a good hold on it." Nevertheless he persevered at it using methods that were comfortable to him, and that mostly meant simply plugging in and helping out.

Jean Helker reminisced about the old '31 Chevy that Paul would drive to pick up kids for young people's meetings on Sunday nights. "It was so old that everyone joked that it didn't have a working motor anymore, but that the Bubnas put their feet through the floorboards and pulled the car down the street." Jean's husband, Bob, was saved during that period, and he credits Paul for persistently bringing him to those meetings. After Paul had so faithfully made the trip in his old car to pick him up, Bob said, "I just didn't have the heart to turn him down!"

The success of the youth program in the St. Louis Alliance Church sent shoots of Christ's vine into surrounding churches. Friendships among Christian young people were robust in the secular public high school that Paul attended. That comradery gave Paul confidence to pursue public ministry, especially in music. He and Dave Harvey organized a trio that consisted of Dave Harvey, Paul Bubna and a guy named Jimmy Strassheim. They often performed at YFC meetings and at church. In the same vein, Paul became a church song leader, and this was when he developed into an accomplished saxophone player, performing both in high school and in church services. According to Dave Harvey, Paul had a "real touch for that instrument, and it just seemed to fit him."

Those postwar years were a period in Paul's life filled with a rich blend of strong pastoral leadership in youth evangelism, comradery with other youth who felt God's call into ministry and an unusual moving of God's Spirit among youth in the city of St. Louis. Altogether it wove a pattern displaying a purpose of God's design, and it strengthened Paul's resolve to pursue in it a bigger picture of the glory of God. However, God does not equate intentionality with preparedness. Soon the light of God's glory would reveal some serious flaws in the material and make Paul's human resolve and zealous effort seem mostly for naught.

Fault Lines

The intensity of Christian activity in Paul's teen years was not so much due to Paul's personality as it was to the belief that the busier Christians were, the more the Lord was pleased with them. Paul was naturally swept into that belief and seemed by all appearances to be very much at home with himself. But there were rumblings that began to expose fault lines in the landscape of his spiritual life. Over a period of time these unseemly lines became more conspicuous. The incongruities may have been mildly annoying to friends, but they were painfully disruptive in the spirit of this young man whose personality inclined him to be somber, reflective and painstakingly truthful with himself.

The outcome of his self-examination was something Paul disclosed to no one—not to his closest friends, not even to his own brother. Only his reflections later in life reveal the depth and pathos of his introspection. Paul experienced genuine anguish from such self-scrutiny. Dr. Paul Tournier once wrote about Paul:

> He indeed knows that he is always more or less on stage, that he strives to seem what he wants to seem in order to hide better what he is, but he does not know what he is hiding or what it is. He indeed knows that no matter how beautiful his life may be, it is only a fresco that he has painted on the door of his secret closet.[5]

Certainly that is what young Paul Bubna sensed about himself during his adolescent years.

Some of his inner tension arose from his parents' marriage. Even in the ideal Christian family an adolescent can feel awkward about his parents' habits and values; in less-than-ideal situations he can feel embarrassment; and, in truly debilitating surroundings, he can feel animosity or possibly contempt for his parents. It's safe to say that George and Georgia's spiritual transformations redeemed what otherwise would have become a contemptible situation for their sons. As it was, it was barely tolerable.

Paul's adolescence, besides involving the normal changes that propel a child into the adult world, awakened in him a clearer perception of his parents' problems. He wrote to his daughter Laurie regarding that time, "My dad's epilepsy started then, and their marriage was troubled. I didn't like being home. It was like a double life—fairly good in public, tough at home." It wasn't often that Paul became entangled in his parents' conflicts, but at a family reunion many years later Paul recounted one vexing experience that could be directly attributed to his parents' habitual noncommunication with each other.

When Paul was seventeen he was permitted to take the car once in a while (a '31 Chevy—as old as he was). He had arranged to go on a date with a girl who lived some distance from their home, so he asked and received permission from his father to borrow the car. But as he headed to the garage on his way out of the house, his father stopped him and told him that he couldn't drive it because the brakes were not in good working order and it might not be safe. When Paul argued that the announcement left him with no time to make alternate arrangements, his father said that he could take the bus. Since the bus would take longer for Paul to get home, his father waived the normal curfew of 11 p.m. and advised him to tell his mother of the new plan, which he did. At least he thought he did.

However, she was so absorbed in fretting over her discovery that her tropical fish were having babies that she did not hear when he told her about the revised plan. So Paul left the house with his mother still fussing over her tropical fish, and he took the bus to meet his date. As his father anticipated, Paul arrived home past the normal curfew at about 1:30 in the morning. When he walked through the door, he noticed his mother still frantic, but to his astonishment, she was crying on the phone with the police because she was sure something terrible had happened to Paul. Upon seeing him she erupted and announced that he was grounded for a month!

Meanwhile George was sitting on the couch, *right there* in the room, completely quiet. He had not explained what had happened, nor had he even attempted to calm her fears. He just sat there in silence watching the sky fall on his son's head. Finally, when Paul appealed his mother's judgment, George intervened and the sentence was withdrawn. But Paul was so perplexed that the next day he faced his dad and asked him why he didn't tell his mother that he would be late due to taking the bus. George shrugged and then answered with utter resignation, "It wouldn't have done any good. She wouldn't have heard me anyway."

This tension and its painful effects on the boys seemed only to increase when the Bubnas moved into the basement apartment of the church in 1947. That year the church had moved to south St. Louis and occupied what had once been an Odd Fellows temple, three stories high and very old. George Bubna agreed to become the sexton in exchange for free rent. There they no longer had a house of their own, which worsened the family dynamics. Don describes the apartment:

> While the basement apartment had four large rooms, it was mostly dark, *as was the experience of living there* as a family. Everything revolved around cleaning and maintaining this large former Masonic Temple. Dad still worked full-time at Penney's, and I worked full-time also for eight months before leaving for college.

Don lived there only a few months before leaving home for John Brown University. He never returned home again, even for a summer, though he would often visit. For Paul, the move required a transfer from Soldan High School to Roosevelt High, and also that he face the prospect of living there without the companionship of his older brother.

Paul and his younger brother, George, Jr., assumed major responsibility for helping their father clean the church, a tedious and never-ending job. Paul's father had a strict, no-nonsense approach to the custodial duties of the church. According to Paul's son Steve, "He told me once that if they failed to complete their part of the job, George would not say so the night before. But he would wake them up at 5 a.m. the next morning and supervise its completion." For Paul, the dismal atmosphere of living in that basement apartment, compounded with the difficulty of reconciling his parents' problems with his intellectual understanding of the Christian life, produced more shadows than light in the melancholic spirit of a young man earnestly seeking to gain momentum in his pursuit of God's calling.

Another unresolved tension had to do with Paul's lack of self-acceptance, which was tied to his relationship with his older brother Don. In high school and even more so in college they seemed to be close, but in fact they experienced none of the emotional closeness that many years later would come to define their relationship. Early in life Paul and Don had both committed their lives—with their parents' enthusiastic approval—to full-time Christian service. In their teen years neither wavered from that goal, but Paul began to experience a tension between his self-understanding and his call to serve God. This tension stemmed in part from unfavorable comparisons of Paul to Don that could be traced back directly to the strain in George and Georgia's relationship. Throughout those all-too-sensitive years Paul was picking up the message that his personality might not be entirely suitable to the calling. Paul shared the conclusion to which he was inevitably drawn:

> Being a classic introvert brought tensions early on. My father was extremely quiet and reserved. My sanguine mother found it difficult to cope with his lack of verbal expression and there was frequent conflict between them; it angered her that my father just didn't talk enough. Friends frequently commented that I was just like my father. So the message was clear: I was quiet and reserved and that was not a good way

to be. This became a tension in life as I began to get serious about preparing for pastoral ministry. My older brother Don is the extrovert. He developed his people skills early and was always at the center of the action. He preceded me to college and by the time I arrived there he was president of the student body. I loved him and admired him but I couldn't miss the comparison. The way he was, I reasoned, is what I needed to be if I was going to make it as a pastor.[6]

During Paul's first two years of college there were many occasions of comparison that cast him into the shadow of his brother. Don's talents were very evident on the college campus as he went about leading student organizations and finessing public relations for students and faculty alike. Don's competence early on won the praise of staff and administration, and after his sophomore year he was deservedly voted into "Who's Who in American Colleges and Universities." This was an award that Paul coveted but never achieved. Illness that led to an "incomplete" in his class work disqualified him from even being considered.

On another front, Don courted and eventually married a "campus queen." Paul courted and was "dumped" by a campus queen who told him that he didn't have a future! And then there was the college choir. In those days it was a big thing to be in the choir. Don became the student manager of the college choir, arranging their tours and also introducing broadcasts when performances were aired on the radio. Paul merely participated in the choir. And so on a daily basis he had opportunity to view his brother's talents being powerfully utilized, all the while tortured by the painful awareness that they were impossible for him to duplicate.

In Paul's mind Don resembled what *real* leadership was, and his success reminded Paul of just how different these two brothers were—and how *unsuitable* Paul was for the calling they both shared. So two things became obvious to him: Don fit the mold for ministry perfectly, and he, Paul, did not. He never talked about this with Don during that time. In fact, he didn't talk to anyone about it. He just thought about it. But he expressed his inner torment in other ways, namely through his growing cynicism and his volcanic eruptions of anger. In the summer of 1952, after his sophomore year, these fault lines in his character would bring him to the brink of an emotional collapse and push him over the edge, plummeting him into a spiritual crash from which only a merciful God could redeem him. That story deserves a chapter of its own.

Notes

1. Paul F. Bubna, "Laying Claim to the Land of Promise" (sermon preached July 21, 1985, from Joshua 18:1-10).
2. Paul F. Bubna, "Learning to Draw Near to God" (sermon preached January 6, 1985, from Leviticus 6:1-7).
3. Paul F. Bubna, "MBHO, or Management By Heavenly Objective" (sermon preached September 18, 1988, from Luke 12:35-48).
4. Richard Harvey, *Seventy Years of Miracles* (Camp Hill, PA: Christian Publications, Inc., 1977), p. 131.
5. Paul Tournier, *Reflections* (Philadelphia: Westminster Press, 1976), p. 9.
6. Paul F. Bubna, *Second Corinthians* in *The Deeper Life Pulpit Commentary* (Camp Hill, PA: Christian Publications, Inc., 1993), pp. 10-1.

The Personality and Passion of Paul F. Bubna

The year was 1995 and the place was Alliance Theological Seminary. I was a student and one morning found myself desperate to understand the inner turmoil that characterized my life over the past several months. I was weary, tired of trying to figure it out and exhausted trying to fight it. I picked up the phone, called Dr. Bubna's office and simply told him I needed to talk. Later that afternoon I met with him in his office, and he shared with me his personal crisis experience that had ushered him into the deeper sanctified life. He prayed with me and then handed me a pamphlet he had coauthored, titled "Christ and the Crisis." My soul was hungry.

Revelations began pouring in as I read the pamphlet along with God's Word. This is what I have written in the margin of the pamphlet:

> *If I am to be anything, above all holy, it must be Christ that does a work within me. It isn't how much I try; rather, it is allowing God to place His desires within me in order for Him to bring about change. My job is to walk in obedience and deny self . . . daily.*

The months of inner turmoil amounted to a calling by Christ for me to come and die. He desired to reign supreme . . . with no limits.

I praise my heavenly Father with every remembrance of Dr. Paul Bubna. The deep truth of "Christ in you, the hope of glory" (Colossians 1:27) began, for the first time, to take shape in my life. The result? Freedom!

—Pamela Reeder,
a student at ATS when Dr. Bubna was
president of the seminary, in a letter to
Don Bubna after Paul's death while
doing her home service in Butler, PA

Chapter Five

Crossing Over

Searching for truth appeals to one's sense of pride, but finding the truth demands submitting to it.[1]

—Paul F. Bubna

Perspective on Spiritual Crisis

In his booklet *Christ and the Crisis*, Bubna wrote,

> If we are to experience the fullness of the Spirit's life within us, there is something that needs to die. Our Lord's call to His disciples was a call to the cross. "If anyone would come after me, he must deny himself and take up his cross daily and follow me" (Luke 9:23). Bonhoeffer wrote from a Nazi prison camp where he later died, "When Christ calls a man, He bids him come and die."[2]

Paul's invitation to the cross and death to self did not begin in the safe confines of home and church. His inner life would remain a dangerous enigma to him until he reached his third year of college. He explained:

> I grew up in an Alliance church. Dr. Richard Harvey was my pastor. I must have heard hundreds of sermons on the deeper life during my growing up years. I went to the altar for prayer

at least once a month . . . but somehow by the time I went off to college I still had no grasp of what the issues were concerning the *inner life*. . . .

Self was enthroned in my heart and it was locked in mortal conflict with the Spirit who had come to indwell me. I was raised in a loving Christian family with strict disciplines and watchful parents, but the self-life in me had been socialized and civilized—and its ugly nature was unchanged. When I left the protective and restraining atmosphere of home and moved into the dormitory at college, I was confronted with an ugly inner reality that threatened to overwhelm my spiritual desires and enslave me. God was ready to take me deeper into His grace and power, but there was something in me that needed to die.[3]

This assessment sets the stage for our consideration of Paul's own crisis of faith, and particularly what that *something* was that *had to die* on one dark night of the soul in the summer of 1952.

Fault Lines Exposed

By the time Paul entered college in the fall of 1950, he knew that intellectually he could hold his own. He possessed analytical skills that enabled him to unravel complex problems and clarify the issues better than almost everyone around him. That ability would later become his "anointing" and a source of comfort and hope to many who came to him troubled and bewildered. But there was a period in his youth when Paul took more delight in using that ability to muddle and confuse than to clarify and encourage. Was he exploring his own gifts? Was he searching for intellectual answers? Sadly, that wasn't the case—by his own admission. His personal judgment regarding that period tells us that it is more likely that he was hiding the brewing turmoil in his inner life by competing intellectually in offensive maneuvers of attack and destroy.

For the first couple of years of college he routinely indulged his sharp intellect in a game of spiritual "upmanship" by analyzing what made others "tick," then shredding them by exposing inconsistencies in their beliefs. Years later he observed that

> . . . one of the most subtle forms of self-deceit is that of equating our ability to see the faults of others with being virtuous. . . . I remember with no minor embarrassment the expertise I had cultivated as a college freshmen to be a critic. My roommate in the dorm was a brilliant and witty young man and we led each other into a pattern of dissecting the lives of people to uncover their inconsistencies and poke holes in their theological systems. We were good at it. Both of us had grown up with a fairly good background in Scripture (knowing just about enough to make us dangerous) and among our peers we were a force to be reckoned with. Our arrogant and offensive style no doubt wounded a lot of people. The real danger, though, was what it was doing to us. It seemed so natural to believe that individuals who were so keen at perceiving the faults, sins, and phoniness of others must surely be on the right path. It was a painful day when God knocked me down and turned the searchlight of revelation upon my heart to uncover the emptiness, dryness and dishonesty that characterized my inner life.[4]

Coinciding with the pattern of cynicism was a personality flaw that might best be described as "intentional indifference." That means that he simply ignored common rules of etiquette. He seemed to care little about his slovenly appearance, floppy shirttails, slouching posture and his abrasive and crude manners. This might have been his nonconformist tendency showing through, but more likely it was another manifestation of his cynicism and, by inference, his unhappiness with himself.

His sharp tongue and crude manners were still only a passive announcement that all was not well in his inner life. Had he only those faults to mend, he might have gotten by with a few adjustments to his image to accommodate the social veneer of Christian culture. However, the fumes and gases seeping through the fault lines in his spiritual life signaled that this was not a problem that would be easily healed. In fact, they signaled imminent and recurring emotional volcanic eruptions he could barely conceal—his anger.

Flashpoint

Strangely, Paul's anger did not submit to his introverted personality. When he was upset, which was often, he did not seethe in quiet anger but gave vent to an explosive temper. Later in his career Paul routinely led a workshop with Don at the internship training seminars for aspiring pastors. One topic of the workshop was anger. Paul would always begin his session with these words: "I am a specialist in this field. I have had to deal with this probably more than anyone I know."

When he moved onto the college campus he not only left the protective environment of his parents' home, but he also entered the uniquely competitive environs of a Christian college. There is a *spiritual charge* on a Christian college campus that can magnify the significance of every decision a young person makes and every impression he develops about himself. Amidst this charge Paul perceived two categories of Christians: the visionaries who were called to lead, and the rank and file who were consigned to be drones and worker bees. His introversion and lack of charisma forced him to believe he was in the latter category. He wasn't flamboyant and he wasn't doing much leading. The prospect of not having the capacity to lead threatened to shatter every dream Paul had entertained about serving Christ. It certainly did not jibe with a conviction bred in him by his mother's oft-prayed affirmation that her sons would do *great* things for God![5]

He Could Really Fight

Paul's expectations of himself—especially in the light of his brother's dynamism on the college campus—seemed to exacerbate the problem of his anger. Dave Harvey detected in Paul a serious struggle with his own identity. "Don was a flashy leader at John Brown University. Paul had a quiet reserve. The tensions [produced by this] brought out the fighter in Paul. And Paul was a fighter; he could really fight."

Throughout high school and during his first two years at John Brown University, Paul found it increasingly difficult to control his anger. He was careful not to allow his anger to be displayed in unacceptable places, such as in the classroom, at church or in other social settings. However, in sports a different rule applied. Paul loved team sports and was active in intramural baseball and basketball throughout high school and college. In whatever sport he played, he quickly gained a reputation for two things: his determination to win and his hot temper if he didn't! Sports competition formed a controlled environment where, in Paul's mind, uncontrolled anger could be legitimately vented. And vent he did. Dave Harvey recalled, "He could get very angry on the basketball court. That's where he really showed his temper."

Consequently, his brother Don, while not very athletic, always tried to join Paul's team in order to discreetly patrol his brother and tone down his anger if possible. Then if all else failed, in the event of an eruption, he did damage control! Don recalled an incident that would long ago have been forgotten but for its bearing on the real problem.

Don and Paul were having breakfast one morning in the dining hall. A tall, blond fellow, who happened to be very good at sports, walked by their table. His team had handily beaten Paul's team the day before, and there was still a bitter taste in Paul's mouth. Sensing Paul's glum expression, Don attempted to give perspective by mentioning something about the man's dedication to Christ. Paul caustically retorted, "What that guy needs is a good, sanctified punch in the mouth!" Don was startled because Paul's skepticism seemed to be directed at the young man's profession of faith. From then on he began surmising that perhaps this was symptomatic of an emptiness that Paul was experiencing in his own inner life.

Of course, the flash point was not always confined to the basketball court or the baseball diamond. On one occasion at a high school football game a young man taunted Paul in the parking lot—and soon paid dearly for his misguided remarks. That might be excused, for naturally at sporting events scuffles occur. But a "black tie" reception is another matter. Yes, the scene of the most notorious display of Paul's anger off the court was the beautifully arrayed reception hall at his brother's wedding on May 19, 1952.

The backdrop for this incident was a rivalry that had evolved on the campus of John Brown University (JBU) between the "engineers" (those enrolled in the technical school) and the "preachers" (those preparing for Christian ministry). Over a period of time it became an intense and even bitter rivalry that aroused passions that might be comparable to the attitudes of competing fraternities at a secular university. To make matters worse, the engineers audaciously sought to impose their domination over the campus by sponsoring a special "engineers' day" on March 17 every year. The rule was that for six weeks before that day, the male students "must withhold the razor or pay the price for failing to sport a beard."[6] Then on that day the engineers would receive the tribute of the entire school. Those who did not acquiesce or offer such tribute were forcibly placed "in stocks" in a contraption rigged in the middle of the campus to humiliate anyone who didn't bow to Caesar! Needless to say, Don and Paul ignored the custom and behaved in a manner that displayed their contempt for the arrogance of the engineers. Their defiance was not overlooked, nor was it forgotten.

On graduation day in the spring of 1952, laudatory speeches were given and diplomas respectably conferred. Don enthusiastically celebrated in cap and gown with his degree in hand. As a capstone to his college career, he and his fiancée, Dee, had arranged to be married that evening in town so that many of their friends could attend. Hence, family and friends gathered in the First Baptist Church for a beautiful wedding, and subsequent to that joined them for an elegant wedding reception held in the basement of the church. Even the illustrious president of John Brown University and other college dignitaries attended the event.

The engineers, meanwhile, knew that time was running out to settle their score with the Bubna brothers. They hastily decided to kidnap Don from his own wedding reception! The plan was to ambush him as he left the church for his honeymoon, take him down to the community festival being held in the center of town and deposit him in a special device called the "bear cage," which could be exited only through a hole at the bottom that opened into a cattle feeding trough—in the middle of the town's main street. The effect would be total humiliation and they would have the last laugh!

But things went awry. The reception never seemed to end, and the engineers became impatient waiting in the bushes outside the building. Finally, out of desperation, they stormed the building and crashed the party.

There are various accounts of what happened next, but by all accounts it fulfilled every bride's worst nightmare! The engineers charged through the doors, grabbed Don and tried to pull him out of the room. He smashed a plate over the head of the first guy, then clung to the chair next to him—along with the dress of the bridesmaid sitting there, ripping her pristine gown.

A struggle ensued that quickly turned into all-out war. Dishes were shattered, chairs were thrown and blood was shed. And not surprisingly, striking back in full force in the middle of the fray was Don's younger brother Paul. With knuckles bared and fists flying he unleashed a volley of punches that appeared to be reserved for just such a brawl! He and some friends even sealed the doors so the engineers could not escape! How the brawl ended is not clear. But the president of the college was aghast at the scene being played out in front of him—and on graduation day, when his heart typically gushed with pride in his JBU students. He finally stopped the chaos, restored order and took down the names of every one of the intruders. They were summoned the next day to his office and threatened with expulsion from college. Dee's father mercifully intervened to prevent their dismissal. Instead they agreed to apologize in front of the church at prayer meeting and pay for all the broken dishes! Dr. Brown escorted Don and Dee to the edge of town to prevent any further attacks.

Paul must have been quite a sight after the brawl, since his normally untidy appearance was now complemented by torn clothes and bleeding fists. Surely he was conspicuous to one young girl who had attended the wedding with her older sister. Paul had not met that girl, but earlier in the day he had sighted her as she entered the auditorium where the choir was rehearsing before the graduation ceremony. She so intrigued him that he said to the guy next to him, "Someday I am going to marry that girl." That statement was not made on a whim. He knew that her older sister was Helen Neuenswander, who was the campus nurse and a close friend of Dee, Don's bride. Paul greatly respected and admired Helen for her wisdom, elegance and poise. He was eager to meet this younger sister, whose beautiful appearance revealed those same virtues.

Helen, however, was not exactly a fan of Paul. She saw his cynicism, caustic attitude and crude manners. In her mind there were many unanswered questions about him. She probably did not share any of these with her younger sister Jeanie, but the debacle at the wedding reception must have burned the image of this preacher-fighter indelibly in Jeanie's memory. Most likely she made a note to herself to beware of someone with such a volatile temper!

The Crash of '52

By now Paul had completed his sophomore year at John Brown University. After his brother's wedding he chose to go to southern California to work for the summer at the Southern California Military Academy. There were good reasons for this. Don and Dee were moving to southern California to work with the John Brown University schools in that region. Since Don and Paul had been roommates during Paul's second year of college and Don had worked at the military academy the previous three summers, it was convenient for Paul to go there. Besides, the long-distance separation from college and parents offered him a much-needed change of scenery. Coincidentally, before he left he had picked up a book by A.W. Tozer entitled

Pathways to Power. The ideas he pondered in that book planted a time bomb in Bubna's self-life, and it began ticking.

Events over the next few months provided ample evidence that *something* was wreaking havoc with his inner life. Night after night, in the silence of the barracks, he brooded over his unhappiness. Little did he understand the nature of the assault that was ripping his soul apart. He did not talk about it because of his quiet and reserved disposition. If others *had* pressed him to reveal the nature of his quandary, he might have only said that some things were out of whack in his life and he needed some time to think things through. But how does one think his way through a crisis of faith?

Every part of his life revealed dissonance and failure. A conflict had been fomenting in his spirit for many months about his anger. His cynicism was one way that he released some of the anger, but he knew that his words were hurtful to people he had no right to judge. On many occasions when he disagreed with an umpire's call in a softball game or was beaten in a basketball game, his scathing words would hurt even those who were close to him. Academically, he regretted his slipping grades; also, he failed to meet deadlines for a column he wrote for the campus newspaper. Socially he had just endured a "failed love relationship" that left him feeling inadequate. Taken altogether, this had the effect of producing profound "self-doubt about the ministry."[7]

His introspection bordered on unhealthy self-absorption. Unable to think his way out of this one, he tottered on the brink of a nervous breakdown, while a deepening gloom was immobilizing his ability to keep such an emotional collapse at bay. He saw himself descending down a spiraling staircase into a black hole. He compensated by clutching at verses from the Bible such as Isaiah 26:3, "Thou wilt keep him in perfect peace, whose mind is stayed on thee" (KJV). He prodded himself by repeating that promise over and over, by singing hymns and by thinking positive thoughts. But peace did not come.

Paul's crisis did not go unnoticed. Don and Paul had been improving their relationship during the course of the year they roomed together at JBU. And Don and Dee's marriage in May of 1952 did not inhibit Don from pursuing a purposeful and growing closeness to Paul. In fact, his new bride valued the relationship as much as her young husband, and they frequently set out a plate for Paul at meal times. They enjoyed attending church together and frequently planned social outings. A favorite pastime was driving to Knotts Berry Farm, where they enjoyed good food and relaxing entertainment.

"I Can't Talk. . . . I Can't Talk"

This amusement park became the backdrop for a disturbing experience one afternoon that summer. They had been walking in the hot sun for some time and were rather weary. However, that does not account for what happened next. As they walked, Paul unexpectedly turned to Don and gasped, "Don, I can't talk. . . . I can't talk. . . . I can't . . ." He began to stutter and his words became incomprehensible. Don and Dee barely concealed their horror at what was happening. They tried to calm Paul down and immediately took him to a first-aid station where they could get him out of the sun. He regained some composure and calmed down. They drove him back to the school where he was staying, while Don pondered what to do next.

In his words, "Paul was reacting psychologically and emotionally to something that I did not understand." Don was only twenty-three years old at the time, so the pastoral skills he had developed were not sufficient to address the depression that was darkening Paul's spirit. "We had no other family there. I felt he needed to talk to someone about what was going on inside." Don contacted a college friend who had herself received "professional" help. She referred him to a physician in the Wiltshire district of Los Angeles. They made the appointment and Don drove Paul there. For two hours Paul was diagnosed regarding the vague and intangible emotional crisis that had erupted in a stifling (though brief) speech impediment. Don wasn't sure whether the visit would be helpful, but filling the role of the older brother he dutifully paid the bill since Paul had no money.

By the time the doctor saw him, Paul had recovered enough to smooth out the external façade. But the doctor, a Christian, sensed the need to engage him in a candid conversation about God and grace. Afterward Paul said little about the visit, but did remark to Don that there was something "odd" about the man. Don recalls, "He [Paul] told me about this 'pipe-smoking Christian' (something negative to us with our fundamental, legalistic background) who talked about 'sin' and 'grace' and 'forgiveness' and 'who we are,' which made a lot of sense to him." That picture of a Christian whose demeanor was very unorthodox but who talked sincerely about the heart of the gospel seemed to open a crack in Paul's darkened world. A sliver of light broke through. Paul's mind began to process fertile, new ideas instead of the chaff he had been churning to no avail for months on end. He left that appointment feeling vaguely hopeful, though not at all healed. His was a wound that could not be easily healed.

Paul's anguish was about rights. He knew he was challenging the prerogative of God to demand the absolute right to reign in his life. A person may feel justified to challenge an authority he does not trust. And Paul had been harboring a growing distrust of a God who would call him into the ministry but not fit him properly into the mold of a minister. His perplexity about his own identity was manifested in sarcasm, lack of discipline and explosive anger. He just could not comprehend that *his own* personality and *his own* gifts were uniquely suited for the work God would give *him* to do. Nor could he believe that his unique, God-tailored service would fully glorify God as well as fully satisfy his own yearning for happiness.

He had carefully constructed a "spiritually correct"—and altogether rigid—framework for serving God and living the Christian life, which depended in large measure on his own inherent ability. Actually, it was someone else's ability—that he didn't possess but perceived was indispensable—that he needed to squeeze into the less-than-ideal mold of his own unsuitable temperament. And then with that patchwork of mismatched material he would, by sheer human willpower, serve God—even if it killed him!

Such a framework credits God with little and requires from the subject a superhuman effort to achieve success. Paul later reflected, "That summer as I sought to stay my mind on God, I found that there was something I was unwilling to be—I was unwilling to be a *failure*. I was willing to be a preacher, or whatever God wanted, but I *had to be a success!*"[8] Hardly a joyful undertaking, especially when these were his terms for playing the game. Hence, what ensued was a life-or-death struggle in an emotional and spiritual crisis that threatened to shatter his religious paradigm, sending it crashing in upon itself and all that was left of his self-life. Later he made this observation, undoubtedly drawing from that personal experience:

> It may not occur to most people that indecision and complexity of life are spiritual problems at their roots. It has been said that all of our problems are ultimately theological problems. We have been made in the image of God and made to know Him and to enjoy Him and glory in Him. When we allow rivals to gain our heart's affection so that we are torn between two things, we experience inner conflict and our external life becomes very complex.[9]

A.B. Simpson could have been describing Paul when he chronicled the Christian's dying-to-self in this manner:

> Let no man think this death of self is easily secured. It is the most difficult part of a satisfactory religious experience. Self dies hard. Crucifixion means rough handling, humiliation hard to endure; it means agony and solitude, the assaults of devils and men; it means the piercing spike and the darkening heavens; but, thank God, it also means resurrection, triumph and God's glory. *Except a kernel of wheat fall into the ground and die, it abides alone; but if it dies, it brings forth much fruit.*[10]

The Fight of His Life

The struggle became unbearably intense one hot summer night. It was the middle of the night, and sleep had eluded him. He paced up and down, back and forth along the corridors of the barracks, perspiring from terrifying anxiety. The darkness outside only intensified the darkness of his soul. His thoughts were not hopeful, but tortured and desperate. How could someone so zealous to serve God feel so utterly abandoned? Hadn't God set him apart from early childhood for the gospel ministry? Hadn't he affirmed by his own conversion and diligence this divine appointment? Hadn't he driven himself nearly to exhaustion in the belief that God wanted him to be the best for His glory? And wasn't *success* what God wanted? Why then was there only pain and failure and confusion to show for all his efforts? From here we will allow Bubna's own words to finish the story:

> I shall never forget the day that I crossed over. It was after my second year of college. I was going through a severe time of anxiety and depression, not understanding what it was all about. My inner life was torn by drivenness, an overly competitive need to win, an unnatural desire to excel, to be somebody, to prove who I was. All my efforts were ending in frustration and my inner world was in disorder and pain. I was working that summer as a counselor at a military academy with the summer camp program. The days were filled with inner turmoil, the nights with little rest.
>
> One night as I paced the floor, I finally threw myself at the edge of the bed and wept my heart out to God. In those moments, I crossed over. I told God, "I am done, and the past is cut off. I don't have to win any more, I don't have to be a pastor or anything else, and I don't have to be anybody. All I long for is to be your person, whatever that may mean." There, in that military barracks in Long Beach, California, peace began to come to my inner life. It was not a fully completed and accomplished fact at that point, but the door was open for God to begin to bring order to my inner life.[11]

In his commentary on Second Corinthians he added:

> I didn't feel there was much to give but what I had was totally yielded to God as best I knew how. Abandonment to God is painful but life changing. I returned [that fall] to college a new person. I didn't understand then that God ministers through our weakness, but somehow I *began to believe* that God could use *an introvert like me.*[12]

Notes

1. Paul F. Bubna, *Second Corinthians* in *The Deeper Life Pulpit Commentary* (Camp Hill, PA: Christian Publications, Inc., 1993), p. 56.
2. Paul F. Bubna, *Christ and the Crisis* (Camp Hill, PA: Christian Publications, Inc., 1995), p. 10.
3. Ibid.
4. Bubna, *Second Corinthians,* pp. 180-1.
5. Taken from Paul's testimony at his mother's funeral, March 1977.
6. *JBU Pioneer* yearbook, 1952.
7. Paul F. Bubna, "Finding Rest . . . Crossing Over" (sermon preached July 7, 1985, from Joshua 1:1-9).
8. Paul F. Bubna, "The Peace of God" (sermon preached June 27, 1972, at the Indonesian Pastors' Conference).
9. Paul F. Bubna, "The Double-Minded Man" (sermon preached July 24, 1983, from James 1:2-18).
10. *The Christian & Missionary Alliance* magazine, editorial, 7/28/1900, excerpt in "Communicate" vol. 10, No. 2, Nov. 2000.
11. Bubna, "Finding Rest . . . Crossing Over."
12. Bubna, *Second Corinthians,* pp. 10-1.

The Personality and Passion
of Paul F. Bubna

The amount of actual time I spent with Paul one-on-one was not very much. Although Paul was my first pastor and a close friend, most of the mentoring I received from him came from afar. I watched him intently. I watched as he preached each Sunday and pastored people. I watched him handle difficult people and lead his church staff. I watched him parent his kids and love his wife.

Paul had an impact on hundreds of church leaders by the way he lived everyday life. He was the same person in the pulpit as he was in the board meeting, on the tennis court or at the dinner table. And I watched, intently, because I knew he walked very closely with the Lord.

As I went off to seminary and then eventually into the pastorate, Paul was there to encourage me and always had words of wisdom and hope. He used to tell me, "Dennis, make sure you always leave people with hope." He certainly modeled that. On one occasion, I called to tell him that the youth pastor on our staff had just been arrested for child abuse, and I will never forget his immediate response to that: "Dennis, if you and your church respond with complete honesty and integrity in this situation, this will not hurt your church long-term." What a word of hope and encouragement in a difficult time! It came true. When the TV microphones were in front of me and the reporters were inquiring about the incident, I did not spit out the usual flippant, pat response: "He's a sinner like everybody else. God forgave him and so do we." Instead, I described how our congregation really was trying to cope with such shocking news. I told them, "We're in shock right now as a church. We have a range of emotions going through this place right now. We're angry. We're sad. We feel betrayed. We feel badly for the victims and the pastor and his own family. Basically we're hanging onto our God and our faith in Him—that He somehow will bring us through this." We didn't lose a single family over the incident, and our solid reputation in the community stayed intact.

Today, I'm the senior pastor of a church of over 2,000, and there is no question that most of what I am as a pastor, preacher and church leader I learned from Paul Bubna.

Just before Paul went to be with the Lord, I asked him to do me a favor. I had named my second son after him, and I asked Paul if he could write my son a letter that I would then place in his hand at his high school graduation ceremony. That is such an important crossroad in a person's life, and I wanted my mentor to speak to my son about life in general and give him some parting wisdom. This letter is still sealed and waiting in my desk for the high school graduation ceremony of Paul Episcopo. When my son opens that letter, the advice will be twelve years old, but I'm sure it will be filled with encouragement, wisdom, humor, a godly challenge and lots and lots of hope!

—Rev. Dennis Episcopo,
senior pastor, Appleton Alliance Church

Chapter Six

Becoming a Kingdom Person

I hold as a primary purpose in my life to be a worshiper of God. By that I am not merely talking about attending worship services regularly. No, my goal is to live my life so that moment by moment I learn to keep God always in view; to live so that all the facets of my life, all of its events, are arranged so God is in view; to structure the values of my life so God is primary and central.[1]

—Paul F. Bubna

God's Person

Paul Bubna returned home at the end of that summer a changed man. He had been freed from the entanglement of self-centered aspirations, so much so that he even considered not returning to college. The college campus had been the epicenter of the spiritual earthquake that precipitated his crisis, and he had no intention of being drawn back into that pain and confusion. More important, he simply wanted to be "God's person." There was a mysterious yearning in his surrender to being "Your person, whatever that may mean." One thing was sure—now he could become that person, with or without John Brown University.

As summer wound down, however, his emotional strength returned. Deciding to make another go at it, he returned for his junior and senior years. Dave Harvey testifies that a transformation had indeed occurred in Paul's life. "I don't know when it happened or how, but only that by the time he had graduated from JBU, Paul was a different man. He had met the Lord in a new way." Paul's descriptions of that period of renewal are scarcely documented. But his attentiveness to God's grace in his life was such that he attributed some very significant external blessings to God's faithfulness. "As I surrendered to be a 'kingdom person' God began to add some of the other things beyond what I could have dreamed."[2] Those "other things" started with a person. That fall semester Jeanie Neuenswander enrolled at JBU.

A Great Complement

Jeanie was born on November 6, 1932, to Irvin and Bethany Neuenswander. Her father was raised in an austere Swiss-German home in Kansas, the oldest of five children. His Mennonite forefathers had suffered persecution in Switzerland before emigrating to America, and those hardships had imparted a serious view of life to the Neuenswander stock.

Irvin became a Christian at the age of fifteen during Methodist revival meetings, and, not looking back, he fixed his sights on one goal in life: "to do God's will." God anointed Irvin's evangelistic zeal, and within three years of his conversion his parents and siblings followed him in professing faith in Christ. At the age of seventeen he enrolled in Oklahoma Methodist University and then straightway entered the ministry as an evangelist and preacher with a United Methodist church. In his early ministry he conducted meetings throughout the Oklahoma territories, where he traveled as a singing evangelist. One of those stops was an out-of-the-way Oklahoma country schoolhouse where he met a young teacher, Bethany Emma Swartz, with whom he quickly fell in love, courted and married in the space of a year. That was 1918. He was twenty-one and she was twenty.

Ministry in the territories in those postwar years was a tenuous venture for a man who needed to provide financially for his own home. So Irvin, applying his varied skills, toiled as a cook in a work camp, operated a produce house and did other odd jobs, all the while continuing his preaching. Over the years Irvin and Bethany were fruitful domestically; the family grew to encompass twelve children. Jeanie was number eight in line. Her brother wrote of their parents, "They had literally sacrificed their whole lives for a house full of kids." They welcomed God's sovereign call for them to be parents and devoted their energies to spiritually shaping the lives of their children. Irvin administered order in the family by exercising constant and consistent discipline. He

> never let any of the eleven of us take control of the "no" word. [However] having done the best he knew, he committed us and our futures to the God he served. . . . He believed that if he could commit his own life to God, he could also commit his children's lives to Him.[3]

Jeanie undoubtedly inherited her father's forceful and disciplined temperament. But she possessed another quality that rightly belonged to her mother Bethany: an attitude of self-denial or setting aside her own private advantage in order to serve the interests of her husband and children. That virtue wasn't Bethany's natural disposition, because in the early years of her marriage she passionately contended for her rights, and communication with Irvin was often a contest of wills. But a painful crisis changed that. Nancy, their ninth child (and next in line after Jeanie), died when she was ten months old. That personal crisis shattered Bethany's confidence in her ability to chart the course for her life or manage her children's welfare. Many years later, just prior to her own passing at the age of seventy-nine, one of her sons asked her to explain what happened to bring such a change in her life. He had particularly noted the change since as a mischievous son he had often been the focal point of his mother's wrath. He relates,

> She laid aside her crochet hook and responded . . . "It happened when you were about ten years old and your sister

Nancy Ann died. Her death came at probably the most difficult time in my life. And with her death I began to die. It was
like God was completely taking me apart piece by piece and
laying me out on the table. And as He put me back together it
was like I had learned what was really important in life. And I
have never been the same since."[4]

Her transformation affected the tone of her marriage and
served as a pattern for the journey to faith of more than one of
her children. One of her sons said that the new commitment that
he had observed overtaking her life caused him nine years later to
realize a new and compelling drive to search out and relate to the
same sovereign Lordship of God that she had found.

The memories that were made in the Neuenswander home
were, by and large, happy ones. Jeanie's older brother Paul
reminisces that when they were young,

> particularly on a rainy or stormy night, we would sit on the
> floor around Dad and he would read or recite poetry from
> Edgar A. Guest or Henry Wadsworth Longfellow. Or at
> times he would play his guitar and sing and yodel the old
> Swiss ballads that he had learned from his Uncle Albert or
> Grandfather Gfeller who played several string instruments.
> Those were especially joyous and unforgettable times.[5]

All that family closeness was anchored to a spiritual purpose in
life that was sealed by Irvin's conversion to Christ and a consistent working out of that faith throughout his long life. A testimony to these happy memories is the fact that the Neuenswander
family reunion, held every two years, still summons all nine sur-
viving siblings, their children and grandchildren to Colony, Kansas, where Irvin and Bethany lived longer than any other place in
their lives, and where they were buried.

Jeanie was positioned near the end of that long line of voices in
the Neuenswander choir—all clamoring for a personal audition
with Mom and Dad. But Jeanie possessed a positive and confident outlook on life and disciplined herself to be free from her
mother's apron strings in a family where any indulging of that
sort might be hoped for only on one's birthday. Her daughter

Laurie reports that her mother enjoyed her childhood. Rather than getting lost in the crowd, she wholesomely asserted herself and didn't hesitate to "take charge" if the situation warranted it. She hadn't read the research telling her how a number-eight child is supposed to behave. Not that it would have mattered. The force of her personality swept her to the front and left a few of her sisters wondering if maybe she wasn't just a little too bossy.

Laurie recalls that when Jeanie was laid to rest in Colony, Kansas, in 1994, her aunts shared feelings about what a "take charge" person Jeanie had been, drawing from childhood memories that had been frozen in time for fifty years. What they saw then had been only a diamond in the rough. But what Laurie saw revealed a fluid and evolving transformation through the course of a lifetime. Through many years that followed her departure from Kansas, Jeanie would reflect an interior image of God's grace that would match her external refinement and assertive zeal. Testimony to the fruit of that maturity is that later in life she would serve as mentor to many women, playing a significant role in their spiritual formation.

Too Good to Be True

Jeanie enrolled in John Brown University in the fall of 1952, following in the train of her sister Helen whose character had so impressed Paul. Paul was quick to note that another blossom from the same flower had sprouted on campus. Without a moment's hesitation he asked Jeanie to the "Welcome Banquet," an event that ceremoniously adopted incoming freshmen and new students to the JBU family. Unattached upperclassmen customarily seized the occasion to scope out prospects for matrimony from the untapped ranks of freshman girls. No doubt they were terrified by the thought of leaving that paradise for the windy plains of Kansas or Arkansas without a mate. Paul had the enviable task of performing as the Welcome Banquet emcee, which would plant him in the spotlight all evening. He was confident that Jeanie would agree to go with him.

But Jeanie had other thoughts. She was wary of this young man who had turned his brother's wedding reception into a shootout at the "OK Corral." So she rebuffed his invitation by saying she wanted to go to the banquet with her roommate and girlfriends. Not to be a solo act, Paul took another girl named Rita—who later would become a close friend of Jeanie. But the whole evening Paul could not take his eyes off the strikingly pretty young woman sitting across the room with her friends. She may have turned him down for one date, but the school year lasted nine months! And besides, he had the distinct impression that she liked his jokes during the banquet! Shortly after that, he asked her to a town football game. This time she consented.

Paul's heart leaped in excitement. Unlike previous quests, which had ended in futility and self-doubt, this relationship contained a responsiveness that had the markings of God's anointing. Forty-two years later, after Jeanie died, Paul affectionately reminisced in a note to his daughter on the beginnings of their relationship that seemed so saturated with God's grace: "I was struck by her beauty. She carried herself with confidence. Her eyes were captivating and her smile lit up my world. From day one I could tell that she believed in me. It seemed too good to be true. *How could someone so beautiful accept me as I was?*"[6] They quickly became a couple, and the relationship grew.

That winter Paul and Jeanie joined a college choir tour that sang in St. Louis. They stayed at Paul's parents' home. Late one night as they sat on the couch watching TV, Paul gathered up the courage to ask Jeanie if she would marry him. Without hesitation and to his delight, she gave an enthusiastic response. He hadn't purchased a ring yet, but he did so in April and gave it to her at Lake Weldington, near Siloam Springs, Arkansas.

Jeanie decided to leave JBU at the end of her freshman year and go to live with her sister Emily in Kansas City. There she worked to save money and prepare for her wedding. That fall of 1953 Paul's thoughts were already far beyond campus life. He habitually drove up to Kansas City every weekend to see Jeanie. While they had originally set a wedding date for after his graduation, the stress of the long-distance relationship prompted a friend with some common sense to suggest to Paul that he simply go ahead and get married! They moved the wedding date forward to December 18.

They asked Jeanie's father to marry them, but he became ill just as the family was leaving to attend the wedding. There was some lighthearted suspicion that the college scene intimidated him. So Pastor Harvey was recruited at the last minute to perform the wedding at the Presbyterian Church in Siloam Springs, Arkansas. Paul and Jeanie picked up their wedding license early that morning. After that, Paul dutifully attended morning classes and then swiftly changed into a black tuxedo for the wedding. Jeanie borrowed a wedding dress from a college friend, while she made all the bridesmaids' dresses herself. Paul's two brothers, Don and George, Jr., along with Dave Harvey, stood up for him. Jeanie's sister Ruth and two of Jeanie's college friends were her attendants. The day was a whirlwind of activity, but rather than causing stress and exhaustion, it produced the sensation in Paul of being swept forward by a draft of God's mercy.

President Brown of JBU gave them (as was customary for him to do) a $100 certificate to honeymoon at the Majestic Hotel in Hot Springs, Arkansas. The honeymoon suite was $12 per night (plus an extra 50 cents for the radio!). The total bill for their stay there was $65. The newlyweds did not know they could charge their meals on their bill and that it would be covered by the $100 certificate, so with the frugality that would be a lifelong trait, they ate out in cheap restaurants. That did not diminish the start or the enduring quality of their marriage. Paul reflected with exuberance almost out of character, "We had a great time. Did we ever!"

They returned to JBU for Paul's last semester of college, where they lived in the married student apartments. They purchased a bed for fifty cents and collected old furnishings, and Jeanie proceeded to turn the dark and dingy place into a beautiful home. Paul washed pots and pans in the school cafeteria on weeknights, worked part-time at a shoe store in town and began preaching on Sundays. Jeanie worked as assistant cook in the college cafeteria, and together they turned their poverty into a benediction of God's favor. Later, Paul (again out of character) exclaimed his joy in tracking God's provision: "We did fine money-wise. And were we ever happy. Wow!"

Living the Calling Before the "Call"

Paul graduated in the spring of 1954 from John Brown University. He immediately began his search for a pastorate in The Christian and Missionary Alliance. Though he had been preaching at Alliance mission points in Oklahoma, there were no Alliance churches open for them to serve in that area. So they moved back to Kansas to be near Jeanie's family. There Paul began pursuing credentials to serve in the Western District of the Alliance.

Most pastors begin their preparation for ordination while simultaneously serving in a local church. The academic preparation for ordination is a rigorous, though somewhat pedantic exercise and takes about two years of study under close supervision of an older pastor. The motivation to press on often comes from an open door to ministry and encouragement from a local body of believers. Paul had neither. What he did have was a conviction that he wanted to serve in the Alliance. Hence, he was interviewed and afterward licensed on September 20, 1954. He was ordained two years later (right on schedule) on September 27, 1956.

A curious thing about Paul's ordination was that he had not received a call to an Alliance church *before* he was licensed, nor during the two years *after* his licensing, *nor for two more years after his ordination* in 1956! But that did not prevent the Licensing and Ordaining Committee from offering him full credentials as a minister accredited by The Christian and Missionary Alliance. The Licensing and Ordination Committee for the Western District included such luminaries as Dr. A.W. Tozer, Rev. Ord Morrow and Rev. Richard Harvey. A.W. Tozer was present for Paul's oral examination, the last step in his ordination proceedings. He made this notation in the margin of his notes: "This boy is on his way to a useful ministry. He is teachable and humble." Paul may not have seen this note for a long time, but if he had, he probably would have asked, "If God can use me, then why hasn't He started yet?"

In retrospect, he was being taught the nature of *the calling* to ministry. That calling to be God's minister did not need the validation of an Alliance church or even the Alliance itself to give it authenticity. Church councils and denominational timetables did not bind God. At that time and at subsequent junctures in Paul's ministry, he was conscious of the essence of his call, and that "it is required that those who have been given a trust must prove faithful" (1 Corinthians 4:2).

Thus Paul's first placement was in a field—literally on a farm in Kansas. Paul hauled hay and dug ditches for his brother-in-law during the summer of 1954 and for several summers after that. According to Jeanie's brother Dan, Paul was indeed a pitiful sight "haying," because "he never really mastered the art of handling bales of hay." But he worked very hard at it and was determined to provide for his new family.

It didn't take long for that family to begin taking shape. Jeanie became pregnant with their first child, Laurie, in January of 1954, while Paul was a senior at John Brown University. Two more children—Steve and Tim—arrived by the summer of 1957, a full year before Paul received his first call to become the full-time pastor of an Alliance church. For Paul and Jeanie, family was God's design for community and the natural means for propagating the gospel, so the modern notion of *waiting* to have children until they could afford them was ludicrous. Years later, when their own children married and were attending Bible school or seminary—or waiting to go overseas as missionaries—Paul shared his conviction whenever his counsel was sought on the matter: "Children are a blessing from the Lord and shouldn't be considered as a financial expense. The question of whether to have children should never be a question of whether they can be afforded. God will provide!"

And for the Bubnas, God did provide—but not without struggle. When their daughter Laurie was only nine months old, she was diagnosed with a congenital hip dislocation. The defect required surgery and an extended stay in a disabled children's hospital in Kansas City. Don remembers visiting with Paul there on one occasion. He related that Laurie "was tied down in her bed with her feet elevated. When we had to leave, she began to cry. Paul had to rush out of the room as he immediately also began to cry. It was a very emotional time." Laurie remained in a body cast—from her upper torso down to her knees—for the better part of a year!

One discovers between the moment of surrender to God and the actual commencement of service just what has been offered up in that surrender. It is one thing to offer our skills and spiritual gifts, quite another to embrace the "*all things* that God is working together for *our personal good*" (see Romans 8:28) during those in-between times when we are not playing to an audience. Paul never discarded or trivialized the "day of small things" (Zechariah 4:10). He was always alert to the connections God was making between his seemingly insignificant responses to situations and God's larger calling upon his life. This equipped him with a realism that helped him forge links between God's will and things that "just happen"—without resorting to empty clichés. Perhaps that is why his church audiences were so attracted to his message.

One humorous incident occurred that summer that illustrates the honesty with which he approached life and his own wrestling with God's promises (taken from a sermon much later in his life):

> There are times in our lives when the promises of God seem almost ludicrous. One that I remember took place during our first year of marriage. I graduated from college and we were looking for a place to pastor. It was a couple of months before we were called to a small parish in Kansas. It was hot; the July humidity was heavy. We were trying to move into a parsonage that was run down and needed a lot of cleaning.
>
> We had dressed up and gone to town to buy some bare sticks of furniture. I had borrowed a trailer from a farmer and we had loaded it with some secondhand furniture and we were making our way back to the town where we were going to live. The mattress that was stacked on top of the other things fell off while we were going down the highway and rolled into a ditch. When we noticed it was gone, we stopped and tried to turn around. Being raised in the city, I was not very adept at driving with a trailer. Trying to turn it

around on a highway, I jackknifed it and part of the trailer came up over the rear bumper of the car and the bolt that was there hung up on the bumper. Worse than that, the corner of it came up against the trunk of the car and dented it—just a little bit but we had just had the car painted. The only way to get the trailer off the back bumper was to jack it up, and the trailer was up against the trunk of the car so I couldn't get the trunk open to get the jack out.

It was about 105 degrees. Somewhere down the highway our mattress was lying in a ditch, maybe in water, we didn't know. On the busy highway we were now stuck with the trailer jackknifed. It was not a very happy situation. Our Lord's statement that "He came that we might have life and have it more abundantly" did not seem to immediately apply to my situation. I am not saying it didn't apply, I am only saying it didn't seem like it applied. We can all identify with circumstances in our lives where God's promise of abundant living seems far from us.[7]

Guarding the Good Deposit

Early in the fall of 1954 Paul was invited by the district superintendent of the United Methodist Church (UMC) to serve two United Methodist churches located in Kincaid and Lone Elm. The background of that relationship was peculiar. At that time Paul's father-in-law, Irvin Neuenswander, was the pastor of a United Methodist church in Colony, Kansas, though he was not a member of the denominational conference. He had his reasons for that.

A number of years prior to this he had left the United Methodist denomination because of their active pursuit of liberal causes and seeming disinterest in the basics of the gospel and new birth. In fact, the district superintendent of the UMC once paid Neuenswander a visit in his home to reprimand him because he had publicly chided the UMC for being a front for liberal political causes. The superintendent pointed his finger at Irvin and said, "If Christ had been alive today, He would have likely been a communist."

And on the question of Christ's deity he assumed a more super-
cilious posture: "Irvin, we all know that people who know how
to read and write know that virgins don't have babies." When
Irvin plaintively asked him if he would be willing to say these
things to the congregation publicly, he retorted, "Of course not.
These are simple, rural people and they would be upset by it. But
you, Irvin, ought to know better!" Irvin did, and shortly after, he
left the UMC, with many in the UMC church in Colony following him to help found an independent community church.

Irvin's ties with the UMC, while opening a door for Paul to
preach, also presented him with a conundrum. He was fresh out
of John Brown University and fairly naïve about denominational
politics. He was even more naïve about the doctrinal compro-
mises that had been worming into and corrupting mainstream
Protestant churches over the past fifty years. But his calling was
from God, and God did not need denominational endorsement
in order for His gospel to be effectually proclaimed. So in the fall
of 1954 the Bubnas moved into the parsonage at Kincaid and
Paul proceeded to preach the gospel faithfully—and to attentive
ears. Showing surprising openness to the gospel, individuals (and
not a few longstanding church members) in both churches came
to faith in Christ and were subsequently baptized.

At first, the UMC district superintendent tried to persuade Paul
to take steps to join ranks with the United Methodist denomination. Paul hesitated. Consequently, over the course of the next
two years he became the target of a different kind of persuasion—
a growing pressure from the denominational office to tone down
his evangelistic preaching. Perhaps Pastor Neuenswander's reputation had tainted any chance of Paul's being fully trusted in that
district of the UMC. So when he would not be bound by the offer
of their fraternity, they sought to use other means to coerce him
into compromising his faith. Bubna stood his ground and rebutted the charges with a clear pronouncement of the authority of
God's Word. The following reference to that period shows his
comprehension of the God of the Bible and additionally a profound insight into human nature:

Our first pastorate was a small country church that was part of one of the mainline denominations. In one of the first copies of the denominational magazine I received I was disheartened to read a quote by a famous bishop who was preaching at a seminary and said that the God of the Old Testament was a big bully. He went on to say to the theological students that he for one could not believe and serve the kind of God depicted in the Old Testament. This is typical of those who somehow cannot put together the goodness of God with God's holiness and wrath. He was not very clear about just what kind of God he could serve, nor did it seem to occur to him that his statements were not so much a commentary about God, as about himself.[8]

While his defense of the gospel would forever endear him to his father-in-law, the pressure from the political wing of the denomination eventually led to Paul's own forced resignation from both churches after two years of faithful preaching. The new believers in those congregations were simply not rooted enough in their faith, nor strong enough politically, to prevent the higher echelon from having its way. Looking back, Paul understood that God had ordained that experience. It was a time when Paul engaged his mind in doctrinal issues that were profoundly basic; his conviction about the authority of the Bible was both tested and galvanized into a reverential respect for the inerrant Scriptures that would thereafter hold sway over his preaching.

Ministry Without Money

In 1956, after his resignation from the UMC, Paul again hauled hay during the summer months and in the fall began attending evening classes in Emporia, Kansas, about a seventy-mile drive from Colony. He realized that he needed a fallback option and so pursued a certification to teach in public school. Meanwhile he had held revival meetings in an independent church in Geneva (a town that no longer exists), and they invited him to return to preach every week. That little church offered nothing that would attract an ambitious young couple to lead it. Charlie Compton, a nephew of Paul's and a teenager in the church, described it this way:

Geneva Church was started as a small group in a tiny unin-
corporated town. They met in a four-room grade school in
the town of Geneva that had only about a dozen homes and
no stores or gas stations. It was almost impossible to find
pastors for two reasons: The church was so small, and the
church was poor—not only poor; it was also made up of
people who were very frugal (the nice word for it).

It is doubtful that money was ever discussed when they negoti-
ated the terms of his service, but they paid him $20 a month. The
Bubnas, while not *wanting* an open door to serve there, accepted
it as from the Lord. And the congregation of Geneva Church
opened their hearts to Paul and Jeanie. A number of individuals
professed faith in Christ and were baptized in a creek near the
school.

Geneva Church became an unexpected delight, and the Bubnas
savored their ministry there, especially among the teens. Besides
Bible studies, they organized youth outings, cookouts, swimming
parties and ball games—often paying the tab themselves. They
cultivated a ministry of "presence" among the teens. And the joy
Paul felt in ministry to them was contagious. Compton reflects,

> My impression of Paul Bubna's ministry at Geneva, Kansas,
> is best described in C.S. Lewis' book, *Surprised by Joy*, be-
> cause he gave me the first real example of a Christian who
> was a *truly joyous* Christian. I had always before known a
> more harsh, legalistic Christianity.

Another boy in that small youth group would someday become a missionary with New Tribes Missions. Don Curtis was
deeply impacted by Paul's presence. He wrote,

> He always accepted me and I could trust him in every way.
> I would go over to his house and sit and visit for hours.
> These were always times of talking about the Lord and life
> problems and questions. One time I was leading a Twenty
> Questions game with the youth and the category was "peo-
> ple." No one guessed mine so I had to tell who the person
> was. I said "Legion." Everyone started laughing, and I was
> embarrassed, as you could well imagine. He made a big im-

pression as he covered for me and eased my embarrassment. I was at the age then that my ego was fragile, and I
really appreciated his concern.

Of the six boys who participated in Paul's weekly Bible study,
two of them were directly influenced to pursue full-time Christian ministry.

The fruitful work in that tiny hamlet promised neither the security of fitting remuneration nor of a parsonage, which was
compounded by the arrival of their first two children, Laurie and
Steve. Pastoral ministry invariably teaches a pastor and his wife
lessons about money and dependence. And contrary to success in
the world, with its corresponding financial reward, faithfulness to
God can sometimes inversely affect one's financial well-being, a
case in point being Paul's forced departure from the UMC. What
would later become a hallmark of Paul's ministry— his commitment to the issue of God's ownership and faithfulness to care for
the pastor—actually stemmed from their financial insecurity in
those early days.

God used an insurance salesman to bring home to Paul the
point that the ministry (apart from God's faithfulness) could
never bestow financial security. He related:

> I remember in one of our first pastorates having an insurance
> salesman make a call at our home. We had two children then.
> I was pastoring a small country church, digging ditches and
> hauling hay on the side to keep food on the table. His sales
> pitch that I needed a financial plan was a solid one. It was
> simply hard to visualize it when our income didn't quite
> cover the essentials. His clincher was the fact that by the time
> our children would be college age, a college education would
> cost as much as $4,000. It turned out that by the time our
> kids got ready for college, it was more like $30,000 or
> $40,000, not $4,000.[9]

Years later he reflected on convictions about money that were
galvanized in those early days:

> When I started in the pastoral ministry I began to meet other
> pastors who were somewhat bitter. They complained about
> how small their salaries were, the burden it was to their fam-

ily. Some of them had children and wives who were complaining and bitter at the church for lack of adequate salaries. As I thought that over, I realized I had to find a way to prevent bitterness from souring my ministry. Jeanie and I talked about it, and prayed, and decided to make a covenant with God that we would *not work for the church at all*. In response to God's call, we would serve God's people, but we would trust God for the supply of our needs.

I believe that is a solid principle in the Scripture. In fact, I am willing to say that God does *not want us to work for money*. He wants us to work for His Glory. I think this applies whether you are a pastor, or whether you are a teacher, or a doctor, or a lawyer, or an executive. There is a liberty when we are working for the glory of God, and trusting Him to provide for our needs according to His measure.

So, through these thirty-four years of ministry, we determined never to complain about our wages or ever to ask for a raise. We believed that if we served joyously as unto God, He would abundantly supply for us. There have been times in our past when we felt that the local church did not give us an adequate salary for our family. Yet we never felt cheated because it was our conviction that we were serving God and that He was going to care for us, and He did! Abundantly![10]

That abundance was manifested in the summer of 1956 when God also blessed them with improved housing. They were invited to housesit for a year in a spacious home in Colony!

Pursuing the Call

In the fall of 1957 Paul accepted a job teaching high school English and coaching basketball in the Colony, Kansas, public schools. English had been his second major at JBU, and he thoroughly enjoyed the chance to teach his favorite subject. The job also provided much-needed financial security for Paul and Jeanie, and now also Laurie (three), Steve (two) and Tim (who had arrived in July). Perhaps more important, it permitted them to continue serving the Geneva church, which offered very little compensation. At the end of the year Paul was actively recruited to stay on the school faculty, but he remained convinced that God had called him to the ministry. So, without ever looking back, he left the security of a teaching position to pursue the call of God.

The administration of the school was so impressed with his demeanor, however, that they asked him to deliver the baccalaureate address to the graduating class of 1958. We must remember that only six years prior to this Paul's life was driven by a compulsion to win at any cost. Paul had once gloated, "I never lost a game that was played fairly!" That attitude could have been readily communicated in the execution of his coaching duties at Colony Public High School. But God was molding a kingdom person who was cultivating in his inner being radically different kingdom values. And what had once been only lip service was being transformed into a passionate yearning for God's glory.

He exhorted the student body on that spring day:

> We need young men and women who are God-conscious! If we are conscious of God's claim on our life, we will have purpose. . . . You say you believe in God with your lips, but do you say it by the way you live? Do you live like there is no God, no moral law, no claim upon your life? "You are not your own, for you were bought with a price; therefore, glorify God in your body, and in your spirit, which are God's" [see 1 Corinthians 6:19-20].[11]

He closed his address by quoting from a poem by an author—himself?—he did not name. It described his journey. Part of it goes like this:

> With station and rank and wealth for [my] goal,
> Much thought for body but none for the soul,
> I had entered to *win* this life's mad race—
> When I met my Master face-to-face.
>
> I had built my castles and reared them high,
> Till their towers had pierced the blue of the sky;
> I had sworn to rule with an iron mace—
> When I met my Master face-to-face.
>
> I met Him and knew Him and blushed to see,
> That His eyes full of sorrow were fixed on me;

And I faltered and fell at His feet that day
While my castles vanished and melted away.

Melted and vanished and in their place
I saw naught else but my Master's face;
And I cried aloud: "Oh, make me meet
To follow the marks of Thy wounded feet."

My thought is now for the souls of men;
I have lost my life to find it again;
Ever since that day in a quiet place
I met my Master face-to-face.[12]

Notes

1. Paul F. Bubna, "The Worshiping Heart" (sermon preached November 13, 1988, from Habakkuk 3:1-7, 16-19).
2. Paul F. Bubna, "The Witness of God's Grace" (sermon preached April 7, 1991).
3. Paul Neuenswander, biographical paper on Irvin Neuenswander, p. 7.
4. Ibid., p. 5.
5. Ibid., p. 6.
6. From memories Paul shared with his daughter Laurie.
7. Paul F. Bubna, "Finding Rest . . . Crossing Over" (sermon preached July 7, 1985, from Joshua 1:1-9).
8. Paul F. Bubna, "God and the City" (sermon preached June 12, 1988, from Nahum 1:1-8).
9. Paul F. Bubna, "The Poverty of Possessions" (sermon preached September 24, 1988, from Luke 12:13-21).
10. Paul F. Bubna, "Acknowledge Him in All Your Ways" (sermon preached September 27, 1987, from Proverbs 23:1-12).
11. Paul F. Bubna, baccalaureate address notes, May 18, 1958, Colony [Kansas] Public High School.
12. Ibid.

The Personality and Passion
of Paul F. Bubna

The Church in the '60s was going through a suspicious phase. Denominational leadership telegraphed distrust to seminarians. Not so for Pastor Bubna. From the get-go he was supportive and helpful. He had an eye on the future, and the encouragement and development of pastors for the next generation was a high priority for him.

When Pastor was in Vietnam we shared messages a few times via cassette tapes. He was always sharing what he was preaching about and what he was learning. On one occasion I remember hearing a tank or half-track rumbling down the street outside his office.

Prior to his leaving Northbrook for Vietnam I had a sense that the morning worship services were becoming a bit of heaven on earth. The times of worship and of preaching were just glorious. When he announced that he was leaving for Vietnam, I was not surprised or disappointed. I felt that he had led me in rich experiences and that in the kind providence of God someone else would fill that role.

Words that describe him: enabler *(in the good sense),* facilitator, encourager—*a come-walk-with-me person. The last thing he ever said to me was at the Council prior to his death. He was in the back of the auditorium and we were both headed to the platform during a business session. He said, "Arthur, come walk with me." I did.*

—H. Arthur Dunn,
intern to Pastor Bubna, Alliance pastor

Chapter Seven

Becoming a Kingdom Pastor

Sometimes I imagine God speaking to me. He says, "Paul, why are you so busy?"

"Lord, there is so much to do. Do you realize all the responsibility?"

And I hear the Lord replying with a bit of an edge on His voice, but with loving patience, "Paul, do you work for Me?"

"Why, yes, Lord, I want to be your servant."

"Paul, remember, if you are committed to My purposes, then success is assured. Paul, I am in control, I am the owner and I am at rest. My heart delights when I see that you are able to stop and rest. In doing so, I know that you trust Me."[1]

—Paul F. Bubna

Open Door in Boone

On a hot, muggy Kansas summer day in 1958, Paul was called in from hauling hay by the Western District superintendent of The Christian and Missionary Alliance, Rev. C.R. Thomas. Although he had Alliance credentials, Bubna had sojourned for four years outside the Alliance fold. That was about to change. Cornerstone Alliance Church in Boone, Iowa, was open, and they were formally extending a call to Paul Bubna to be their pastor.

Boone, a town of 10,000 residents—many of them farmers—
was located at a busy rail junction where train whistles and the
roar of three or four locomotives rumbling through town could
be heard at any time. The Alliance church there had been started
in the '30s through a tent crusade and had moved from tent meetings into a more permanent Quonset hut structure off of Main
Street. In that dingy building were three rooms—two at the front
and one at the back, partitioned off from the sanctuary. There
was no basement, and coal stoves heated the church. Nearly
thirty years had come and gone since those tent meetings had
stirred revival, and in 1958 there remained only the smoldering
embers of revival fire at Cornerstone Church. The Quonset hut,
for want of vision, had become a permanent worship center, and
the church was beginning to reflect its dark and dreary ambience.

Paul was the first young pastor the church had ever called, and
he may have felt some ambivalence about his prospects in Boone.
Yet it was an open door, so he and Jeanie took that as God's cue
to enter. Their first priority was to revitalize the atmosphere in
worship. The church welcomed the exuberance of their young
pastor and his wife. One member, Alida Cronk, remembers those
days. "We had wonderful services. In the morning there would be
vocal solos, and in the evening we had an orchestra with trom-
bones, horns, violin, cello, clarinet, piano and even a saw." It
should be noted that the church also heard the distinct sound of
Paul's saxophone, which, in his early days of ministry, he played
during worship services. Cronk continues, "There would be ten
to twenty people, or as many as could fit on the platform, who
would play in this orchestra. We became popular and were even
invited to play for evening meetings and youth groups all across
town."

Changing the atmosphere in a church is not nearly as challenging as changing an attitude that was debilitating the membership. Bubna quickly discerned that he was preaching to a
congregation that was struggling to believe that God would, or
even could, bestow on them a brighter future than the one reflected by their dismal surroundings. So he patiently nurtured

their faith and finally led them to believe that God would supply the money needed to build a new facility. True to His
promise, God raised up both the vision and the resources for a
brand-new building. In 1959 volunteers from the church do-
nated their labor and worked at night under spotlights to build
an attractive sanctuary that seated 250 people, along with a
Sunday school unit in the basement. They held their first service in the new facility on February 21, 1960, and a memorable
dedication service was held on April 3. In his annual report for
that year, Paul reflected, "As we look over the blessings of the
past year, we must lift our hearts to God in thanks!"

His emphasis on financial stewardship, which would become a
perennially anointed pulpit series, was in large measure shaped
during those days at Cornerstone Church in Boone, Iowa. A personal experience also sharpened his conviction about money and
God's faithfulness. Their son Joel was born in June 1960 with a
visual defect—he was cross-eyed. So Paul and Jeanie began saving
up for the surgery that would be necessary to correct the problem. The week before the surgery, Herb and Jessie Nehlson, missionaries to Burkina Faso, spoke at their church and made known
a financial need for the *exact amount* that the Bubnas had saved
up for Joel's surgery—already scheduled for the very next day.
When they went home that Sunday night, Paul and Jeanie spoke
about the need, and before going to sleep they both felt led by
God to give the money to the Nehlsons. The next morning when
they awakened their son for the surgery, to their amazement his
eyes were healed!

The next year Paul resigned from Cornerstone Church to accept a call to Northbrook Church in Minneapolis. However, he
would carry stories of faith from Boone, Iowa, that would lay
the groundwork for his emerging "life message." In his farewell
letter he expressed heartfelt appreciation to the Boone church
for the opportunity they gave him to minister among them: "I
came to you young and inexperienced, and I thank God for a
group of men who have shown kindness, patience and under-

standing, and who have faithfully stood by their pastor in love and prayer. May God bless you for it."[2]

Seven years of ministry in rural Kansas and Iowa had quickened and confirmed Paul Bubna's call to pastoral work. The uncomplicated longings, dreams and heartaches of country people motivated him to step outside of his introverted disposition and freely feel and express the God-instilled emotions of love and affection for those in his charge. Those years were redemptive for Paul in addressing his motivation and heart-surrender to God's sovereign call, and in yielding to God's timing in circumstances related to that call. Leaving the flock under his care was accompanied by a sincere reluctance to part from those for whom he felt such deep affection and to whom he felt deeply indebted. Yet God was kindling in him a vision for ministry in a much larger world, one that lay beyond the hamlets of rural life, past the harvest fields surrounding Geneva and Boone. That vision was to preach the big picture of God's redeeming purpose in the world and to pastor a congregation toward building a "Great Commission" church. And Paul was primed to explore that vision and develop the gifts that would be essential to pursuing his call in a larger arena.

This Man God Has Called to Be Our Pastor

Steve Armstrong remembers the first time he saw Paul Bubna. Paul and Jeanie had brought their four children—Laurie (six), Stephen (five), Timothy (four) and Joel (one)—to Northbrook with them to candidate for the position of pastor at the Northbrook Alliance Church in Minneapolis. Steve's father, Harlan Armstrong, was the chairman of the elders and search committee. While only in his early thirties, Harlan was a deeply sensitive and spiritual man. He invited the Bubnas to stay with them during the interviewing process. Steve Armstrong recalls, "I don't remember the other candidates, though I am sure there were others. It's just that Paul clicked immediately with my dad, and my sister and I clicked with their two oldest kids. Dad went

back to the board and told them that *this is the person* that God
has called to be our pastor and they needn't look any further."

One peculiar image that Steve retained from that visit is how
very heavy Paul Bubna was at that time. "That didn't seem to be
an issue for anybody. Yet I remember that Paul, even then, when
he first came to the church, would often sit slouched with his
arms over the armrests of the chair. He was a big guy, slouchy,
and he [projected] the picture of an undisciplined [lifestyle]. But
again that didn't matter to the leaders of the church. They called
him and he accepted the call." It was a call that neither they nor
he would ever regret.

Paul made an immediate—and lasting—impression on the
Northbrook congregation that overshadowed any concerns
about his appearance. That impression was that he possessed
complete and unswerving devotion to God and to serving Him,
and it was reinforced over the course of the next fifteen years by
the consistency of his devotion, particularly with respect to his
own wife and family. One congregant, Bob Jueckstock, noted,
"His character was above reproach and nowhere was the demon-
stration of that character more evident than in the lives of his children. God's love was deeply instilled in the lives of the Bubna
children by a dad and mom who walked with the Lord." The effect was a huge impression made on the church by the *entire*
Bubna family. This is best communicated by vignettes and humorous stories that illustrate the dynamics of Bubna family life in
the context of their ministry in the Northbrook church.

Marriage in the Manse

Jeanie was always elegantly dressed and comported herself
with a demeanor that reflected her devotion to Paul and his love
for her. Her support of Paul ensued with her actively promoting
his goals and vision for the church. She was socially polished, and
when it was possible, she accompanied him when he made contacts with new attendees. When Kerm and Merilyn Klefsaas visited the church in 1963, Jeanie was at Paul's side when he called
on them in their home the next evening. It was a good thing. In

Kerm's words, "If Jeanie hadn't come with him, nothing would have been said all night." As it turned out, Paul actually fell asleep during the visit, while his industrious wife briskly proceeded to promote her husband's ministry, answer questions about the church and become better acquainted with the talented couple (who eventually became leaders in the church). They finally decided that, since Paul had found such a comfortable chair and was exhausted from his work of the previous forty-eight hours, they would not rouse him until it was time to leave!

Paul often tended to be quiet and reserved in social settings. Of course, he was always willing to listen and demonstrated a heartfelt gift of mercy when engaged in one-on-one counseling. But when thrust into social chitchat, he was a paragon of silence. He once said, "I am a quiet person. I am able to have long conversations with people without saying a word." And he admitted, "That bothers some people. It bothers my wife when we've had a long conversation and I haven't said anything."[3] Nevertheless, Jeanie complemented Paul's social reticence with her own assertiveness, which she readily employed on her husband's behalf and in ministry of her own initiative. Their relationship bears a closer look.

Paul and Jeanie's marriage could be described as a process of melding contrasting personalities into an instrument of service that was more effective than either could render independently. Their relationship would become an integral component to Paul's success as a leader. No one disputes that. Paul could not have made the impact that he did without Jeanie. And Jeanie's goal in life was to amplify her husband's gifts as a pastor and leader. How their relationship worked is not entirely clear. Paul was introverted and quiet; Jeanie was self-assured and outspoken. Early on in their marriage those differences posed a real threat to their happiness. Paul related that initially Jeanie could take his silence for only so long, and "then she'd say, 'Talk to me.' And when she said, 'Talk to me,' I *didn't* want to talk to her. I didn't want to talk to her *at all* when she was saying, 'You've got to talk to me.' " At another time he added, "[Jeanie] was very quick to make judgments. . . . She was quick to make judgments on my decisions and ways of doing things. I was tempted to withdraw."[4]

Antidotes for this potential malady in their marriage were quite simple. Common courtesies and routine affirmation formed the mortar in their relationship. Their communication included a constant flow of compliments—"I love you," "You look beautiful, dear," "That was an excellent sermon, honey." And it wasn't a façade. As son Tim commented, "I would have to agree: *She* always was [beautiful], and *they* always were [excellent sermons]!" They openly displayed physical affection for each other with hugs, hand-holding and physical touch. Paul was chivalrous to a fault: He always opened the car door for her whether they were getting in or out of the car. In fact, he opened *any* door they walked through together. He always helped her put her coat on, pulled out her chair and simply treated her with gentlemanly courtesy.

While routine courtesies formed the mortar, other antidotal measures evolved out of deep spiritual convictions and shaped the very foundation of their marriage. Jeanie was indeed a very strong person, but she *wanted* Paul to lead. And Paul wanted to lead. This was a biblical conviction. And, as Paul related to Laurie, "I am glad she was unhappy when I didn't lead. This helped us identify what was happening and deal with it. She became a great cheerleader." Likewise, Paul's esteem for Jeanie enabled her to pursue her calling with vigor. The following is a conviction he applied to both home and church:

> A loving husband should be sensitive to all that God has built into his wife. He will understand her gifts and abilities. Some of them are greater than his. He sees what God has built into her life. And as a faithful steward and responsible leader, he does whatever he has to do to help her grow into all that God wants her to be. . . . It seems to me that the same picture is to be lived out on the stage of the world by the Church. . . . I am deeply concerned about this. I am concerned because very often the message that women get in the church is that they are devalued, that men do not recognize their gifts, tend not to listen to what they say, do not

view them as people to whom God is speaking. It is very easy for the same twisted, degrading spirit that has characterized the fallen human race to take up residence in the Church.[5]

Very Much in Love

Laurie observes that she, her siblings and the entire church family perceived that Paul and Jeanie were

> very much in love. They adored each other and were very happy together, which made our home a wonderful and secure place to be. . . . Their relationship was very special—a precious gift to each of us children, and our children after us.

An anniversary letter to Paul from Jeanie (after he'd lost over fifty pounds subsequent to his heart incident in 1968) allows us to peer inside their marital disciplines and witness a deepening affection for each other:

> My Dearest Paul—I've not only grown used to your ways, but I've grown to love and admire everything about you. You are a very handsome man and I'm proud of that and appreciate very much the way you keep yourself—but that is only your outward shell. When I look inside, I see the fruits of the Spirit operative in your life and I thank God for the depth of your inner life. If God should choose to take one of us home early, it seems my mind can't even comprehend life apart from you. But somehow I feel after twenty-one beautiful years of loving and growing together, we've only begun, and that in the years ahead, God has yet greater plans for our life together.[6]

Jeanie's admiration for her husband parallels a reciprocal permission and freedom Paul gave to his wife to journey beside him and even make spiritual judgments about him. There may not have been another man alive who could have brooked a woman of Jeanie's talents and remained undeterred by her assertiveness and energy. However, to Paul, her disposition and loyalty remarkably complemented his reflective and sometimes introverted disposition. Paul may have been inclined to remain in the shadows had it not been for Jeanie's absolute certainty that his abilities demanded a wider ministry. There were moments, no doubt, when her critical assessments (especially of other people) challenged his nonchalance, and her relentless prompting disturbed his passivity. But the divinely imprinted synergy in their marriage stirred deep gratitude in Paul for Jeanie's role in his life. Once, when preaching about worship, he drew this analogy from his marriage:

> Remembering has a lot to do with worship. Maybe you haven't thought about that. The same is true in human relationships. If I should totally lose my memory of all past happenings, I would not be able to love my wife as I do. My worship of her—and I am using the word "worship" in the proper sense—is inseparable from the memories that are part of our lives together. When I sit down to write a love note and begin to recount those memories, I am flooded with gratitude and affection and worship and find that the momentary irritations that are part of living together seem inconsequential when seen in the light of those memories.[7]

It Takes a Family

Paul's brother Don remembers Paul and Jeanie always wanting a large family. By the time they were called to the Northbrook neighborhood of Minneapolis, God had already blessed them with four children. But Laurie wasn't content with three brothers as her only siblings, so she prayed desperately for a little sister. God answered that prayer by adding Gracie to their family quiver in April 1965. Thus it was Northbrook that became a fixture of "home" for the Bubnas.

Laurie, the oldest of the Bubna children, remembers the house on Camden Court in Brooklyn Center, Minneapolis, as "home." It was just a few doors down from the church, and since there were no relatives (on either side of the family) nearby, the church became like an extended family—"and a very happy place to be." Laurie recalls,

It was a growing church during those years, so the folks were definitely busy in ministry. But I never remember feeling that the ministry consumed them. Mom and Dad were careful to protect time for the family. They set aside one regular night each week that was just for our family. After dinner we would head down to the bottom level [of the parsonage] for a fun evening together. During the colder months Dad would always build a fire; sometimes we would roast marshmallows; it seems like we always had popcorn (and fudge when we were lucky!). We didn't have TV during the years we were growing up, so family night usually centered around board games like Monopoly, Life, Password and so on.

Another prominent memory about those years was of Mom's hospitality. It seems like we were always having company, and I loved that. Mom would get up early Sunday morning to put a nice dinner in the oven and would often invite someone at the morning service to join us for a meal. We met more interesting people that way! Then almost every Sunday evening after the service we would have several families over for goodies and a visit. I loved those times of connecting with friends. Looking back, I realize that Sunday was never a "day of rest" for Mom. She seemed to love every minute of it, though. I don't know how Dad did it either. But hospitality was definitely a regular part of the Bubna household.

Don also recalls Jeanie's zeal for hospitality by noting,

Jeanie made the parsonage very warm and went full-steam ahead with her ministry of hospitality. For most of her married life she was the one inviting people into their home. Paul was more of an introvert. He felt this was right and cooperated with it, but it was not what he was most comfortable with.

Paul was intentional about developing the minds and hearts of his children to grasp spiritual truths in life. He routinely led family devotions after breakfast or in the evening. These spiritual moments were neither awkward nor starched, but rather blended into the flow of daily life in the Bubna home. Of course, that's the adult version. Typical of most families, the children were less than thrilled about the routine on school days when they were preoccupied with other things. Certainly compared to A.B. Simpson's father, who stood his children in a line every Sunday afternoon and quizzed them on the *Shorter Catechism of the Westminster Confession*, Bubna's training was quite relaxed. He was careful to ask questions that solicited thoughtful responses from his children, confirming that they understood the Bible story for that day. Paul's personality inclined him to be mostly indirect, but ever alert to what the children were thinking.

An important element in the devotional routine was prayer. And a high priority was prayer for the world. Tim recalls the large yellow map taped to the wall in the kitchen with pins marking the locations of missionaries serving around the world for whom the Bubna family regularly prayed, by name. Pertaining to family and spiritual issues, Paul commonly focused attention on the larger matters of the Christian life. Stephen recalls that his father's prayers during those family times always focused on *being* and *walking* in relationship with Christ, never on *doing* things that might make one's appearance acceptable to God or others. Steve looks back to his teen years when he chafed at restrictions at home and took issue with pat answers at church. His father's emphasis on being in relationship with Christ was definitely clearer and certainly more comforting than his mother's scrutiny of his behavior.

Laurie concurs. "I always felt like Dad understood my heart and my way of thinking without my having to explain myself. I also felt like Dad *delighted* in me—not that Mom didn't—but it was just a very special attachment to Dad." Years later, after Jeanie passed away, Paul asked his daughter Laurie to accompany him to Russia where he was invited to speak to missionaries. She was ambivalent since she was reluctant to leave her family, but she felt that her dad needed her, so she went along.

> We had a great week together with the missionaries, and in the plane on the way home, Dad asked me, "What was the highlight of the trip for you?" I mentioned several of the ministry things that had happened that week. Then I asked

Dad what the highlight of the trip had been for him. He just smiled and said, "Spending the week with you." I'll never forget that!

Question and Answer

One technique Paul incorporated in mentoring his children was "the question." Asking questions without offering any answers became a trademark Bubna technique. He designed them to prod his children into thinking about the future and ultimately their "life investment" (according to Tim, one of Paul's all-time favorite phrases). Of course, as the children grew older, they adopted their father's tact and loved asking *him* questions. But he retained his purpose—and the upper hand. Rarely did he give a direct answer, but instead purposely guided them to draw their own conclusions.

When asked a question, he was customarily slow to speak and used very few words. The seemingly interminable lapses in their conversations were not a small frustration to them (and to anyone else who knew Paul). Tim elaborates:

> When I say "slow to speak," I mean that a five- to ten-minute lapse between the question and the answer was *not* uncommon. I recall times when I figured that he had not heard my question and I went back to reading the paper or something. And then when he began to respond, I would think, *Who is he talking to?* But it was always worth the wait!

Even in matters about which Paul held strong convictions, he preferred to respond to his young adult children's questions by discussing the issues around the questions, raising more questions and then asking what they thought. Paul never let them off the hook and consequently cultivated in his children a valuable skill—making wise choices.

Steve remembers a period during junior high school when he succumbed to the temptation to use his intellectual freedom to challenge his superiors. He was participating in a kids' program that met before the Sunday evening service, and he routinely challenged the teacher's knowledge of the Bible. At issue was not his quest for knowledge but his arrogance about what he thought he already knew. One evening the leader gave a Bible quiz that included the question "What is the unforgivable sin?" Steve saw that as his opening and immediately jumped in, protesting that there was no unforgivable sin. What ensued was a toe-to-toe verbal altercation.

Finally, in desperation the teacher asked, "Do you want to go on or keep arguing?" "Keep arguing!" Steve shot back. Suddenly the side door of the room was flung open and in strode his dad. He grabbed Steve by the ears, literally picked him up out of his chair and spirited him out of the room in a most humiliating fashion! "I deserved it," Steve reflects. Disrespect was something Paul did not tolerate in his children!

Punctual Paul

When it came to appointments, deadlines and planned outings, Paul was punctual, sometimes impatient and always unwilling to keep others waiting for him. He could also be uncharitable when it came to waiting for others. (This irritation would trigger a relational crisis in his staff many years later.) Son Tim shares this not-so-fond memory about an experience of Paul with his sons at the Minnesota Twins ballpark:

> In the '60s we went to a few Twins' baseball games every summer. Dad could not stand the lines of cars exiting the parking lot [after the game], so we would leave at the end of the eighth inning—always with us kids complaining. On one of these occasions, the Twins were trailing, and as we pulled out of the stadium, we heard on the radio (above the roar of the crowd) the game-winning home run! It was *not* a happy ride home.

Mentoring the Message

Paul's quiet and reserved temperament seemed to be ill-fitted for the ministry of equipping energetic young believers to follow and serve Christ. Yet his inner life overflowed with a spiritual vitality that attracted young Christians seeking a role model. He was not consciously aware of the significance of his example for many years. He wrote,

> In the early years of pastoral ministry I didn't clearly see that what would matter in the long run was the few people into whom I could pour my life. I was busy learning to run the machine and running the machine is what gets a pastor good press.[8]

God was weaving the message of the Scriptures into Paul's personal journey in such a way that it wasn't difficult for him to lay the foundation for his personal mentoring from the pulpit. And so he did, where he hammered home the importance of *vulnerability* and *God-dependence*. He theologically challenged his listeners to allow their weaknesses to become God's strength and exhorted them to minister fearlessly *out of weakness* because that is how biblical ministry works. He proclaimed,

> [The Apostle] Paul was able to pour out grace and love to people, not because he had all the answers, but because he was a captive, a man with a rebellious will that had been broken. . . . Whenever we carry in our hands our own weapons of self-righteousness, we destroy any possibility of Jesus Christ being clearly seen. It is when we carry in our hands the broken weapons, when we walk by grace alone, that Jesus Christ is communicated through our life and attitudes.[9]

Paul, in a very remarkable way, identified with people who were willing to be vulnerable by being honest about failure. He shared,

> One of the most encouraging meetings I ever attended was a testimony by a businessman who had come to speak. "Folks, I want to tell you how God has worked in my life. I've been in five different businesses and I have failed in all five of them. And I want to tell you how God helped me *in my failure*." I sat right up. Here's somebody I can relate to![10]

How did his own pilgrimage embolden him to minister on this footing? On January 28, 1973, he concluded a series of sermons on Second Corinthians (a series he revisited a number of times in the course of his ministry) with a message entitled "Weakness and Strength." In that sermon he declared how Christ prepared for ministry by becoming weak and vulnerable. Likewise, the Apostle Paul adopted this same posture of being willing to live in weakness if it would make others strong in God's grace. The message culminated by Bubna relating his own journey through weakness. His personal crucible became the reference point and impetus for this conviction:

> From my youth I felt threatened by people. Personal relationships and communication were difficult. . . . I always tended to avoid any new situation, like meeting people I didn't know. In my youth I felt called to either be a pastor or missionary. This burned in my heart. And I had peace about it until I got to college and began to face the demands of what it would mean.
>
> In the middle of college I had a nervous breakdown because I couldn't put it all together. Like the Apostle Paul, I came to the end of my resources. To believe that the God who raises the dead was able to use me—[I realized] it just had to be Him! Then God set me at peace to go on and, if need be, to fail in the eyes of men, if only I could please Him. I was called [by God] to invest myself in the very area where I felt most weak and inadequate.
>
> One of the results of this kind of weakness has been an ability to be sensitive and to feel things deeply with other people.[11]

He would experience this kind of weakness repeatedly in his later life, and this reflection later broadened into a conviction penned in his material on mentoring:

> In the development of a leader one of the key ingredients is the experience of learning to live beyond one's own strength, power and resources. To be regularly put into situations where divine empowerment is the requirement for success. Part of the learning experience is to gain value from failures as well as the successes. . . . The role of the mentor is to coach the mentored to risk and to see God carry him or her beyond his or her own resources, but also

to give the mentored permission to fail, and to nurture him
or her through the experience, ultimately to risk again.[12]

Story of a Mentor and Protégé

Paul's legacy in many people's lives can be traced to a point of
weakness and desperation, a time when Paul instinctively identified with their pain and then accompanied them through it, em-
boldening them to hope in God. Such was one very fruitful
mentoring relationship that Paul embarked on with a sixteen-
year-old boy.

The point of entry was one of the most painful in both their
lives. Harlan Armstrong, the head lay-elder in the church, was
Paul's closest friend and co-laborer at Northbrook. In the summer of 1967, Harlan sensed that he was losing touch with his
son Steve. The boy was drifting spiritually and seemed to be
losing his grip on values he had been taught as a child. He was
visibly annoyed at the restrictions and rules at home and just
wanted to do his own thing. So in late summer Harlan asked
Steve to join him on a canoe trip. He and his wife June had determined that they would even sacrifice their twentieth anniversary celebration so that Harlan could spend that time with
his son and hopefully repair their relationship.

Steve was not much interested in being with his dad, but he did
really want to go on the canoe trip. It occurred to him that his dad
was willing to sacrifice his own "big day" to do this. So they went.
And they had a great time. Steve was allowed to have his space,
and while his dad led devotions, no pressure was put on Steve to
contribute. The result was a deepening bond between father and
son. They returned home on a Sunday night. The next evening
Steve waived an invitation to a family game night and rushed off
to see his friends. Accordingly, his parents suspended the game
night and went shopping for a new car.

Coming home, Steve became immersed in traffic that was backed
up for miles due to a car accident on the main four-lane highway.
Inching his way past the accident, he observed that one of the de-
molished vehicles was identical to his parents' car—a big Pontiac.

The front end was pushed so far into the seats that they could not be seen. He assumed his parents were home and made no connection. However, he noticed as he pulled into the driveway that his parents' car was gone. When he asked his sister where their mom and dad had gone, she told him, "To shop for a new car." He was greatly relieved since the car dealership was in the opposite direction of the accident. Strangely, though, a neighbor who had never been in their home before was sitting at the kitchen table; a couple of minutes later Pastor Bubna pulled into the driveway.

Opening the door, Steve greeted him enthusiastically and told him he had heard he preached a great sermon the previous Sunday. Paul stood silently in the doorway. Finally, gathering the children close and with great heaviness of heart, he informed them, "Kids, I have some bad news for you. Your mom and dad were involved in a bad accident and . . . [pause] your dad is with the Lord." While his sisters collapsed in tears, Steve, confused and angry, bolted for the door.

Immediately Paul stepped between him and the door, grabbed his arm and gripped it more tightly than anyone had ever held him. And he would not let go. Steve's frightened, darting eyes caught Paul's steady gaze and fathomed in it a deep well of sorrow and compassion. This man was not just announcing grievous news; he was grieving himself. Steve eventually settled down and Paul loosened his grip.

Then and there began a long journey shared between a frightened sixteen-year-old boy, whose father had been killed by a drunk driver in a senseless tragedy, and his father's best friend— his own pastor. They did not set aside a formal time each week. Steve would not have benefited from that sort of regimen. But whenever he felt a twinge of anguish or grief or anger, he would stop by the church and they would work through it together. This mentoring continued for many years, until it evolved into a relationship mutually shared between two colleagues working together, side-by-side, in ministry at Long Hill Chapel in New Jersey.

At the Heart of It: Integrity

Paul once wrote, "Only integrity of heart can give the freedom needed for the mentor to share his or her inner life with the protégé." This concept was a key to Paul's relationship with John, a lay leader in the Northbrook congregation. It was not until his small son was healed from an allergy that plagued the family that John's spiritual desires were awakened. John began to watch Paul closely, gaining insights from his example. Paul was happy for the impact he was having on the young man's life. But being reserved by nature, he found it difficult to initiate interaction. Hence, God used John's probing questions to uncover essential tools in the mentoring relationship: transparency and spiritual intimacy. Paul describes John's role in equipping his own mentor with this perspective:

> When we had conversations together (most often by his initiative), he began to probe into my personal life; not in a distasteful manner, but I sensed that perhaps John had a need to know me at that point that was beyond my comfort zone. As I look back I see that my relationship with John began to promote growth in my life that was probably as great as what was taking place in him. An issue uncovered by our friendship was my need for greater honesty with myself. Clearly, integrity was the issue.
>
> God used his passion to find inner wholeness and his strong desire to be effective in his home to uncover my need to relate to people on a deeper level. There was an unforgettable moment that may have been the turning point. We were visiting in my study one afternoon and John was bombarding me with a variety of questions, many of them quite personal. Out of the blue he looked me in the eye and said, "Paul, have you had struggles with lust as you have matured spiritually? You have, haven't you?" I told him that lust was a common frailty in fallen human nature, and that it had been an issue in my growth.
>
> John pressed his point. "Paul, surely you must know that as a young believer I have struggled with lust. Yet we have been friends for several years now and you have not even

once let on that it has been an issue with you. I have watched you and tried to model your lifestyle. Paul, I need to know what makes you tick. If you have overcome lust, I need to know how!" What followed was a conversation that I think was helpful to John. It was just as helpful to me. I had never spoken with anyone so intimately about my inner life. I began to see that you can't share your inner life and help others grow if you aren't honest with yourself and comfortable with your heart's relationship with God. It is called integrity.[13]

While Paul communicated integrity in these mentoring relationships, he also communicated it in the manner in which he was willing to learn from laymen whose experience in administration and management qualified them to be mentors to him in those areas. Men like John Gordon, a small-businessman, and Harry Kiel, an executive with the phone company and, later, a member of the Board of Managers of The Christian and Missionary Alliance, were leaders at Northbrook who pressed Paul to think strategically about ministry. Paul's willingness to allow them to be the experts earned him the right to speak to spiritual issues in their lives. Harry Kiel reflects, "The Lord has blessed me with only the overwhelming memories of gratitude to Paul for his spiritual input in my life."

The Mentoring Ministry

When the Bubnas lived in Minneapolis, there were about a dozen Alliance churches in the Twin Cities. In those days, before Alliance Theological Seminary was a full seminary, The Christian and Missionary Alliance subsidized seminary students who wanted to go into Alliance ministry. Bethel Theological Seminary was one of the approved schools, and it was located in Arden Hills, just east of the Brooklyn Center section of Minneapolis where Northbrook Alliance Church was situated. The Alliance insisted that a local Alliance pastor should mentor the students they subsidized. Paul was one of the younger pastors, but his spiritual maturity was well-known. He was the mentor of choice in the Twin Cities area, so many prospective Alliance pastors sat under the tutelage of Pastor Bubna.

One intern was Arthur Dunn, a graduate of Nyack College who had become a Christian during his junior year of high school. He attended Bethel from 1968 to 1971. Dunn has had long-term pastorates in Oregon, Maryland and New York since his days as an intern under Pastor Bubna.

Art's impressions of his experiences at Northbrook under Pastor Bubna show the impact of a godly leader on a young person:

> Pastor Bubna was my pastor from September 1968 until he left for Vietnam. I was a seminary student at Bethel Theological Seminary. I was assigned to Northbrook with Pastor Bubna overseeing my field education. I attended one of everything a pastor did with him—one funeral, one wedding, one trustee meeting, etc. Here are some of my remembrances:
>
> I remember during one sermon that he said he found a note outside the church that was apparently from one teen to another. Teens started squirming. He never did read the note in the sermon, but that was a real attention-getter.
>
> One Sunday an alarm clock went off during one of his sermons. A youth, maybe one of his own sons, had placed it in the choir loft. It wound down, and he went on.
>
> When Pam and I taught the junior high Sunday school class, we had a project of teaching them how to listen to a sermon. Pastor Bubna was an exceptional communicator who always—and I mean always—had a great opening sentence. We took the Sunday school class into the balcony and placed a chalkboard at the front of the balcony, off to the side. I would write clues on the board as to what to look for, such as "Be on the alert for Pastor's FIRST sentence." Then I would outline the sermon as it unfolded. Pastor Bubna was really supportive of this project and was amused that we even attracted some adults to this learning experience.
>
> On one occasion he took me on a visit to a nursing home. On the way he shared how this was some of the hardest work he did. He carried a heavy burden for those who were suffer-

ing. However, he was quick to add that the people we were to call on that day were such a blessing to him that he felt they gave more to him than he did to them.

He didn't share a lot about his family with me or in the group setting with the seminarians. However, one day he met with us on his day off and got on the wrong side of Mrs. Bubna. He made it quite clear that we had to stick to our allotted time frame. He said Mrs. Bubna had chastised him about his long hours of work and the small amount of time he was resting and taking time off. I thought it was kind of amusing that such a highly respected pastor could get in the doghouse with the "missus."

In late 1968 or early 1969 Pastor Bubna preached one of the finest messages I ever heard on the theme of discouragement. I took notes from it on a three by five card and carried the card in my Bible for years. I was a first-year seminarian and was greatly impressed with Pastor Bubna's transparency regarding discouragement.

One time Pastor Bubna invited me to preach at Northbrook in an evening service. He said he was on vacation. When I arrived I was horrified to see him there. He said, "I am on vacation, but I like this place." He very graciously introduced me before the sermon and was so encouraging and affirming when it was all over.

I have always called Pastor Bubna "Pastor." Even when he was the president, he was "Pastor."

Northbrook Makes an Impact

The total span of Paul's ministry in Northbrook covered fourteen years, interrupted by two and one-half years spent overseas. It was a period of his life that was filled with joy and a place where he hit his stride as a father and a pastor. His intellectual grasp of the Bible was appreciated. His personality, far from being unsuited to the ministry, meshed beautifully with the purposes God was laying before him. He was cognizant of the miracle of being used *as he was* by God. He shared with the congregation on one Thanksgiving, "I want to express my personal thanksgiving to God for the fellowship of the saints, for people who love me—

who know me *like I am.*" He utilized his journey through weakness as a powerful instrument to develop future spiritual leaders. His tenure in Northbrook gave him ample time to see the fruit of his labor—lifelong attitudes and habits changed, human relationships reborn, God being incarnated in the lives of sensitive Christians and the church being the Church—serving, comforting, helping, equipping, loving and blessing the congregations of other churches—just as God intended the Church to be.

Yet his vision was still growing, because a large world was out there beyond Northbrook, and it was dying without the gospel. He often alluded to that world in his prayers and moments of personal reflection. On one occasion he shared,

> I thank God for a purpose larger than myself—one that encompasses time and eternity and the great scope of redemption. I thank God for missions, and the joy of being involved in something as big as the world—something as big as heaven![14]

In 1970 he would experience the joy—and pain—of being personally engaged in the Great Commission in the most conflicted and dangerous place in the world: Vietnam.

Notes

1. Paul F. Bubna, "Acknowledge Him in All Your Ways" (sermon preached September 27, 1987, from Proverbs 23:1-12).
2. Paul F. Bubna, letter of resignation to Cornerstone Church, Boone, Iowa, dated October 2, 1961.
3. Paul F. Bubna, "Drawing Near to God" (sermon preached in 1985 at the Canby Grove Conference, Pacific Northwest District of The Christian and Missionary Alliance).
4. Ibid.
5. Paul F. Bubna, "Male and Female in Christ" (sermon preached February 22, 1987, from Galatians 3:23-4:7).
6. Jeanie Bubna, anniversary letter to Paul Bubna, December 18, 1974.
7. Paul F. Bubna, "The Worshiping Heart" (sermon preached November 13, 1988, from Habakkuk 3:1-7, 16-19).
8. Paul F. Bubna, "Integrating Mentoring into Ministry," chapter from an unpublished manuscript, 1992.
9. Paul F. Bubna, "Captives for Christ," The Northbrook Pulpit, 2 Corinthians 2, n.d.

10. Paul F. Bubna, "Life Can Be a Ministry," The Northbrook Pulpit, 2 Corinthians 1, n.d.
11. Paul F. Bubna, "On Weakness and Strength" (sermon preached January 28, 1973, at Northbrook Alliance Church).
12. Paul F. Bubna, "Mentoring the Next Generation of Leaders," chapter from unpublished material.
13. Paul F. Bubna, session on mentoring for Alliance Theological Seminary Internship Workshop, n.d.
14. Paul F. Bubna, "Harvest Festival Chat" (sermon preached around Thanksgiving, 1969, at Northbrook Alliance Church).

The Personality and Passion
of Paul F. Bubna

While I was a student at the University of Wisconsin (UW) in the early '60s, I joined the Madison, Wisconsin, Alliance church. The membership fluctuated wildly due to students and professors coming and going, and I ended up being the only member left in the church. Every Sunday I welcomed 50 to 100 visitors.

After graduating, I moved to Eau Claire (Wisconsin), where I became the youth Sunday school teacher at Fay Street Alliance Church. We brought carloads of kids up to northern Minnesota to work in Native American missions and helped build dorms at Big Sandy Camp. I helped establish Campus Crusade at the UW-Eau Claire campus.

In 1968 I was invited to be the young adult Sunday school teacher at Northbrook Alliance by Pastor Paul Bubna. One notable member of the class was Jon Pederson, whom God raised up to lead a street ministry in the West Bank area of Minneapolis. With Pastor Bubna's encouragement, I became a writer and wrote the counseling manual for Jon Pederson's lay ministry, and later a book called The Onion describing this unique ministry among street children and college-aged youth, which was operating mainly through the Minnesota Free University.

Pastor Bubna accompanied us at many programs held at the Extemp Coffee House and at Jon's house. Pastor was very comfortable with counterculture youth and had a valuable gift of communication. As you may expect, the young people thought of Christianity as "a bunch of frigid rules." They had never seen the spiritual side that changes people's lives. Pastor talked convincingly about grace. He was welcomed into their intellectual discussions. "Grace," i.e., "fundamental fulfillment," was an interesting new concept to many of them.

While Pastor Bubna was ministering in Saigon, my friend Jon and I were invited by Pastor Don Bubna (Paul's brother) to lead a discussion on reaching unregenerate youth for Christ, especially young people with unconventional lifestyles and beliefs. This involved all *district ministers and was held at Big Sandy Camp in late 1970. It included a discussion of "Freak Society vs. Plastic Society," as some termed the incompatible factions among youth and adults within the Church.*

Many of the young people we ministered to were against the war during the days of the Vietnam "conflict." Hundreds of kids found Christ, but many remained antiwar. Neither Jon nor I was an antiwar protester, but because we ministered to kids who were, we were not extended the same "grace" we had experienced from Pastor Paul.

—Don Moses,
Northbrook parishioner

Paul and his father, George,
at a picnic.

Paul as a young boy on a picnic at Rockwood Reservation
Park near St. Louis, 1942.

George and Georgia Bubna, early 1940s.

The Bubna family home, 1909 Arlington
Avenue, in St. Louis, 1934-1947.

This was the family's home church in St. Louis, Missouri, from 1942 to 1947.

Paul in college at John Brown University (JBU) in Siloam Springs, Arkansas, probably 1953.

Paul and Jeanie's engagement picture, January 1953.

Paul and Jeanie's wedding at the Presbyterian church in Siloam Springs, December 18, 1953. The officiating pastor was Dr. Richard Harvey.

Paul at JBU graduation in the spring of 1954.

Paul with his parents, George and Georgia, at his graduation from JBU.

Paul and Jeanie in front of Colony Methodist Church, Colony, Kansas, in late summer or early fall of 1954. Jeanie was expecting their first child, Laurie.

The house where Paul and Jeanie lived in Kincaid, Kansas.

Paul with their first three children in the summer of 1957: Laurie, 3; Stephen, 2; Tim, baby.

Paul as assistant coach of Colony High School varsity basketball from 1957 to 1958. Earl Clemens was the head coach.

Family picture in front of the Alliance church in Boone, September 1959.

Paul, Jeanie, Laurie, Steve and Tim, 1958, probably in Boone, Iowa.

The three Bubna boys—George, Paul and Don—with their parents on the patio of Don Bubna's home in San Diego, California, probably in early 1960.

Family picture in the parsonage at Northbrook Alliance Church in Brooklyn Center, Minnesota, in the spring of 1962. Joel is the baby.

Family picture in Paul's office at Northbrook in 1967. Gracie is the youngest.

George and Georgia Bubna with Laurie, Steve, Tim and Joel in front of the parsonage at Northbrook, 1963.

Family picture outside International
Protestant Church (IPC) in Saigon,
1970 or 1971.

Paul and Dan Mitchell, a journalist/
foreign correspondent in Saigon,
during the early 1970s.

Vietnam field conference in front of IPC in Saigon in the early 1970s.

Paul and his mom in the last year of her life in Glendale, California, 1976.

George, Don and Paul in Glendale, California, in 1977.

Don, George and Paul at Mission Colony when their mother lived there, around 1976.

Staff at Long Hill Chapel, Chatham, New Jersey: Don Swope, Elaine Thomas, Paul, Dan Bergstrom and Steve Armstrong.

Don, George and Paul in Riverside, California, around 1989.

Paul Bubna during his time as president of The Christian and Missionary Alliance.

Chapter Eight

The Great Commission Gets Personal

If you can keep your head when all those about you are losing theirs, you probably don't know what is going on.[1]

—Paul F. Bubna

Startling News

On a sheet with cryptic notes likely intended for a student audience in the late '70s, Bubna addressed the question "How does God lead?" Across the top of the sheet was the word *testimony*. Part way down the page Paul was obviously directing his attention to overseas service. There appeared these words in bullet-style script:

Inner urging of long standing—Committed to missions—
Openness to go—But a closed door—
Kept prodding—Then an opening—At a point of challenge
and struggle.

A fire to serve God had been kindled in Paul Bubna's heart when he was a young boy in St. Louis. He never interpreted that fire as simply a calling to pastoral ministry. From the beginning it was a call to be engaged in the work of proclaiming God's redemptive grace *anywhere* in the world. The Great Commission and pastoral ministry were seamlessly woven together in his

mind. The main reason for the local church to exist was to promote missions; the main outcome of missions was to build local
churches.

Communicating the significance of missions and overseas
church planting had been a vital aspect of his ministry at
Northbrook. But few were aware that for Paul Bubna *personally*, missionary service had been an "inner urging of long
standing"! Bob Jueckstock recalls that, in the fall of 1969,

> in one of our elders' meetings, Reverend Bubna shared how
> the Lord had laid it on his heart to pray for the forthcoming
> missions conference that, in his words, "five couples would
> respond to the call of God on their lives to full-time Christian
> service." When Ken Swain, missionary from Vietnam, gave
> the invitation at the close of the conference, we were not sur-
> prised that five couples responded, dedicating their lives to
> full-time ministry. The surprise was that Pastor Bubna and
> his wife Jean also responded—and, shortly after, began mak-
> ing preparations to leave for Vietnam.

"Surprised" is putting it mildly. They were utterly astonished
when Paul and Jeanie announced that they were resigning from
Northbrook in order to pastor the International Protestant
Church in Saigon.

When asked by a local newspaper reporter to explain why he
wanted to go there, Bubna replied,

> My wife and I felt that God would lead us into foreign
> work some day. We tried to keep our hearts open for such
> an opportunity. We made ourselves available. We heard in
> 1967 that the former pastor was coming home. We applied
> again this summer and were appointed by the board in
> New York. We hate to leave our many friends here, but
> we're looking forward to this opportunity.[2]

In another interview Paul revealed two events that had converged and energized that purpose in his mind: "I suffered a serious heart attack on January 30, 1968, at the same time as the Tet
Offensive in Vietnam. Six [Alliance] missionaries who were serving lepers were killed at that time. I knew them personally. While

at Northwestern Hospital, I felt there was a reason I was saved miraculously. Now I know."[3]

His brother Don affirms,

> Having already had a heart attack, his first heart surgery and five children, he did not seem like a prime candidate for overseas ministry. To his surprise, his physicians told him that the Asian diet would be excellent for him since it was largely rice, chicken and other low-fat foods. His preaching skills and Jeanie's marvelous abilities and commitment to hospitality seemed to make it a natural choice.

The following "covenant with God" that Paul helped to formalize many years later undoubtedly was taking shape in his mind during that period of his life:

My Covenant with God

As a new creature in Christ through the finished work of Christ, and as part of The Christian and Missionary Alliance, I covenant with God to give myself to the following disciplines in order to hasten the coming of our Lord Jesus Christ through the completing of the Great Commission.

I will forgo my personal, selfish ambitions and yield fully to Christ so that He may fill and work His good will in me.

I will set my heart to be an intercessor for the unreached peoples of the earth wherever they may be found.

I pledge to be a steward of all that God puts in my hands with the Great Commission in view.

I will bring the first and best to God in tithes to my local church and trust God to enable me to give over and beyond that to reach unreached and responsive peoples worldwide.

I will become a full participant in the body life of my local church and in its endeavors to reach the community where God has planted us.

I am willing to move beyond my comfort zone to enable new congregations to be planted through our local church. I affirm my willingness to have the Lord of the Harvest to call forth workers from among my family or circle of friends, beginning with me.

I realize that the above commitments may well call for a significant change in lifestyle and values. As God enables me,

I will be willing to change and be a change agent in my sphere of influence.

The tidings of their ensuing departure were both startling and difficult for those close to Paul. Steve Armstrong, his young "mentoree," was shocked and sickened by the news. Paul had become his surrogate father. Kerm Klefsaas was attending a football game with Paul when Paul leaned over and said, "Kerm, we are going to Vietnam." Kerm was overcome with sadness, akin, he said, to a funeral experience.

With Fear and Trembling

The Bubna children faced the biggest challenge. Paul and Jeanie broke the news one night a couple of weeks before Thanksgiving 1969. It was during Northbrook's fall mission conference, and the speaker that evening was a missionary from Vietnam who had shared how the house where he had lived in Saigon had been threatened in the Tet Offensive a year before! With that story still unfolding in their imaginations, their father pronounced, first privately to Laurie and Steve, then to all the kids at the dinner table, "We are going to Vietnam." Paul later reflected on that announcement, "We all had some challenging lessons to learn about what it means to follow Christ. Our children, *with fear and trembling*, prayed with us. And we faced our new task together."[4]

The children felt just about every emotion possible—except elation. Laurie hated it and felt vulnerable. She did not want to leave her friends in high school, where she was in the middle of her sophomore year. Steve, age fourteen, was stunned. Tim was totally confused. He relates, "We didn't know that the folks were even considering ministry elsewhere, much less overseas, and less yet in a war zone!" His first question was, "Who are us kids going to stay with while *you* are over there?" He wasn't in denial. It was just that during that particular year they were housing the daughter of missionaries in Africa because the MK school she'd attended only went up to the tenth grade. Twelve-year-old Tim naturally concluded that the Bubna children would be split up and assigned by number to different homes—like orphans in the storm.

Nine-year-old Joel, however, remembers the experience as being pretty radical, or as children would say today, "totally awesome." He continues, "Dad and Mom sold everything—furniture, beds, etc.—basically, they cleaned out the house. There were five barrels packed in the basement, three of them headed for Malaysia [to the MK school] and two to Vietnam." The youngest Bubna, Gracie, was probably the most composed about it. Of course, she was a preschooler and would not face the separation of boarding school for at least another year. On the brighter side, the children had never been in an airplane before, and now for the first time they would get to fly—and over the ocean to boot! And as a bonus for them, a two-day stay in beautiful Hawaii was being planned, and they had heard that was definitely a cool place.

The next six weeks were a whirlwind of preparations—filling out passport applications, attaching passport photos, visiting dentists and doctors (including ten vaccination shots for each member of the family), selling household goods and packing a total of fourteen barrels and one steamer trunk. They parted with everything except for two "prized possessions"—the piano and a stereo cabinet someone had made for them. These were entrusted to friends for safekeeping.

There is something mysterious about moving overseas. The initial exhilaration of adventure into the unknown is like an anesthetic before a painful surgery. The cutting is invasive but the numbing effect of the anesthesia makes it temporarily a pleasant experience. Likewise, while a move overseas begets sadness over leaving friends and relatives behind, that pain is numbed by the thrill of going to a new and exciting place. The effect is a dizzying romance with a fantasy that keeps flitting from one scene to the next with nothing particularly clear—only a stream of varying neon colors and shapes. And the whirling of packing, paperwork and well-wishing people conveniently prevents a family from having to deal with colliding and lurking inner emotions. Not until they've landed does the anesthesia begin to wear off and reality issues a wake-up call. However, for Laurie, oldest of the Bubna children at age fifteen, the anesthetic did not take. Those emotions were real from the moment she was given the news that evening. And they were terrifying.

On January 1, 1970, they departed from Minneapolis. Many friends and church family came to the airport to see them off. Laurie remembers finding her seat on the plane, then looking out the window at her friends waving from the terminal. She began crying quietly so as not to upset her parents. She relates, "I wanted to cry forever." After a brief interlude on the West Coast and Hawaii, they landed at the Ton son Nhut Airport in Saigon. Then after only a few days the four oldest children boarded another plane at the same airport, one that would take them—without their parents—to Dalat School in Malaysia. The same pain that Laurie had barely managed to suppress returned with hurricane force. Just days before, she had been torn from her home, friends and church family. And now, before she could catch her breath, she was cast away from her own parents—the only security she had left in the world!

Again she squinted to see through the plane window. "The pain I had felt in leaving friends behind in Minneapolis deepened into an unbearable ache as I thought of leaving my parents. Not only was I going to be separated from them for four long months, but I was leaving them behind in a war-torn country." Through her tears she watched as her mom and dad were reduced to mere specks on the observation roof. As the plane angled into the sky and headed toward a place where she knew not a single soul, she remembers feeling "utterly and totally lost." It was good that she could not see her parents' eyes, now gushing so badly that the sunglasses they were advised to wear at the airport were useless. Once in the car Jeanie wept all the way home.

The following year, when Gracie was old enough to go to school, her Uncle Don and Aunt Dee were at the airport with her parents. Don gives this account of that experience.

I remember going with all the Saigon missionaries to the airport in August of 1971 to tell their kids good-bye as they embarked on a flight to Penang, Malaysia. This was Gracelyn's first time away. She would be entering first grade. When the kids all went through security at the airport, all the adults went up to an outside observation point on the roof of the airport. When the children finally emerged from the terminal, flight attendants escorted them across the tarmac holding hands two-by-two. Gracelyn and her friend were out front leading the pack. No tears, only excitement. Some of the older kids were crying. All of the adults, including Uncle Don and Aunt Dee, were in tears. It was the most emotional scene I have ever experienced in my overseas travel. I began to see the cost of the missionary enterprise.

Saigon

Saigon
   City of war, black market, traffic jams, bribes, refugees, GIs, rockets, plastic bombs, Hondas, people.
Americans
   Here by choice to serve, here by assignment counting the days, here to escape.
   Running from heartbreak, disappointment, failure, responsibility.
The Church
   In Christ, yet also in Saigon, diverse, striving to be one amid hatred, seeking to love in the midst of greed, corruption, lust; but not of it, learning holiness, not isolation.
The Body of Christ
   Learning to be open, honest, accepting, forgiving, healing, communicating Christ.

We hope this poem may communicate some of the emotion, adventure, blessing, and struggle that characterize our ministry in this strategic city. Our hearts are at times broken by the awful suffering and waste of war—then again amazed at how God is using these times and this place to shake men loose from their complacency and defenses

and confront them with spiritual reality. While we cannot
grasp it all, is not suffering a friend that leads us to God?[5]

These words and poem capture Paul's view of that city after re-
siding there for a short time. His family had been dropped into
the French oriental capital of South Vietnam, a city swarming
with American and Vietnamese soldiers, refugees and foreign
personnel. Transportation vehicles representing a mishmash of
cultures and disparate eras packed sometimes narrow streets,
weaving in and out in no logical pattern. It was quite a challenge
for the Minnesotan pastor to navigate the streets of Saigon—
avoiding ox carts, pedicycles, rickshaws, bicycles, jeeps, taxis and
little children walking unattended in the maze of traffic. While
there was no speed limit, traffic was so congested that in Paul's
words, "I have only had my Volkswagen out of second gear a
couple of times."[6] Perhaps the only thing more daunting when it
came to getting around was squeezing the family into their Volkswagen bug. Son Joel laughs about that: "Who can forget the VW
bug for seven—cruising the streets of Saigon with all seven of us
packed in it, and having to all jump out and push-start it when it
stalled!"

While Paul's ministry would be in English, it still demanded
some familiarity with the culture and language. Accordingly, Paul
enrolled in language school and tenaciously studied the culture.
Among foreigners, Americans overseas perhaps struggle the most
with sorting out the dissimilar cultural cues and nuances of body
language in the host culture. Still, adjustments in perception and
behavior are a prerequisite not only to getting around in that culture but also to earning the right to be heard there. Paul was a
quick study, however, and in a short time could make these observations:

> The Vietnamese customs are not just different from ours but
> in many ways exactly opposite. They give their family name
> first while we give it last, the man walks through the door be-
> fore the woman, one gives the gesture "to come" with the
> fingers extended down instead of up, and to talk with one's
> hands in his pockets is not a gesture of informality but direct

insult. . . . We Americans dress up so people will think well of us, but a Vietnamese dresses up so that others will know how much he thinks of them. So if you go to see someone and are dressed informally, you are communicating to that person that you do not think highly of him.[7]

Paul wished to have access even to areas of the country that were off-limits to civilians. So he applied for and received press credentials obtained through the Post Publications in Minneapolis. Now, in addition to being a pastor he was also a freelance correspondent with an agreement to submit articles on the war in Vietnam. He took full advantage of that privilege and responsibility. In the spring he used his press credentials to fly by army helicopter into Cambodia, where he took pictures of a Viet Cong arms cache that had recently been uncovered. He wrote informative articles that were published in the *Brooklyn Center Post* newspaper in Minneapolis. Yet all of this was window dressing for his real work—shepherding the international community through the Saigon International Church. It was thrilling for him to anticipate the prospects of ministry in the name of Christ, the Lord of history, "in this place where world history is being made and where church history is being written with the blood of the martyrs."[8]

The International Protestant Church

In 1950 The Christian and Missionary Alliance in Vietnam became burdened for the English-speaking community of Saigon. Although Vietnam was a French province at the time, growing numbers of English speakers were arriving in the country. When Vietnam won her independence in 1954, more English speakers arrived, not only from America but also from many countries. In 1960 chaplain Harry Webster conceived of the project to develop an international English-language church. In 1964 Reverends Gordon Cathey and J.H. Revelle launched the building of a beautiful facility in a quiet but central location of the city. The compound accommodated the church, church offices, two large apartments and a couple of smaller ones, a small bookstore and a fellowship center where servicemen could come for training and fellowship.

The atypical configuration of the congregation that Paul and Jeanie had come to serve stretched and changed some presuppositions about church ministry. Laurie gives this description of her parents' work at the International Protestant Church:

> The ministry in Saigon was unique, not like a typical congregation because it was so transient. And people didn't have "homes"—they just lived in little apartments or barracks. So Mom did lots of entertaining in our apartment—which, of course, was "her thing."

By "transient" she meant that people rarely stayed longer than two years, most leaving after one year or even six months.

People attending the church included US Armed Forces, American Embassy personnel, physicians, college professors, political advisors, missionaries in transit, journalists and an English- speaking community that comprised over a dozen nationalities. Paul wrote,

> If the nationalities are many, the denominational backgrounds are even more varied, and represent a wide spectrum of doctrinal thought and practice. Yet, it would seem, because they are far from home and cut off from the pressures of their own culture and because they are a distinct minority (religiously, culturally and linguistically), they are not so anxious to defend their distinctivenesses as they are to share those things which are common. This release from defensiveness somehow frees people to face the central fact of the Person of Christ and cuts away the religious veneer so that Christianity may be seen as a relationship to God in Christ.[9]

Bearing Fruit

It was not long before they incorporated their gifts and passion to serve in that unusual and stimulating environment. Within a few months Paul had traveled to Nhatrang Bible School in the north, to Cambodia and to Dalat School in Malaysia, where he and Jeanie visited their children. They also hosted the Vietnam Field Conference at the International Church in Saigon, where Paul was invited to be the conference speaker. The field chairman reported, "The refreshing breath of the Holy Spirit has swept across our hearts as Rev. Paul Bubna, Pastor of the Saigon International Church, ministered the Word of God to us."[10] In the next two years Paul preached in field conferences in Laos, Thailand, Hong Kong and Singapore.

And before they departed to return to the States in the summer of 1972, he ministered the Word to the Indonesian field conference. In a letter of thanks afterward, the field chairman wrote,

> Right from the beginning of your ministry we could sense God's Spirit working in our midst. Your heart-searching messages each day from the book of Second Corinthians have been a source of real spiritual refreshing and renewal in our lives. . . . Because of God's anointing upon your ministry, lives and attitudes have been changed, and there has been a oneness and willingness to minister to the Body of Christ. . . . As you leave for the States, we trust that God will continue to use you in a mighty way for His glory.[11]

Paul was a pastor. Accordingly, they adopted the congregation entrusted to them by God with as much zeal as they had felt for any church they had been privileged to pastor. So it might be expected that the thing most satisfying to Paul was the ministry he extended to individuals attending their church. He and Jeanie reported at the end of the first six months,

> Our greatest thrill has been to see the FIRST fruits of our ministry here . . . a Navy commander renewing his commitment to Christ, a young GI confessing his failures and setting his face to stand true, a hardened government negotiator sobbing his way to forgiveness, a young family shedding their disillusionment with the church to return home committed to revival, a police expert ending his long search for God by finding Him here at the "end of the world."[12]

With the Bubnas' arrival in 1970, Americans were already beginning to pull out of Vietnam. That planned evacuation was accelerated in the ensuing months. But that didn't affect the attendance at the International Protestant Church, which was filled to near capacity every Sunday. Jeanie prepared food for guests from the English-speaking community nearly every evening and warmed the hearts of diplomats, executives, military brass and mechanics alike. And for the last few months of their stay in Saigon, Paul's Sunday morning messages were broadcast live on the AFVN radio station, resulting in weekly phone calls and visits by men and women seeking emotional and spiritual help. Paul experienced great joy in sharing Christ with those who so honestly confessed their pain and despair. And they opened their hearts to God's counsel through this anointed man.

Mentoring at the End of the World

Paul's passion to equip young leaders to serve the Church did not diminish while he was in Vietnam. His effectiveness as a mentor had always been predicated on vulnerability. He once said, "The crux of the ministry is both the realization of our utter dependency upon God and our willingness to be transparent enough for that dependence to be evident."[13] The following account reveals this common denominator in the lives of those he ministered to personally:

> One of our close friends in Vietnam was a missionary who was a very talented young man. I think when he is going strong, he can produce more work and results than anybody I've ever seen. But he is a young man who at various times in his life has been struck with seasons of depression. A depression that completely incapacitates him—he cannot work or think; he cannot do any of the things that are a part of his ministry. He just has to hole up and try to wait out the thing until he is lifted out of depression. This has come upon him several times. It came upon him last year again and perhaps was one of the worst seasons he's had. I think one of the reasons he has allowed me to be close to him is because he knows I had a similar circumstance in my early ministry.
>
> I flew up country into a village where he ministers to be with him for a few days. He asked me to come, and we spent

these days together and shared in the Word and prayer. One day as he was expressing to me his awful frustrations he said, "Paul, down in the village there is a Bible school and the leaders in the church know that I am supposed to be down there. And here I sit in the house and I can't do a thing. It has been two months." He continued, "They are sitting down there wondering why I can't come down and teach; why I can't preach; why I can't do all the things I've come here to do. It is frustrating."

I said to him, "Why don't you go down there and tell them why you can't come? Why don't you just pour out the whole thing and let them pray for you?"

He was utterly aghast at the thought. "You don't want them to see me like I am, do you? You want them to know how weak I am?"

I said, "Do you suppose they are weak?"

Here is a young man who had a great image. This man comes across like success, power and strength. And in the moment of his weakness he didn't want them to know. I almost had to drag him, but I got him down there. And for the *first* time, his Christian brothers saw him *as he was*. They grabbed him and they loved him! That man is having a new kind of ministry today. He is successful and talented, as he was before, but a new door has been opened into the hearts of a tribal people because he is no longer the missionary who has all the answers, but like them, has no resource but the God who raises the dead. Part of the thing that makes a church begin to go is when we are willing to be what we are. It's there that God can be seen—in our weakness.[14]

Fruit of Obedience

The move to Vietnam certainly created upheaval and some trauma in the Bubna family, especially since they undertook it with five children and in the midst of a fruitful career as an American pastor. The sacrifice they made begs the question "Was it worth it?" We offer these vignettes as a response:

Paul Bubna and Tom Stebbins had been meeting weekly to pray for revival in Vietnam. The country was either on the threshold of peace when the gospel could be taken to every village, or the doors were beginning to close and missionaries would be forced to say farewell to their Vietnamese brothers, leaving the Church to the mercies of a sovereign God. In everyone's mind, more time was needed. In early 1970 Rev. Doan Van Mieng and Rev. Pham Van Nam, leaders of the National Church of Vietnam, reported that while the preaching of the gospel was reaping good results, "we feel that the Vietnam Church is still very weak for such a great responsibility of carrying out God's love to the tribes in and out of the country, and we really need your prayers to fulfill our duty."[15]

Conditions worsened and by spring 1972, the political instability and terrorism in the countryside began spreading to the cities. On April 26 of that year, Nathan Bailey, president of The Christian and Missionary Alliance, received a cable from Rev. Tom Stebbins that read:

> NATIONAL CHURCH REQUESTS WORLDWIDE ALLIANCE UNITE
> FASTING PRAYER MAY SEVENTH FOR VIETNAM SOLUTION.

Dr. Bailey relayed this cable to the Alliance worldwide, adding,

> Reports from the field indicate enemy activity in all areas of Vietnam, with some places much more critical than others. . . . These are perilous days for the survival of South Vietnam and I cannot stress too strongly the urgency of this request.[16]

On the appointed day, around the world and in Vietnam, believers gathered to intercede for the war-ravished country. In Saigon, Christians, many of them missionaries who had served throughout Vietnam, united in prayer. One observer gave this account:

> It is thrilling to hear 150 people raising their voices in supplication for God's blessing on this country. They invoked His promise to help all that call upon Him in need . . . by whatever method He chooses to use. . . . Those who prayed firmly

believe that God will answer their prayers—and that He will be glorified in Vietnam.[17]

God did answer—and continues to answer to this day—by shaping a body of believers that now numbers over .5 million strong (the largest national Alliance church body in the world). Paul gave this account of the fruit that he witnessed in answer to the intentional and resolute supplication being offered on behalf of Vietnam:

> We were pastoring the International Protestant Church in Saigon in 1972 when a much-prayed-for revival broke out at the Nhatrang Bible School. As the students fanned out into the village churches on the weekends, fires of revival were lit across the countryside. Among just one of the tribes sixty churches were affected, with some 6,000 Christians being greatly stirred and evidencing a change of heart.[18]

Paul heard firsthand reports that in the villages a renewed fear of God and sensitivity to sin emerged. Fetishes and idols from the old life were brought to public bonfires to be burned. He beheld in wonder the awesome work of God in answer to persistent prayer at a pivotal time in the history of the country. He had been furnished a glimpse of the glory of God in a place filled with violence and bloodshed.

He also discovered among the Vietnamese a startling faithfulness to God in the midst of suffering. In a sermon delivered later at Northbrook, he preached,

> It is an awesome thing to stand in the presence of pastors in Vietnam who have the Viet Cong knock on their door every night and threaten them. I was in a conference where a young pastor stood up and said, "Men, I need your advice. Every night the Viet Cong come knocking on my door, demanding food and threatening me. What shall I do?" They discussed it and the vote was that he should stay where he was. I thought, *I am glad they are not voting on me!* There are few pastors in Vietnam who haven't lost members of their families. The suffering of the body of Christ isn't done yet, *anywhere*.[19]

The Family First

Perhaps the greatest impact of all was the working of the Holy Spirit in his own life and in the lives of members of his family. Don assesses that period in Paul's life: "Their worldview changed. After Vietnam, I never remember any talk about any do's and don'ts of legalism. Now it was about the *big* issues. It was about life in Christ."

For Paul Bubna, nothing in his priorities had changed since as a lad with his mom he had claimed his life verse, "Seek ye first the kingdom of God" (Matthew 6:33, KJV). The family was not first, but within the kingdom, Paul knew his first responsibility was to his family.

The decision was made to leave Vietnam after two and a half years, even though it was the hope and expectation of the area director that they would stay for four years. Paul answered the Southeast Asia area director's inquiry communicating "keen disappointment" with a letter that included these words:

> If God is sovereign in our lives and in the Church, then I think His will for me will not conflict with what He asks me to do for my family. We feel deeply at this point that our children need our parental guidance, and it is upon this basis that we have made our decision.[20]

Their children were deeply impacted by the clear message about the high priority they held in their parents' lives. Joel reflects,

> I remember a sermon Dad preached at LHC [Long Hill Chapel] many years later. He was talking about the importance of priority concerning the children God entrusts to us. He used an example of their time in Vietnam. They knew that son Steve was really having a hard time at Dalat. [Dad] said one day he and Steve took a walk and he said to Steve that though they felt that God had called them to Vietnam he had first called them to be our parents. If Steve thought it was just too much and he couldn't make it, it was no problem—they would drop it all in a minute and head back to the States.

Steve recovered sufficiently to stay for the duration overseas, but other general concerns about the children's welfare precipitated a return home.

What impact did these experiences have on the Bubna children? Today, Laurie [Berglund] mirrors her mother's role, serving as the wife of the senior pastor of a large missions-minded church in New Jersey. Steve, after teaching science in an inner-city New Jersey school, now pastors a missions-minded church in his parents' homestead town of Colony, Kansas. Gracelyn and her husband are active lay people in their church in Alaska. Both Tim and Joel are now missionaries, one serving in South America and the other in West Africa. Joel was particularly molded into a vessel fit for such a high calling by the impressions left upon him during the Vietnam experience. He summarizes,

> In my life those years were formative. Looking back, the fact that Dad and Mom, two years after going through open-heart surgery and with five children, were ready in obedience to God to sell everything, leave friends and family and take their children into war-torn Vietnam, spoke a loud message. And they never acted like any of it was a sacrifice. On the contrary it was a joy and nothing short of reasonable service.

Farewell, Vietnam

Laymen and missionaries alike came to the airport to bid the Bubnas farewell when they left Saigon for Singapore en route to Malaysia and Dalat School and then on to the States. It was difficult to believe that their ministry was finished there. As in churches they had bid farewell to in the States, here also they were leaving people to whom they had become closely attached. There was another emotion, however, one that a person doesn't understand unless he has lived in a conflicted country where political power struggles and terrorism encroach every day into the thoughts and sometimes experiences of normal life. Paul Bubna comprehended the peril threatening the country of South Vietnam. Perhaps he never felt more gratitude for the freedom Americans have than after takeoff. As the plane carrying them climbed into the sky, leaving the land of Vietnam behind, Paul remembered, "It was like a burden rolling off our backs—like we were flying to freedom."[21]

God was calling him back to the States (initially to Northbrook, then to Long Hill Chapel) to paint with bold strokes the big picture of God's purposes for the Church. He gave an address entitled "The Kingdom and the Task" at Nyack College in 1980, where he clearly perceived that his role as a pastor was fused to the Great Commission:

> Though I am not a missionary, I want to assure you that I am a missionary person. The establishing of the Church of Jesus Christ in every culture in preparation for His return is the basic commitment of my life.
>
> Having been a pastor for twenty-five years in a local church, I do not see myself in any way disconnected from the missionary task. Rather I see that my life investment has been given to the building of the basic foundation of the foreign missionary task. My role as a pastor has been given to make the local church a workshop where God the Holy Spirit, the Lord of the Harvest, can thrust forth laborers into the harvest field. Missions has to do with the one thing in all of history that is going to endure the test of passing time. The Church is going to last. Everything else is going to go.[22]

Having been there and back again, there was no doubt in his mind that the missionary task was *everyone's* task. To the Nyack student assembly he proclaimed:

> Some of you here today plan to be missionaries, probably the majority of you do not. And yet the secret of the effectiveness of the Church in completing the missionary task may lie as much with you who are not going to be missionaries as it does with you who are. . . . If we are committed to Jesus Christ, honesty calls for us to put our values, our ideas of success, the ultimate fulfillment of our lives [where they can] be hinged upon God's great purpose in history.[23]

Notes

1. Paul F. Bubna, "Faithful Managers of God's Grace" (sermon preached November 6, 1986, from 1 Peter 4:1-11).

2. Mary Jane Gustafson, "Pastor Bubna and Family Leave Today for Vietnam," *Brooklyn Center Post*, January 1, 1970.
3. Sandra Day, interview, *Minneapolis Tribune*, fall 1969.
4. Paul F. Bubna, "Banquet Talk," Brooklyn Center.
5. Paul F. Bubna, prayer letter, October 1970.
6. Paul F. Bubna, "Vietnam: First Impressions," *Brooklyn Center Post*, March 18, 1970.
7. Ibid.
8. Paul F. Bubna, newsletter, February 6, 1970.
9. Paul F. Bubna, "Many Members . . . One Body," news magazine of the Vietnam Field, The C&MA, Summer 1970, #7.
10. Vietnam Mission of The C&MA, "52nd Annual Vietnam Conference Report," May 15, 1970.
11. Field Conference Program Committee, Indonesia Mission of The C&MA, July 3, 1972.
12. Paul F. Bubna, summer newsletter, 1970.
13. Paul F. Bubna, "Every Member a Minister" (sermon preached January 3, 1988, from 2 Corinthians 1:1-11).
14. Paul F. Bubna, "Life Can Be a Ministry," The Northbrook Pulpit, 2 Corinthians 1, n.d.
15. Rev. Pham Van Nam, Chairman of Vietnam Missionaries, and Rev. Doan Van Mieng, President of Vietnam Church, "A Brief Report on the Mission Work of the National Church of Vietnam," spring 1970.
16. Nathan Bailey, presidential report, April 26, 1972.
17. Bernard R. Sarchet, USAID-UMRTAID to Education, Saigon, "Prayer in Vietnam," part of article series in *Rolla Daily News* (MO), May 1972.
18. Paul F. Bubna, *Second Corinthians* in *The Deeper Life Pulpit Commentary* (Camp Hill, PA: Christian Publications, Inc., 1993), p. 118.
19. Paul F. Bubna, "Life Can Be a Ministry," The Northbrook Pulpit, 2 Corinthians 1, n.d.
20. Paul F. Bubna, letter to Rev. Grady Mangham, March 27, 1972.
21. Paul F. Bubna, tape to brother Don, June 13, 1972.
22. Paul F. Bubna, "The Kingdom and the Task" (message given at Nyack College, February 22, 1980).
23. Ibid.

The Personality and Passion of Paul F. Bubna

Paul Bubna was my mentor. I remember one Wednesday midweek service that Paul taught. He had us come up with a list of what he termed the "miserable Ds"—words like depression, disappointment, discouragement, despair. Then he asked us what we thought the answer was to these conditions. Of course someone said, "Jesus." Paul was very patient and kind and let it go until he finally had to tell us he thought "praise" was a way for the believer to handle some of these things in our lives.

By this time, I was one of the leaders in the church and would come by Paul's office from time to time to talk, encourage or pray with him. I came by his office a week or two after the above Wednesday evening teaching session, and Paul was discouraged. In my typical shoot-from-the-hip manner, I said, "Paul, remember your teaching a few weeks back about praise? Why don't you do that?" He looked at me, and I remember that little Paul Bubna grin, and he said to me, "Now you're meddling." This was a very godly man and a very human person. I have never known anyone quite like him. I miss him.

—John Gordon,
Northbrook parishioner

Chapter Nine

Life—One Day at a Time

When we quiet our hearts to listen to God, when we allow the Scriptures to speak God's intent to us, when we allow God to have the first word, then our prayers can answer God's word to us, and we can pray the prayer of faith. The last words of Jehoshaphat's prayer depict the powerful results of fasting and prayer: "We do not know what to do, but our eyes are upon you."[1]

—Paul F. Bubna

Bubna's fragile heart may have aided in qualifying him for the role he was to play as a Christian and a leader. For Paul Bubna, misfortune could occur at almost any moment, particularly in the form of a heart incident. Over the course of the last thirty years of his life, two heart surgeries and multiple bypasses were not without complications. The hard reality of his condition made him profoundly aware that God's purposes for him encompassed the actuality that his steps on any given day could lead him precipitously near the edge of eternity and the end of his earthly journey. In his words,

Coronary disease is interesting in that just about any symptom that you have can indicate a coronary event. Headache, neck ache, backache, shoulder or arm pain, nausea, stomachaches—any of those could be symptoms. So, in any given month there is usually some moment when the range of symptoms suggest that this might be my next coronary adventure, and perhaps the last one.[2]

His journey through physical pain and uncertainty is a journey that can best be documented in one chapter, though it spans thirty years of his adult life. It started one winter day in the Bubna home in Minneapolis.

In January 1968, at age thirty-five, Paul Bubna was hitting his stride at the Northbrook Alliance Church. Eight-year-old Joel, like any boy who has been granted exclusive time with his father, delighted in the prospect of a game of pool with his dad one afternoon. The game never really got started, however, before Paul began experiencing chest pains. From downstairs he made his way up the steps to tell Jeanie, who was in the kitchen with Laurie. She quickly gave him the phone to call the doctor while she ran upstairs to change clothes and collect whatever things she could take for Paul. Meanwhile, Paul, doubled up in pain, was bent over the kitchen table while he held the phone waiting for the doctor to take the call. Laurie recalls,

> I remember how afraid I was as I stood there and rubbed his shoulders, wondering if he would die. When he and Mom left the house, Mom reassured us that Dad would be fine, and that the doctor told him on the phone that it *couldn't be a heart attack* because Dad was *much too young for that!* As it turned out, the doctor was quite wrong.

Surgery and Beyond

In medical terms, he had suffered "an acute inferior myocardial infarction and coronary occlusion," or in laymen's terms, a heart attack. Tests revealed an advanced stage of arteriosclerosis that did not indicate a good prognosis. In July, after extensive tests, Dr. N.K. Jensen performed heart coronary bypass surgery. The myocardial operation involved a "triple implant procedure with bilateral mammary and epigastric arteries." Strictly speaking, it was not bypass surgery but a procedure in which they took healthy arteries off the chest wall and connected them to the heart. It "was one of the first cases of its kind."[3]

After the corrective surgery and a long rehabilitation, Bubna was able to resume ministry, only now he added to his work a prescribed regimen of daily exercise. That regimen became almost an obsession with him. Sharon Benham, who worked as a secretary at Northbrook, commented that Paul regularly "jogged around the sanctuary of the church" to make sure he didn't miss a workout. One doctor described his regimen this way: "He is a regular physical activist, jogging every day, doing rope jumping, etc., etc."[4] A cardiologist to whom he was referred wrote in a summary dated September 21, 1976, "He became a physical exercise nut and has been jogging religiously."[5] His diet also changed, and in the span of a few months he lost fifty pounds.

Paul knew that he was at high risk. His father had valvular heart disease and died on the operating table in 1969 at the age of sixty-five. Don remembers that day well. He and Paul had flown to San Diego to be near their father, who was having heart surgery at the UCSD hospital. They shared some precious moments with him before he was wheeled away to surgery. Eight hours passed without any word; then nine, ten and eleven hours went by. Finally, someone came out and directed them to go upstairs where the doctors wanted to meet with them.

Don and Paul entered an elevator, pushed the button and were standing there when Paul took out a nitroglycerin pill, popped it in his mouth and turned to Don. "He didn't make it," he said. Don reflected on that moment, "He just seemed to know before anyone told us that Dad had died." This occurred only a few months after Paul had undergone heart surgery. So the enormity of that experience and its ramifications in Paul's thought processes is unimaginable. Surely the timing and manner of his dad's passing intensified his resolve to do everything in his power to fight the disease.

Postoperative life for Paul Bubna was an education in living with the reality of a condition he was "too young to have." And unlike surgeries that cure the ailment and end the pain and discomfort, like an appendectomy or tonsillectomy, Paul's bypass surgery led him on a journey with a protracted infirmity that would be his unwelcome companion for the rest of his life. He soon began experiencing an ongoing and wide variety of chest discomforts, headaches, aches and pains in his shoulders and abdomen and even nausea. He never forgot the doctor's insight when he inquired one day about the seriousness of his condition:

> I was trying to ask him in a painless way about how serious my heart ailment was. I tried to pose the question about whether my present condition was terminal or not. He smiled, and then said something that was embarrassing. He said, "Paul, you're a pastor, right?"
>
> I said, "Yes."
>
> He said, "You ought to know that all diseases are terminal. In fact, being born is terminal!"[6]

That answer, while quite profound, offered little comfort to a thirty-five-year-old coping with heart disease.

In January of 1975 he was admitted to the hospital with pain under his diaphragm that he had had on numerous occasions before, but which this time did not go away. The doctors did not think it was of coronary origin and discharged him in four days. Again in September 1976, he was admitted to a coronary unit when he began to experience episodes of angina while jogging. He described the pain as a "raw feeling in the trachea, like those first few breaths on a bitterly cold January morning."[7] Tests showed that he had "complete occlusion of the lateral portion of the circumflex coronary artery, but the rest of his arteries looked pretty good."[8]

After long discussions with the doctor, Paul and Jeanie decided that at that time he would not have a coronary angiography to determine the exact status of his coronary arteries, though that option was left open. The doctor, however, prescribed changes in his medication, depending on the level of discomfort he experienced while on brisk walks. He also recommended that if Paul experienced more chest discomfort, he should discontinue jogging and abstain completely from competitive sports. The consulting doctor recognized that "this regimen is a very tough course for him to follow. However, I am confident that he will cooperate in every way that he can." He also added this at the conclusion of his report:

> I want to say that I very much enjoyed working with this man. He seems a very bright, concerned, empathetic person who has been burdened more heavily than usual by his disease and has invested a lot of time and exercise and psychologic effort in reassuring himself that his surgery has helped his disease a lot. But he remains unconvinced.[9]

The Valley of the Shadow

In the fall of 1977 Bubna accepted a call to be the senior pastor of the prestigious Long Hill Chapel in Chatham, New Jersey. There was no lack of professional stimulation in the high-stakes environment of that metropolitan area and in that exciting and challenging church of 900 members. He was engaged barely four months at Long Hill when he experienced a second coronary, and five months later a third more serious one while he and Jeanie were vacationing in the West. An angiogram indicated that the arteriosclerosis was further advanced. By now Paul lived with greatly diminished energy reserves—not that he could not do his work, but when he attempted anything really strenuous, the resource simply was not there. Dr. Bob Francis, his local doctor and elder at Long Hill Chapel, was (in Paul's words) "getting all over my case" about getting it treated.

So in September of 1978 Paul and Jeanie went to Philadelphia to see if Paul might qualify for a second bypass surgery. Surgeons in Philadelphia examined him and concluded that his condition was too critical and beyond surgery. When they received word that Paul was being turned down, they were both devastated. Paul later told how he and Jeanie returned to their car and sat there in the parking lot for some time with the engine off—weeping and pouring out their grief over this news that portended only a hopeless finality.

It simply did not make any sense! The door had been opened wide to serve in a vibrant church where Paul anticipated having the greatest impact of his career. He had formed a new staff, with Dave Schroeder coming from Armonk, New York, to be pastor of adult education and to give oversight to the youth pastors. Steve Armstrong had come from Minnesota to be pastor of counseling, and the team was taking shape. Ironically, now they were being told that Paul's heart condition was so severe that the best surgeons in Philadelphia refused to risk their reputations on it.

Laurie recalls hearing the news of her dad's deteriorating condition shortly after her daughter Jessica was born in the summer of 1978, when she and her husband, Marty, were still living in Dallas, Texas, where he was in seminary. She was fearful that her dad would die before he saw her baby. She writes,

> I could hardly wait to get home for Christmas. But once we were there, it was so sad because it was the first time I had ever seen Dad depressed. He seemed sad, withdrawn, a little hopeless (for obvious reasons). And he wasn't particularly open to talking about it. That was a very difficult Christmas. I remember how awful it was saying good-bye at the Newark airport. I held it together while we hugged our good-byes, but as we headed down the jet-way to the plane, I burst into tears and cried the whole way home. I had this feeling in my gut that I would never see him again. I always wondered if he was thinking that too.

It was becoming evident to everyone that there was not much time left. Joel recalls, "Steve was the first one to leave [after Christmas], and we had an awful sick feeling as we stood in the driveway saying good-bye, knowing that we would likely not all be together again."

The one recourse Paul could rely on was his disciplined routine. So that fall and early winter he simply resumed his work as much as he was able, fully aware of his weakening condition. He recounted those days:

I set about to fulfill my ministry as best I could. By conserving my energies I was able to cover a good part of the ministerial obligations. It was evident after a few months that I was weakening. But more than that I was getting sick—sick in the sense that I was losing hope, beginning to believe that I would not be able to fulfill the ministry to which God had called me.[10]

Anointing for an Ailing Spirit

The elders were not surprised when, in January 1979, their pastor asked them to pray for him and anoint him with oil. Paul perceived that some of them were reluctant to do it since they had anointed him before. They were convinced that if he was expecting a miraculous healing and it did not occur, then he would be pushed into even deeper depression. He quietly told them that while he was physically sick, there was another sickness from which he desperately needed release—a sickness in his spirit, a feeling of despair, of wanting to give up, of complete hopelessness. He knew that if he did not receive deliverance from that, it would destroy whatever good he hoped to accomplish in the days left to him.

With some apprehension and somberness they formed a circle around his chair, laid hands on him and anointed him with oil. They were uncharacteristically emotional as they cried out to God and openly wept with soul-wrenching earnestness for this man who came to them in weakness—so opposite the posture of a leader demanded by the culture of metropolitan New York. Yet even in weakness Paul was instructing them in the ways of God. He would later write, "Physical suffering can test our spiritual resources, but it is the spiritual and emotional anguish that threaten to cave us in."[11] That moment of human anointing became a divinely anointed and life-changing moment.

What came to me was the deep assurance that God had called me, that whatever His purpose was, that heart disease or sickness or anything else could not prevent Him working the good that He intended to do. I yielded my body to Him afresh for Him to use it however He would to accomplish His purposes. At that moment I began to get well. Totally aside from whatever the condition of my blood vessels was, I began to experience hope and His inner strength to walk on.[12]

Hope and Fear

Shortly after the dramatic anointing, a member of the church told Paul that Dr. Dudley Johnson, a heart surgeon at Mount Zion Hospital in Milwaukee, might be willing to perform the surgery. The X-rays were sent to Dr. Johnson and the news came back that he was optimistic and willing to proceed. Paul felt encouraged that a doctor was finally offering hope. While they did not offer any guarantees about how long the surgery would lengthen his life, they did say that many who received this kind of surgery lived for five years and even longer. After much soul-searching, Paul and Jeanie felt they should go for it, and the date was set for February 26, 1979.

Paul had already undergone one heart surgery and knew too much to "go under the knife" again without foreboding. His hope was naturally mingled with fear, and in a tape to his brothers before the surgery, he described these emotions in his inner life:

> It's interesting how God gives to us, as He promises, strength for the day, and prepares us for what He has us go through. I am not saying this to communicate that this last year has not been stretching, because it has. Lots of times I have really experienced deep fear. Since we have made this surgery decision, I have been awakened at night and my mind gets to going. And sometimes I can't sleep because I am just scared. And then I've got to get up, get going on prayer and get things settled down. But when our focus of faith is on the Lord, my testimony is that God gives peace. And He certainly does that.

In a sermon, he related a childhood experience that seemed to have a bearing on his present struggle:

When I was a little kid, I had a bad gum situation—you know, where my teeth wouldn't break through—and the gums were swollen. They took me to the doctor and the doctor cut my gums. It was a bloody mess. And while I don't remember all the details of that, I remember it was a *terrifying* experience. And ever since then I have had a terrific claustrophobia about being tied down. It's an irrational fear. But every time they put me on a table and strap me down so that I'm in somebody else's power, I just have a terrible irrational fear. The angiogram tests and those kinds of tests have just been a terrible experience for me. This last one—with my heart stopping and all—has not helped that situation. While I can look to the surgery and trust God and even look past it with hope, yet when I look at the situation itself—the *moment of getting on that cart* and being strapped down and the conscious moments I have *waiting*—it is really a difficult thing for me to look forward to.[13]

They flew to Milwaukee on February 23 for tests before actual heart surgery. Joel recalls the evening before surgery:

That evening we were all together in the room and we talked and had a time of prayer together. . . . He said he needed time to really fight it out with the Lord before he tried to sleep. The next morning we were in the hall outside of Dad's room and Bob Nanfelt [an elder from Long Hill Chapel] was trying to find a psalm or some word to encourage Dad. We prayed together and then went in. But when we approached his room we heard him *laughing*—and found him watching Archie Bunker!

Healing for an Ailing Heart

The wait seemed interminable to the family while surgeons attempted five bypasses. Every couple of hours someone would come out to report on progress and then disappear. Finally they rolled Paul out of the operating room and down the hall where his loved ones stood waiting. He had gained twenty-two pounds in water weight and looked terrible, but he was still alive. The next day everyone but Jeanie left, assuming the crisis was over.

But the news turned bad that night. What the doctors in Philadelphia feared had come true—four of the five bypasses had already closed, leaving only one that still functioned. His brother Don flew to Milwaukee to be with Jeanie and remembers that Saturday night when he and Jeanie "ate a little and talked a lot. It was very dark."

The next morning brought surprising news: Dr. Johnson was guardedly optimistic about the future. Remarkably, a few days later Paul was able to walk out of the hospital, although in great pain. On the way to the airport, exhausted, he gasped to Don, "Don, every part of my body feels violated. How did I ever allow them to do that to me again?" It was a long flight back to New Jersey.

The Bubna family and friends from Long Hill met them at the airport and Paul was taken home and settled in to rest. Jeanie, Don and the children attended the evening service that Sunday, and Jeanie gave a beautiful testimony of gratitude to God and the church and provided an update on Paul's condition. Then Dr. Francis, their family physician, stood and spoke to the congregation. He was not given to speech making, but with astute discernment and measured words this dignified physician compared Paul to Epaphroditus in the book of Philippians.

Epaphroditus was a messenger sent by God to minister to the church at Philippi. He was also very sick. Dr. Francis pronounced, "Perhaps God has given us one among us who is sick." For a church accustomed to leaders who embodied strength and charisma, this word was prophetic and prepared the church to receive from their new pastor a message born in weakness. In many ways, Paul's illness rallied the Long Hill Chapel congregation to follow him and to embrace him as truly a messenger sent by God.

The healing in Paul's spirit that occurred when he was anointed in January was sorely tested a couple weeks after the surgery, when he was scheduled to undergo medical tests to determine the success of the operation. On a handwritten sheet of paper dated March 10, 1979, Paul recorded a devotional reflection based on Psalm 139. This is how it appears:

Psalm 139

In many respects this seems like the most spiritually significant day of my life.

Everything about my life points me to praise—

God saved my parents.

Gave us a Christian home.

God called me early to acknowledgment of Himself.

He has gifted and placed me as a pastor in His body.

He has blessed me with a healthy, joyous family.

He has opened a special and significant door of opportunity.

Yet God has uniquely used the areas of weakness—psychologically, physically and educationally—to make me the kind of person through whom he could bless [others].

The heart ailment I have sought to accept as a gift from [Him] to bring gifts of discipline, carefulness, sensitivity to others, a sense of time and eternity! At every turn we have sought to accept this as a loving discipline of God—letting Him use it.

Events of recent months have made this all the more restrictive. Yet God has used it. All of this has brought us to seek a medical adjustment to the problem—so as to offer more strength. Yet in spite of the apparent, initial success of the surgery, God has allowed almost daily evidence to surface that indicates our complete and utter dependence upon Him. I know I need this.

The difficult decision to have surgery

The dashing and resurrecting of our hopes—

The hope of forming new bypasses

All of these have caused me to put my hope in man.

Today I am faced with an angiogram

a test of which I am very fearful

a test which may show much less hope than we thought.

I must prepare myself for the day

Search me, O God, and know my heart! (Psalm 139:23-24)

Paul was required to undergo an angiogram every six months after his surgery. He dreaded these tests, remembering a time during such a test when his heart had stopped beating and they had resorted to shock treatment to save his life. Six months after his surgery the dreaded moment arrived, and Paul lay strapped to the table while the test was performed. He noticed the physician calling another doctor over to view something on the monitor. Paul's spirits plunged since he assumed it was more bad news. But it was not bad news at all. In fact, the doctors were amazed—the test was showing that the bypass that had remained open was supplying blood to a part of his heart that had been oxygen-deficient for years and had actually improved his condition!

Interpreting the Lord for the Body

In the late '50s when Paul began his ministry in Boone, he was a picture of health. Naturally, when he preached on the topic of healing he was eager to uphold the Alliance doctrine on healing and challenge unbelief. He proclaimed,

> God's provision for sickness is the atonement. We have as much right to trust God for healing for the body as we do forgiveness for sin. . . . Jesus "healed all that were sick" (Matthew 8:16, KJV). There is no record where he did not heal any. You must convince yourself from the Word that it is God's will to heal. . . . "If it is thy will" immediately throws doubt on this. It is God's will. . . . You must believe just as you do for salvation—not only believe that God will, but reach out and take it! Let the Holy Spirit do a work in your life. . . .What about doctors? They are good, of God. But for the unbeliever. Either you believe God can't [heal] or that He wills not to [heal]. There is no scriptural basis for either.[13]

Toward the end of this message he delivered the following hard-hitting rhetoric:

> Is it not dangerous to doubt God? If redemption was purchased at so great a price, should it not be [efficacious] to all men [who ask]? "He is not willing that any should perish." Then is He willing that they be sick? If we doubt God on the one point and permit unbelief to creep in, will it not be easy to let doubt creep in about God's ability to save

souls? Will it not result in lack of power in the matter of souls being saved? Let us not tolerate unbelief in our lives, but seek God's face.[14]

Paul's illness had the effect not so much of changing his conviction about the doctrine of healing as drawing out deeper implications for emotional and spiritual healing and placing the doctrine in the context of God's purpose to be glorified in the *whole* life. Thus "if it be thy will" does *not* indicate a lack of faith but rather submission to God's greater purposes beyond the immediate physical infirmity. He preached in 1991,

> If we look to God in our weakness, one thing we need to be keenly aware of is that God's purpose in our lives is His glory. He wants to conform us to the image of Christ. When we come to God with our weakness, with our need, with our sense of lostness and inability, He wants us to come, not just for what we want, but with God's glory in mind. We are positioning ourselves to receive God's grace when we humble ourselves, when we persistently trust Him, but also when we are bringing underneath the desires and longings of our heart to say, "Lord, not my will first, not my comfort, not my health, but Your glory." Because ultimately what God wants from us is to be like His Son and to know His Son.[15]

Thus Paul widened the parameters of the doctrine without denying its power or efficacy in the life of the believer. He stated,

> When we take Christ as our healer, we are not limiting ourselves to any particular manifestation. When the life of Christ is indwelling us and His resurrection power filling us is taken as our resource, God is able to cause us to triumph in our situation, to use our physical suffering and pain as a means to build endurance and spiritual maturity and through all of that, to fulfill His purposes in us in spite of our sickness. . . . If we come seeking *it*, seeking only healing for our illness or disease, we may in the inscrutable providence of God go away unchanged. But if we come seeking *Him*, taking *Him* for our spirit, for our souls, for our bodies—taking Him as our Savior and our Holiness and our Redeemer—we shall

not be disappointed, because He is able beyond all circumstances, beyond all diseases, beyond all frailties, to enable us
to fulfill the good purpose He has for us when we allow Him
to be the Lord for the body.[16]

Paul was able to interpret God's ways in his own life in the
midst of his prolonged battle with heart disease by bringing a
richer, more complete and more biblical perspective to bear on
his situation. He said,

> I don't think medical people would necessarily say that I
> have been healed. In terms of the medical model, I am not
> sure there is adequate proof that I have the circulation that
> I need to function as I do. Out of this whole experience I
> have sensed God's call to live one day at a time, to walk
> moment by moment, to take Christ as my life, the Lord for
> my body.[17]

An Estimation of Life Begotten in Weakness

Although Paul knew that each day could be his last on this
earth, he contested gloomy prognostications with their implied
suggestions that he take a *very* early retirement or at least roles
with reduced responsibility. Instead, he gave everything he had in
God's service up to the very end. And in order to sustain the rig-
ors of an often stressful job, he knew that he had to be in a physical condition that would fortify him to meet each day's demands.
Those of us who worked or traveled with him quickly learned
that Paul didn't exercise every day to make social contacts or stay
in the loop with his younger, athletic staff. He did it to stay alive.
And he pushed himself mercilessly to sustain that discipline.

That discipline underscores an important element in Paul's
thinking, which his heart condition most certainly helped him to
define. That idea is this: Life is about "being" and not "doing."
Paul lived with the attitude that his hold on life was tenuous at
best. He witnessed, "I live life more short-term, often a day at a
time. It affects the way I look at life's situations and how important or unimportant they may be."[18] If tomorrow is not an endowment, then doing the will of God is not predicated on a life

expectancy of seventy or eighty years. It is not predicated on one's visible accomplishments. Paul's estimation of life and doing the will of God may be summed up in this statement he made in his farewell address to the Long Hill Chapel congregation on April 7, 1991: "I am keenly aware that, when all is said and done, the impact of one's ministry has not so much to do with what has been done, or even what has been said, but *what one has become.*"[19]

Despite his tenuous hold on life, Paul was neither pessimistic nor morbid. Even though in this chapter we have pulled together some thoughts he shared about his health, please note that these quotes span several decades, a period when he delivered probably more than 3,500 messages. Rarely did he reference his health, and when he did it was always to teach about the sovereignty, provision and glory of God. Many people who sat for years under his ministry knew he emphasized sanctification through suffering, but they had little understanding about his own medical history, daily vulnerability or regimen of physical discipline just to keep his heart pumping.

Values Clarification

Paul habitually transformed every point of pressure or challenge in life into a classroom where God was the instructor. And he was continually learning in that classroom and making adjustments in his life to adapt to the truth being shown to him. The most important lessons dealt with sickness and suffering. He declared,

> What suffering does do is clarify our perspectives about what is important and what is not. The more an individual suffers no matter what may be the nature of that suffering, from religious persecution, social ostracization, from sickness and disease, no matter what the nature of suffering, that suffering brings a keen awareness of what is permanent and what is passing. If that suffering is properly responded to, it quickens spiritual desire and perception.[20]

That quickening of spiritual desire and perception in Bubna's life produced the conviction that he could not afford to be bound by fear and misgivings about the future. In fact, for him the uncertainty of life made heaven all the more real and palpable. He testified, "One of the most obvious things that the resurrection of Christ does is remove the deadline from our lives. We are not very old when the awareness comes that we are mortal, that life is not forever, that death is a part of the human experience."[21] It is not surprising that he also noted, "With the passing years has come the growing awareness that life's deepest desires can never be fulfilled in this fallen world. I have been made for something that I cannot yet fully see."[22]

Notes

1. Paul F. Bubna, "Powerful Prayer" (sermon preached July 23, 1989, from 2 Chronicles 20:13-28).
2. Paul F. Bubna, "Paul, the Expendable Man" (sermon preached August 21, 1988).
3. Dr. J. Parod, MD, discharge summary of Paul Bubna's medical history, February 23, 1975.
4. Dr. M.F. Lynch, MD, consultation, January 14, 1975.
5. W.D. Kimber, MD, letter to Dr. J. Parod, MD, September 21, 1976.
6. Paul F. Bubna, "Zephaniah: Messenger from God" (sermon preached October 29, 1989, from Zephaniah 1:1-9; 14-18).
7. W.D. Kimber, MD, report on consultation, September 20, 1976.
8. W.D. Kimber, MD, letter to Dr. Parod.
9. Ibid.
10. Paul F. Bubna, "The Lord for the Body" (sermon preached June 6, 1988, at General Council).
11. Paul F. Bubna, Second Corinthians in The Deeper Life Pulpit Commentary (Camp Hill, PA: Christian Publications, Inc., 1993), p. 5.
12. Bubna, "The Lord for the Body."
13. Paul F. Bubna, "The Great Physician" (sermon preached January 25, 1959, at Boone, Iowa).
14. Ibid.
15. Paul F. Bubna, "The Healing Grace of Christ" (sermon preached January 6, 1991, from Exodus 15 and Isaiah 53, 61).
16. Bubna, "The Lord for the Body."
17. Ibid.
18. Bubna, "Paul, the Expendable Man."
19. Paul F. Bubna, "Farewell Address" (sermon preached April 7, 1991, at Long Hill Chapel, Chatham, New Jersey).

20. Paul F. Bubna, "Tempered by Testing" (sermon preached August 7, 1983, from 1 Peter 4:12-19).
21. Paul F. Bubna, "Resurrection Is for Living" (sermon preached March 31, 1991).
22. Bubna, *Second Corinthians*, p. 66.

The Personality and Passion of Paul F. Bubna

I recall the time Paul confronted my misguided assumptions about God's will one day early in my career at Long Hill Chapel. I nervously entered his office after spending half a day poring over the files of my predecessor in the young adult ministries program. I had been told that Steve's gifts and abilities were legendary and that his leadership had birthed a number of important ministries that powerfully impacted the chapel. In reviewing his files, those assessments were confirmed in my mind, and I began to inwardly agonize, sensing myself succumbing to a deepening gloom about my prospects for success at Long Hill.

I anxiously lamented, "Paul, I'm not Steve, and I am not sure that I can ever do the kinds of things that he did here. That's not who I am. And besides that I am not sure there is anything I can do that will impress the people in this church." I hesitated because I felt I was dangerously exposing myself to someone who could end my tenure in this new position very quickly. I feared that perhaps Paul had completely misconstrued my résumé and had blindly assumed that I would jump into the job with the same high energy level and creative genius that Steve had exhibited. I paused, feeling my career suddenly imperiled, while Paul picked up his pen and appeared to fiddle with it.

Being new to his staff and unaccustomed to these pauses in the dialogue, on that day in particular I felt my stomach beginning to knot! But then he turned and gazed at me, and with eyes full of kindness and confidence, he made this observation: "Ron, when you leave this church, I think you will discover that your impact on people's lives will be not so much what you do here, but who you are and who you become."

Time and again this Bubna perspective rebutted assumptions held by many of us in that work-driven culture of metropolitan New York. Our fleshly ambitions dictated that we could to some degree earn God's approval (or Paul's) by doing tangible, external things. His pil-

grimage had trained him to live by another criterion, a spiritual principle we desperately needed to learn if we were to escape the trappings of momentary success with its attending egotism, or conversely, self-pity when that success could not be achieved.

—Ron Jones,
colleague, friend

Chapter Ten

Pastor Paul at Long Hill Chapel

God does not want us to work for money. He wants us to work for His glory. I think this applies whether you are a pastor, or a teacher, or a doctor, or lawyer, or an executive. There is a liberty when we are working for the glory of God, and trusting Him to provide for our needs according to His measure.[1]

—Paul F. Bubna

Afterwards over three years of being without a senior pastor, the people at Long Hill Chapel (LHC) were wondering whether anyone in The Christian and Missionary Alliance would meet their needs. Although founded in 1946 by former Alliance missionary Rev. Anthony Bollback, the church, located in upper-middle-class Chatham, New Jersey, had a somewhat tentative identification with the denomination. As the largest church in the Metropolitan District, Long Hill was a strong supporter of missions—the Alliance program and many others.

Under the capable twenty-three-year leadership of Rev. Leroy Webber, the church had reached over 1,000 attendees and had planted several other congregations in the vicinity. The enormous outreach of LHC in ministries of compassion, giving, sending, preaching, children's programs and music re-

ceived national attention in the Alliance and throughout the
Northeast generally. The successor to Rev. Webber would
need to be an unusually gifted man.

Such a man was serving as interim pastor but was not available for the permanent job. Dr. Robert W. Battles had served
The Christian and Missionary Alliance as a successful pastor in
New York City and as secretary of the denomination. His wit,
charm and poetic sermon delivery satisfied the Sunday morning crowds, but in his retirement years, Dr. Battles was not able
to give full leadership to such a dynamic congregation.

Because the church had such strong lay leaders the programs
continued to minister effectively, but everyone knew a shepherd
was needed. Was there such a person in the Alliance? Several candidates were brought by the district superintendent, but for various reasons seemed not to be the Lord's man for the job.

In the fall of 1977 Long Hill Chapel's pastoral search committee had abandoned hope of finding a Christian and Missionary
Alliance pastor for their unusual church. Rev. Richard Bailey, superintendent of the Metropolitan District, was about out of suggestions, but realizing the search committee was looking outside
the Alliance, asked to present one more name for them to consider. He had heard about the pastor of Northbrook Church in Minneapolis, who had also served as pastor of the International
Church in Saigon, South Vietnam, and thought he might be a
suitable candidate. In fact, shortly after Webber resigned from the
church, Bailey asked Pastor Bubna to candidate at Long Hill Chapel, but Paul did not feel free to accept at that time.

Even in 1977 there were several reasons to reject the idea out
of hand. Long Hill Chapel was clearly a long way from the
Midwest culturally. People who moved to the East usually had
a hard time adjusting to the harsher spirit and quicker pace of
life in the northeastern megalopolis. And Chatham's citizens
were among the most urbane and sophisticated people one
could imagine. Furthermore, it was known that Pastor Paul
Bubna had suffered a serious heart attack less than ten years
ago. Was he fit for such a high-pressured situation?

Despite misgivings on the parts of both congregation and candidate, the pastoral search committee listened to tapes of Bubna's sermons and then sent a delegation to Minneapolis to hear the man. They returned with mixed reports. They were thoroughly unenthusiastic about the bearing of the outer man, but quite impressed by what they could sense about the inner man. His preaching, praying and spiritual authority were something quite exceptional. So they decided to take a chance and recommend him as a candidate. They knew it would be a tough sell because in Paul Bubna they did not see the profile of what they thought the Long Hill members expected. Webber was a tall, charismatic extrovert with a booming voice. Bubna had a great speaking voice, but was an introvert.

Nonetheless, the church was more than ready to hear a candidate, so Paul and Jeanie flew to New Jersey to candidate for the senior pastorate of Long Hill Chapel. The preaching went well, as expected. People were impressed by Jeanie as an excellent helpmate for Paul and a good role model of a Christian wife. And Paul handled himself well with the various boards. Their years in Vietnam had weaned the Bubnas from their monoculturalism, and they easily understood that their missionary skills would be useful in that new setting.

The rest is history, as they say. Paul, Jeanie, Laurie, Steve, Tim, Joel and Gracelyn Bubna would become the new pastoral family. Little did they know how much the move would affect all of their lives. Little did the church know how deeply that unique family would impact their people and thousands of others.

Immediately, everyone wanted to get to know Pastor Bubna. His fantastic feedings from God's Word attracted a spiritually hungry congregation. Even more, his quiet inner life of devotion demonstrated a model quite unusual for the frenetic, urbanized East. Was this man for real? He was a mystery not easily known.

However, as elder Bill Aichele said,

> We recognized early on that Paul was uniquely gifted by God in expository preaching. We received great practical teaching week by week. He not only talked the talk but walked it as

well. He and Jeanie complemented each other with their spiritual gifts. He claimed he had the gift of mercy and hers was hospitality, which she freely demonstrated.

Bill remembers, "One time, shortly after they were with us, we had an ice storm in the area and Louise and I were without power for several days. Without hesitation, Jeanie invited us to move in with them until we had heat in our home."

Another layperson in the church was Barbara Schultz, who had become a Christian the same year the Bubnas moved to Chatham. Paul's impact on her was typical of the way he affected the "folks of the chapel," as he called them. "Through his Spirit-led preaching/teaching, I, as a young Christian, had my eyes, mind and heart opened to biblical principles that helped me to grow in Christ—principles that gave me a solid foundation preparing me for my day-to-day Christian walk."

Barbara was one of the many Chapel volunteers who weekly tended to the beautification of the building and property. She recalls, "Over a period of time Pastor Bubna kept telling me the plants in his office were always dying despite the fact that he fed them. What did he feed them? Water, a little coffee and any other liquid he had handy. When I offered to be the caregiver, he readily accepted. I thought that a rather novel way of recruiting someone for a job!"

Christian holidays were holy times at the chapel. Paul loved the celebration and the decorating of the sanctuary that was part of it. The chapel ladies began decorating for Christmas right after Thanksgiving, adding a little each week. Remembering his nearly childlike enthusiasm over that process leading toward Christmas, Barbara said, "He took great pleasure in observing the progress we made, and his joy was complete when on Christmas Eve he called new believers forward to light the candles down the center aisle."

A Man of Few Words Who Loved Words

One of the many ironies of the person of Paul Bubna was that, despite his quiet nature, he loved words. Paul seemed to be one of the few Christians who took seriously the Lord's admonition about being careful with idle words. His stewardship of language was every bit as pronounced as his stewardship of all of life. Rarely did one ever hear Paul engage in meaningless chatter. No one is sure whether his introversion made him disinclined toward small talk or whether his reluctance to engage in small talk made him appear to be more of an introvert than he really was.

Paul surely could be the life of the party with his extremely quick wit, but one had the sense that when he did take on that role, it was for a higher purpose, like making others feel comfortable. He was quick to enjoy a good laugh, and that put others at ease. Although he was basically a quiet person, rarely did others sense he was judging them. Rather, if people felt awkward because of his slowness to answer questions, it was more of feeling discomfort for him than for themselves, a discomfort he never really had.

One of the frustrations of some of the members and more than one of his staff was Paul's reluctance to be directive with guidance. Because others trusted his wisdom and walk with God, many people would go to Paul for counsel with weighty matters. Rarely did folks go away able to say, "Here's what Pastor Bubna thinks I should do." More likely, they would go away with several ways to look at the issue, usually a bit less self-centered than when they came.

Pastor Bubna never felt obligated to be the answer man for other people. He did not claim any special insight, and he refused to act authoritatively when he did not have a deeply held conviction. And more than most people, Paul was able to discern the difference between absolute truth, his convictions, his opinions and his biases.

As a man who loved words, Paul can be remembered for having certain words that fell often from his lips. Those words included: *careful, holy, sanctuary, inner life, mentor, the main thing, missionary, folk, oh-wow, it seems to me, glory, vision.* His parishioners can no doubt still occasionally hear echoes of "The Scriptures tell us . . ."

Paul the Preacher

While it is true, as we said earlier, that Paul Bubna despised labels, there was one label in which he delighted: Pastor. No other title left him comfortable. He was Reverend, President, Doctor, but he really did not relish folks calling him by those handles.

In May 1984, when Nyack College awarded him the honorary doctor of divinity degree, his congregation at Long Hill Chapel took great delight and even some pride in that recognition. Many of the members said that if ever anyone fully deserved such an honor, it was Pastor Bubna. To celebrate that honor and announce it, the chairman of the elders at that time, Bob Nanfelt, came to the platform on the Sunday morning after the conferral and introduced Paul to the congregation as if it were the first time. Bob waxed eloquent about the many great achievements of Paul Bubna and then presented him to the congregation as "Dr. Paul F. Bubna." The congregation became untypically rowdy and greeted him into his own pulpit with a rousing applause, which lasted a few minutes. In his typical low-keyed, under-impressed-with-himself way, Paul waved them to sit down and as the noise subsided said, "Fear not! It is I, just Pastor Paul."

As pastor, Paul had some interesting practices. He was always thoroughly prepared every time he spoke. Usually he had manuscripts of his Sunday morning sermons prepared about three weeks in advance. He was always working on at least three sermons at a time. By the middle of the week, ten or so days in advance of preaching a sermon, he had his message polished in final form. He would study for a week, dictate the sermon on tape and then have his secretary type the message in a two-page booklet format so that the manuscript would be up to eight half-pages long. Then during the week leading up to the delivery he would read over the script several times, and on Saturday afternoon at home he would lie in front of the fireplace during the winter or out on the patio in warm weather while he memorized the message.

When he delivered the sermons, he would have the manuscript in his Bible, but he rarely referred to it. Of course, on most Sundays he also delivered an evening service sermon. There he sometimes used a manuscript, but he often preached from notes.

Usually Paul preached series of sermons based on books of the Bible. Occasionally he preached topically, such as his practice of preaching three or four sermons every summer on Christian stewardship. For Paul, stewardship of life was a vitally important concept. Stewardship of finances was part of it, but he focused more on giving our talents, gifts, time, energy, relationships and family to the Lord. He was never afraid to challenge his people to give, even financially. Paul was a firm believer that God owns everything, including our bank accounts.

Sometimes his sermon series went on for over a year, such as his popular "Through the Bible" series in which he preached one message on each of the sixty-six books of the Bible. Paul had the uncanny ability to analyze and distill the message of a book down to its essential emphasis and then to make that message urgently relevant to today. Even complex books like Ezekiel or Leviticus became alive and understandable under the pastoral tones of the master teacher, Pastor Bubna.

Sometimes Paul would choose a section of a book to address a contemporary problem. For instance, at Northbrook Alliance Church in Minneapolis in the late 1960s, Pastor Bubna was increasingly concerned about the onslaught of situation ethics and the "anything goes" mentality that was being spread. Not wanting to be reactionary or legalistic, he turned to First Corinthians and developed a short series based on chapters 8 through 10. The messages were titled "The Christian and the Questionable," "The Cross and the Questionable" and "Convictions and the Questionable."

He used the issue of meats that had been sacrificed to idols to show how the Apostle Paul solved a social issue by imparting godly principles, principles that could be used to make decisions about entertainment, fashion, friends and other social concerns.

If anyone truly has preached the whole counsel of God, it was Pastor Bubna. He touched on all the books of the Bible and adroitly wove into each sermon references and verses from many parts of Scripture. He loved to illustrate points by using biblical stories. He might be preaching from Matthew about Jesus stilling the storm and then allude to the storm that must have been going on in Esther's heart knowing she would have to talk to King Xerxes. Then Pastor Paul would rhetorically ask what storms in our lives needed to be stilled and whether we could trust Jesus with those situations.

Paul seemed to like himself best when he was in the pulpit. Not always comfortable in one-on-one conversations, he became completely comfortable in the pulpit. His natural introversion became extroversion. His soft voice became thunderous at times. His overly careful, almost-at-a-loss-for-words dialogue in counseling would be contrasted with a quick pace of pouring out ideas and admonitions. He pastored from the pulpit; he counseled from the pulpit. Paul agreed in part with Dr. Tozer's idea: "If you feed the flock on Sundays, you won't have to baby-sit them during the week." But Paul couldn't completely subscribe to that theory because of his compassionate nature.

The Fragile Vessel

No account of Paul's Long Hill years would be accurate without noting how his uncertain health condition affected him and his 1,000 parishioners. Paul's fragile heart may have aided in qualifying him for the role he was to play as a Christian leader, but it also kept everyone a bit on edge, despite Paul's own serenity.

Ron recalls one Sunday morning when Paul shared with his Long Hill Chapel family that he had just passed a milestone that would likely go unnoticed by the church, yet to him it represented a triumphant occasion. Those who were not personally close to Pastor Bubna may have expected a reference to his involvement with the Alliance or to his work at the chapel. But his testimony opened their eyes to another dimension of his life. He began to explain his personal exercise routine. He shared how his exercise bicycle was a lot more than a pedestal on which he worked up a sweat while crafting the core of his sermons week after week. That 5:30 a.m. daily routine was critical to his long-term commitment to strengthen his heart. He thought that it was likely that the cause of his death would be a cardiac arrest—and also that it would not be surprising if it would occur while he was riding his stationary bicycle. So day after day, month after month, as he pedaled away, he occasionally wondered to himself—as the miles began to pile up—just what the odometer would read on his bicycle on "that day."[2]

On this occasion he was referring practically to "that day" when presumably someone would find him dead beside his machine. At first he speculated whether the gauge would read 1,000 miles. Then when he passed that mark, he speculated if he would reach 3,000, then 5,000. *Perhaps,* he thought, *on "that day" the odometer will read 7,689 miles.* His example using an unrounded-off figure made his condition all the more poignant to the congregation!

Paul was never given to pessimism. In fact, he possessed an indomitable optimism about life. Yet he did not have the luxury of *presuming* he could lay a claim to tomorrow, a claim most of us take for granted. So when Pastor Bubna presented that picture of the reality of *his* daily life, the folks in the pews all momentarily entered into his world. And then they joined him in his euphoria. That Sunday at dawn, he proudly announced, he had passed a milestone that was quite extraordinary. The gauge on his stationary bicycle had just turned 10,000 miles.

The Caring Pastor

Even though Paul's preaching gift was so evident to all, he never considered that his spiritual gift was prophecy. At Long Hill Chapel he and several others on the pastoral team gave a Sunday evening series on spiritual gifts. This required many hours of dialogue, as the team wanted to know each other's gift(s) and to be able to share a theology of gifts on which they all agreed. They chose to focus on the seven gifts listed in Romans 12:6-8. During a staff meeting, one pastor said his gift was exhorting, another said his was teaching, and all expected Paul to say his was prophecy. Instead, without hesitation he declared that he had known for a long time that his gift was mercy. And as the team considered that, they realized it fit. Paul was at his very core a man of great compassion. He cared deeply about people.

One of the ways he wanted to bring new life to Long Hill Chapel in the late 1970s was to help those sophisticated, upper-middle-class Christians learn to show their care for one another. The chapel had already ventured into the trendy cell group idea with their Chapel Life Groups, but Paul was not satisfied with them. Some of them were just social clubs, while others were primarily Bible studies in which, as he said, folks could hide between the pages of Scripture.

So Paul created the concept of CARE Groups, the acronym standing for Congregations Affirming, Relating, Encouraging. To ensure that the leaders would help the groups be adequately relational, Paul chose people given to hospitality to host the groups, while others, usually elders and wives, were chosen to lead the group experiences. A curriculum of monthly meetings based on the "one anothers" of Scripture was drawn up, and the leaders would meet with one of the staff pastors one Sunday night a month prior to the CARE Group meetings to go through the lesson together. Paul and Jeanie were among the CARE Group leaders.

Pastor Bubna led a very disciplined life in every area, including his office. His days were structured in advance. He scheduled pastoral visitation and insisted that everyone on the pastoral team be involved in calling on folks. Hospital patients were the first to receive attention. When Paul learned that a staff member had failed to visit someone in the hospital, he would become literally incensed.

In the office he allowed himself to counsel people one or two times, but then he turned them over to someone else. Pastor Bubna always required people to do some homework before coming back. If they failed to do it, he refused to see them again, thinking they were not wanting to get better, but merely to feel better for having the cathartic benefit of talking about their problems. He figured they could do that with someone else. Often he told folks that they should be taking their problems to someone in their families.

Paul was very cautious about counseling women. He refused to see women alone in counseling situations and told his male staff members never to close their doors with a woman in the office. He discouraged drop-in counseling or visits, but when pressed he would spontaneously meet with someone in the lobby outside his office.

Staff Ministry

Pastor Bubna knew that God had called him to be a mentor to others. It was a role he was not comfortable taking at first, but he knew it was part of the ministry God had prepared him to do. In fact, he enjoyed talking about the ministry of mentoring and very effectively led workshops on mentoring. But he was not always comfortable as a mentor. He hoped his staff members would sort of catch on without a lot of direct teaching and leading of them. Usually, he attracted energetic, gifted young men and women who had a lot of potential and even more questions than they had potential. They all nearly idolized Paul, but they also wanted more from him than he was comfortable giving.

One of his most effective ways of mentoring was in the midst of real life situations. I (David) recall a harsh lesson about visitation. A certain fellow named Wally adored Pastor Bubna and treated the rest of the staff like hirelings. Wally became ill, and Paul asked me to visit him. It was evident that Paul had touched a sore spot because my reluctance showed through my body language. Paul asked what was going on, and I said that I would have a difficult time ministering in a loving way to Wally. I told Paul how Wally was contentious in my Sunday school class, disagreeing whenever possible, trying to make me look foolish.

Paul then, uncharacteristically, said, "You know what, Dave? Maybe this isn't about Wally at all. Did you ever consider the possibility that you have a tendency to turn anyone who disagrees with you into an enemy?" Paul then took me to Wally's house, ministered compassionately to him, and then said,

"Wally, Pastor Dave here has something he wants to say to you." Paul was not about to let me harbor hard feelings toward a parishioner if he could help it.

Paul's most comfortable mentoring strategy was providing words of encouragement. For example, a letter written on November 6, 1985, to staff members begins this way:

> As I worshiped this morning and thanked God for many things, my heart was filled with gratitude for allowing me the privilege of being one of His servants—and of serving together with the kind of team I do. I had in mind to write each of you a note telling you of my gratitude, but on second thought decided I'd like you to know my feelings about each of you.

Paul wanted not only to affirm each member but also wanted them all to know how he valued each one, hoping they would, in turn, learn to respect each other and truly minister as a team. He wrote a paragraph to and about each of seven staff members and an intern. A few examples will reveal how Paul's ministry of encouragement and affirmation served as a mentoring strategy.

> Ron, you have made a very significant difference in my life this past year. Your ability to pick up the administrative detail and manage it well has brought a new liberty to my lifestyle. Your unique way of allowing each person to be themselves is helping us be a happier and more effective team. It's fun to see you growing as a preacher. Bloody sweat and all.
>
> Tom, you are growing rapidly. I'm glad you are feeling stretched—thanks for your steady commitment and your willingness to be involved in the dynamics of your staff even though it stretches you, and all of us. I'm encouraged by the way you are quickly sensing my heart for ministry and letting us know you are on the tee—all the way. Your gifts of preaching and teaching challenge me to carefulness in my handling of the Word.
>
> Melinda, you have been a delightful intern. Efficient, effective—but above all grateful and responsive. You are becoming an effective and servant-minded disciple of our Lord. We are glad you are part of the team.[3]

Pastor Bubna held weekly staff meetings, usually to plan the ministries of the next Sunday and to discuss how the many other ministries of the church were going. He demanded punctuality and became quite upset when a staff member was late. He felt it was disrespectful to the other members of the staff and a sign of lack of discipline in one's life. With one staff member he became so upset over repeated tardiness that it became a spiritual battle in Paul's life. Another staff member asked him why he had seemed to lose his joy and what was troubling him so much. Paul reluctantly shared that he could not get the victory over bad feelings about this other wonderful staff member whom everyone loved. Eventually, reconciliation occurred, but the situation shook Paul's confidence in his walk with God for quite a few months.

As part of his mentoring responsibility, Paul was eager to see his pastoral staff members grow in their ministry skills, especially their use of Scripture. Long Hill Chapel had attracted a number of ministers of God who led or served parachurch organizations. One of them was Barbara Boyd, who authored much of the Bible and Life Curriculum for InterVarsity Christian Fellowship. When Paul realized her unusual teaching ability and experience, he invited her to bring a series of inductive Bible study lessons to the staff. Though she hesitated about being a teacher to her pastors, Barbara complied with Paul's wishes, explaining carefully that she would do it under his authority. Then she proceeded to make the life of Samuel come alive as she showed how to study the Old Testament inductively.

Barbara Boyd's assessment of her pastor gives a parishioner's insight:

> Because I was in ministry centered in Scripture, it was a marvelous gift of God to me to be a recipient of Paul's ministry Sunday by Sunday. Why? Because he taught God's Word with spiritual authority. He had saturated himself in Scripture. He had looked carefully at the large picture of a book, then focused on one part. He had put himself, as Stott says, "under the Word of God," meditated before God on the facts and their meaning and then applied them

to us in a relevant way. We knew that God had spoken to us.

Although I can't remember ever having any counseling as such from Paul, I always had the sense that he understood me. What a wonderful gift for a pastor to have! It is one of the aspects of the Lord's shepherding that is so dear to us. It is part of feeling accepted, to be understood. For then I can be myself; then I am free to be the best I can be.

I am grateful to God to have been one of the sheep in Paul Bubna's care.

So were several thousand other folks who loved Pastor Bubna.

Notes

1. Paul F. Bubna, "Acknowledge Him in All Your Ways" (sermon preached September 27, 1987, from Proverbs 23:1-12).

2. Paul often used this phrase to portray God's timeline, an idea he picked up from a quote of Martin Luther, who once said, "There are two days on my calendar: Today and 'That Day.' " Bubna reiterated, "Martin Luther was saying that there is only one day that a person can live for God, that is 'today.' However, there is a powerful hope that motivates the believer to live 'today' fully for the glory of God, and that motivation is 'That Day.' The call to preparation certainly indicates a day of reckoning, a day of accounting." (Paul F. Bubna, "Joel: The Apocalyptic Man" [sermon preached September 14, 1986, from Joel 2:1-11]).

3. Paul F. Bubna, personal letter on Long Hill Chapel stationery, November 6, 1985.

The Personality and Passion of Paul F. Bubna

I really got to know Paul Bubna when he became the first full-time president of Alliance Theological Seminary (ATS). I saw a pastor devoted deeply to the seminary community. When he was on campus, he attended every chapel. To him worship was a high priority. Often he lingered in the hallways so he could get to know the students. He learned the name of every student and addressed each one by name. Students knew his office was always open to them; they were comfortable going into his office for an encouraging, friendly chat. He filled the role of pastor for the ATS community; he showed me how it should be done.

He reminded us to "pray first." We knew he practiced this, as he rose early every morning to ride his stationary bike and pray. His prayer list, mounted on the handlebars, included us all. He often walked the trails along the Hudson River. As he met people along the path, he endeavored to introduce them to his Lord. He demonstrated how we should exercise, pray, walk and witness.

Paul came to the seminary from many dynamic years in the pastorate. He admitted that he was not an academic. Thus he spent his first year probing and scrutinizing. When I served as academic dean, I always felt he respected my perspective. Paul supported the faculty when their academic freedom was under attack, but not without a solid understanding of the issues. He risked his own reputation for us. He loved theology and would consult faculty in their areas of expertise. He wanted to know what the faculty knew and what they thought. I sensed that Paul was our champion, a thinker, a team player and a consensus builder.

Paul modeled servant-leadership for me. I recognized Paul as a family man. I remember how he loved his family, and especially his wife, Jeanie. As Jeanie's health deteriorated, I observed how he cared for her every need, true evidence of his servant heart. I will never forget his example. After Jeanie's passing, he spoke about healing in my class, a difficult topic in any case. He opened himself up to the students and challenged them, "Ask me anything." He was totally transparent. Pastor/president Paul Bubna enriched my life.

—Dr. Harold P. Shelly,
colleague at ATS

Chapter Eleven

The ATS Years

*It is possible to be intelligent, industrious, studious, even eru-
dite, and still be preoccupied with the trivial. It is possible for
a church to become totally absorbed in trivial pursuits. . . . In
a good many churches what is transcendent and eternal has
slipped away and is seldom missed.*[1]

—Paul F. Bubna

An unexpected turn in Paul Bubna's life occurred in 1991.
No one, especially Paul, could imagine him as anything
other than a pastor. He had no other aspirations. But he
did have a higher priority than being a pastor, and that was doing the will of God. And the will of God seemed to be leading
him to become president of a seminary.

For others who had seen Pastor Bubna's enormous impact
on aspiring pastors and missionaries, it did not seem unreason-
able at all that he should be considered for the presidency of the
denomination's seminary. For Paul Bubna, such a possibility
could only reinforce the idea that God's ways are indeed mysterious. But one thing he enjoyed so much during his ministries
was mentoring pastoral and missionary students. And he would
have those opportunities in abundance at the seminary.

An Unexpected Call

Though by the early '90s more people were calling him Dr. Bubna because of his stature as a denominational leader, Paul did not consider himself to be an academician or an administrator. So when the call came for him to become president of Alliance Theological Seminary, the national seminary of The Christian and Missionary Alliance, Paul struggled to be sure it was the call of God. He knew the seminary's history well.

Pioneered in 1960 as the brainchild of C&MA President Nathan Bailey, Foreign Secretary L. L. King, Home Secretary Leslie W. Pippert and others, Jaffray School of Missions (JSM) was first led by former missionaries Jack F. Shepherd and G. Linwood Barney. This innovative school was the first graduate-level program in the United States to specialize in world missions. The Alliance leaders placed the program on the campus of Nyack College and attached JSM to the college's charter.

As was true of The Christian and Missionary Alliance, Nyack College and other Alliance entities, Alliance Theological Seminary was conceived and piloted to be a culturally cutting-edge institution. Sensing that traditional seminaries were not producing effective, aggressive, Spirit-led ministers for this nation or nations around the world, Alliance leaders in the 1960s created JSM as a new model—one that would serve the needs and interests of the Alliance.

During the "adolescent" phase of the seminary, the institution was known as Alliance School of Theology and Missions (ASTM). Along with the name change was an overt effort to provide a curriculum for training home-field pastors in addition to the existing cross-cultural emphasis. During this phase, the leaders sought to give greater academic credibility to the seminary by seeking professional accreditation.

Having achieved accredited status, not only with Middle States as part of Nyack College, but also with the Association of Theological Schools, the seminary was able to promote itself as an equal to any other traditional seminary program. Thus the name was changed to Alliance Theological Seminary (ATS).

Paul, the Seminary President

Administratively, while the president of Nyack College was technically president of the seminary, The Christian and Missionary Alliance Board of Managers looked to executive directors of the school to give it leadership. That pattern continued until 1991, when the trustees of the college and seminary decided ATS should have its own president. They wanted a man who had a proven track record as a pastor, as well as someone who had a passion for missions.

Two of the most influential trustees were Don Seibert and Bob Nanfelt, who had both served as chairman of the board at different times. They were also elders at Long Hill Chapel and had been greatly blessed by the fourteen-year ministry of Pastor Paul Bubna. They could envision no better role model for seminarians. The question was: Would the seminary faculty accept as president a pastor who did not have a background in higher education nor any advanced degrees?

Another question was: Would this pastor be willing to make such a career move at age fifty-nine? One thing settled the question for Paul Bubna—his intense commitment to the future of The Christian and Missionary Alliance. Paul believed that pastoral and missionary candidates needed more than the head knowledge seminaries could impart. His experience with interns had demonstrated that he could have a significant influence on students. Mentoring was obviously an area of ministry he believed in, because all over America and on many mission fields were ministers whose lives he had impacted.

During his five years as president of ATS (1991-1996), Paul was able to lead the seminary in some significant changes that still bring blessing to that school. Foremost, but perhaps least apparent to new onlookers, was the change of culture his presence encouraged. Never did he pretend to be a typical academic administrator. He led from his strength: his pastoral nature. Don Bubna reports that Paul "wanted to preserve and nurture spiritual formation with a pastoral touch throughout the life of the seminary." He began doing that by building caring relationships for the faculty and staff members. One of the things that most surprised him was that highly educated professors are normal people who need and want to be loved and understood. The ATS faculty opened up to Paul's pastoral style like a flower in mid-May.

He had feared that faculty might be standoffish and skeptical about his leadership because of his lack of academic credentials, yet within months he found such complete acceptance that he sensed the faculty were truly his team. Winning them over did not happen without some pain, however. When Paul came on the scene, Rexford Boda was president of Nyack College. He graciously handed over the title of president of the seminary to Bubna. But that did not automatically make Paul the leader. For its first thirty years, executive directors led the seminary, including such notables as Jack Shepherd, Wendel Price and Terry Wardle. Dr. David Hartzfeld was currently in that role and was truly the leader of the faculty. Paul sensed that David's philosophy of seminary education was rather classical and that his own more practical philosophy might clash with Hartzfeld's ideas. His hunch was right. For the first year the two men tried to work together, but one of the failures of his leadership, as Paul himself viewed it, was his inability to help David make a transition ideologically and personally.

Pray First

One of the ways Paul won over the faculty and students of the seminary was just by being himself. His intense spirituality and heart for God shone through. Jeff Quinn, who served as vice president for administration under Paul, recalls:

> Early in Paul's ATS presidency, signs began to appear around its facilities. Seminary residence halls, offices and classrooms were all conspicuously adorned with these signs. One could not enter an ATS building without seeing them. These simple signs all carried the same two-word message: "Pray First."
>
> Paul had quietly worked with a group of seminary students who had posted these signs. Whether the signs were Paul's idea or the students' was never certain. The message carried by the signs, however, was clearly one of the central themes of Paul Bubna's leadership.

That September, as ATS students gathered for the opening chapel of the semester, Paul Bubna delivered a message entitled "Making Prayer Our First Work." Even at this early stage of the school year, the phrase "Pray First" had become embedded in the consciousness of the seminary. In both serious and lighthearted ways, ATS students, faculty and staff reminded one another that all their endeavors were best begun with prayer.

With two words, the heart of Paul Bubna had begun to impact Alliance Theological Seminary.

Don Bubna believes that Paul's early acceptance by the faculty was in part due to his diligence to be a presence among the people. Paul was regular in attending the Monday morning faculty/staff devotions and chapels. Don also recalls:

> I was with him the very first day he became active as president. On that same day he began a three-day workshop with Alliance pastors from across the US with the view of reinventing internship for the seminary. He clearly showed his priorities by attending all of the sessions and interacting with all the pastors.

Participating so enthusiastically in the internship program was not merely a strategy for Paul to gain acceptance in the seminary community. He was passionate about its potential and believed that internships were among the most important learning experiences the seminary could provide. Jeff Quinn recalls Paul's commitment to the internship program:

> From the beginning Paul Bubna worked to understand all aspects of the seminary's program. In his heart, however, he remained a pastor and he felt most at home in seminary matters that dealt most closely with the life of the Church.
>
> This was evident as Paul became involved in the seminary's student internship program. Working closely with his brother Don and a team of pastors and ATS faculty, Paul endeavored to bring fresh life into this program. He spoke often that "pastors are formed in the local church," and he believed that the internship program could become a transformational part of ATS students' education.

With the help of an anonymous donor, Paul arranged to bring a group of pastors from across the country to the ATS campus. These pastors came from churches large and small, rural and urban. They were all men who shared Paul Bubna's passion for mentoring young ministers. Paul's goal was to involve them in the planning and development of the revised internship program.

On the day of the planning workshop, Paul was animated and energized. The pastor who was now seminary president would, for three days, be back in the world that he knew and loved. The workshop proved productive, supplying the planning team with good ideas for the direction of the internship program. For Paul Bubna, the workshop was a happy confirmation that his new ministry would often lead him back to the life of the Church.

Providing Facilities

One of the early challenges Paul faced was a sagging enrollment made more complex by the lack of affordable housing in the area for students. Most seminary students are married and come with young families. ATS had three apartment buildings but needed more. Paul worked with the trustees to build two new buildings on the Nyack campus. Today these buildings are known as Shepherd Hall and Barney Hall, in honor of the first pioneer faculty members of Jaffray School of Missions.

A greater challenge to the seminary's becoming an autonomous, professional institution was its lack of a building for classes, library and offices. When denominational leaders planted the school on the Nyack College campus, they made a minimal investment of funds. Over its first three decades ATS was able to build an addition to a college facility on the north campus. The space provided offices, classrooms and a library that would comfortably accommodate a school of about 100 students and 10 faculty members. However, the school had grown to over 300 during some semesters. With a very small endowment and several million dollars of new debt to pay for the new residence halls, no solution for the dilemma was in sight.

When I (David) became president of the college in 1993, it was evident that two schools were growing on a campus that could not adequately host one. Tensions were often high, as both administrations needed space. The seminary often got the short end of the deal because they were technically guests on the college campus. Then one day in late March of 1995 I received a call from Alliance treasurer Duane Wheeland. "David," he said,

> We have a problem. Is there any way the college can use the old headquarters building in Upper Nyack? Because it stands empty and is not being used for legitimate charitable purposes, we are about to have to pay a huge tax bill. If Nyack could occupy it by the end of this weekend, you would save the denomination several hundred thousand dollars.

In 1989 when the denomination moved its national office to Colorado Springs, the building was under contract for sale, and the buyer had deposited ten percent of the $6 million sales price. It was virtually a "done deal." However, the president of the purchasing company came over from Asia and said he did not like the location, so they abandoned the deal, including their deposit. For the next five years the building sat empty and for sale. The asking price had been cut in half to reflect the real estate market, but aside from a few nibbles, no serious buyer had inquired. The Alliance had already paid one year of taxes and was finding the facility to be a financial burden.

I got off the phone, called our treasurer in to conference with me, and we agreed: "This is ATS's big opportunity." But could a whole seminary be moved in just a few days? We called Paul Bubna into the conference and said, "Paul, how would you like ATS to occupy a $6 million complex this week?" We explained the deal, and immediately he caught the vision for it. Of course, he had the prospect of "selling" the ATS faculty and staff on the quick move. By that time his role as leader was firmly in place, and within a few days the seminary made its exodus from the college campus. In the subsequent years the denomination has deeded the property to Alliance Theological Seminary, and the facility has been significantly enhanced to be a state-of-the-art learning environment. Many people comment that it appears to have been designed specifically to meet the needs of a modern seminary.

Looking over the three-mile span of the Tappan Zee section of the Hudson River, Alliance Theological Seminary is strategically located as the only fully accredited evangelical seminary in the megalopolis between Boston and Philadelphia. A question had been raised a number of times as to whether the seminary ought to relocate to a less expensive area—perhaps follow the denomination to Colorado—but the faculty and administration have been unified in saying the multicultural environment in the New York City area should not be vacated. Even though salaries cannot hope to reflect the economy of the area, the seminary personnel are willing to sacrifice to maintain their strategic mission.

So, under the leadership of Paul Bubna—this man hardly qualified to be a seminary president—Alliance Theological Seminary expanded its housing opportunities for students and acquired a whole new campus, ready for the challenges of the new millennium.

Cutting-Edge, Church-Based Seminary

President Paul Bubna believed that seminaries existed to serve the Church, and in the case of ATS he was intent on seeing a close relationship develop between The Christian and Missionary Alliance and its theological seminary. He made that clear in a number of ways. For example, in an address entitled "ATS . . . Looking Ahead," which he gave to the ATS faculty in the fall of 1992, barely a year after he became president (April 1991), Paul said:

> It is easy to say if ATS serves the evangelical community well by being an excellent educational institution, it will serve the Alliance in the process. That statement is basically true, but in my mind, inadequate.
>
> It is not enough to take a passive stance toward the Alliance mission; to say, "We have built a fine evangelical seminary, it is here for The C&MA to use as they will." I believe we need to take leadership in helping our constituency to buy into seminary training, to stretch ourselves to package our

offerings so they will meet the market where it is, and to
live on the edge of losing our accreditation if that is what it
takes to get the job done.[2]

One thing he had in mind that would link the seminary more
closely with the local churches was an innovative proposal he
called Creative Curriculum 2000. He explained to the faculty
that it would "involve having the first year of seminary training in
local churches." The benefits of such a unique program, blending
seminary and church in training future pastors, he explained this
way:

> By allowing the student to begin studies in his or her own lo-
> cal church or one nearby, we can minimize the issue of prox-
> imity.
>
> The training of the local pastor to oversee the studies of
> the student, the interaction of the pastor with the regional
> faculty member and the presence of the student interacting
> with the congregation will allow the seminary to have a pro-
> found impact on the local church. At the same time this inter-
> action will help our own campus faculty to keep abreast of
> trends in local church life nationwide.
>
> Students arriving on campus will come with a better un-
> derstanding of local church life, which they can integrate
> with their studies.[3]

Before Creative Curriculum 2000 was implemented, other parts
of the seminary agenda began to fall into place, including the
availability of the new campus in Upper Nyack and the regional-
izing of the ATS program on other college campuses. Nearly a de-
cade later, the plan is still viewed as a creative way to achieve important goals that have defied seminary philosophy for centuries.
In fact, ATS has been working toward a similar plan with some
key Alliance churches.

Seminary Under Fire

In all of his years as a pastor, Paul Bubna had never had to take
a stand in a theological battle in which the orthodoxy of his organization was suspect. Seminaries are rightfully a bit more under

the watchful gaze of the Church than a local church, so when a few ATS professors in the early '90s sought to engage in dialogue about the plight of the lost and the nature of hell, ATS soon found itself under fire. They wrote a few books that presented several points of view on these topics. Some readers took the perspective that the seminary must be endorsing less-than-orthodox views or it would not allow such books to be written by its professors. Word began to rifle around the denomination that a few professors at ATS were not adhering to biblical doctrine.

Paul found himself in a dilemma. On the one hand he wanted to be trusted to keep the seminary theologically sound. On the other hand, after interviewing the professors in question, he knew he had to support his faculty. He took the position that while the two professors in question may not have been as wise as serpents, they were as harmless as doves. His exoneration of them, however, did not satisfy everyone. Paul wanted the matter dealt with decisively, so he urged that a denominational hearing be arranged, and if discipline would be needed, so be it.

The matter was then brought to a district inquiry since the Metropolitan District of the Alliance credentialed the professors. After careful scrutiny by the district committee, the professors were declared innocent of wrongful doctrine. However, everyone involved learned a lesson on the limitations of academic freedom in a denominational seminary. For President Bubna this was a very painful episode because his merciful spirit recoiled at the dissension it brought between brothers in the Lord.

Dealing with Tragedy

When Paul and Jeanie Bubna moved from Chatham, New Jersey, to Nyack, New York, in the summer of 1991, the family knew something was wrong with Jeanie. Her disease was a baffling one. First she lost her usual zip. Some of the ladies from Long Hill Chapel who helped the Bubnas move and settle into their Upper Nyack home were shocked when Jeanie the dynamo needed to take frequent rests and uncharacteristically had to depend upon others. The early thought was that she was suffering from chronic fatigue syndrome. Then she began to lose control of her muscles and nerves, leading to the diagnosis of Parkinson's disease. But the symptoms did not quite fit that either.

On August 22, 1993, Paul wrote to his children to explain the diagnosis and his response to it:

> It was just before the [family] reunion that the doctor confirmed the diagnosis for Mother of Progressive Supra-Nucleur [sic] Palsy. At that point we had little idea of what that meant and it was not until after the reunion that we received pages from a medical journal sent by Paul N. The language was so technical that it took a while to get a hold of it all. In fact, it was not until we arrived home a couple weeks ago and I read more carefully some literature that had been sent by Mary O., that I realized how quickly this disease moves.
>
> As you probably know now, the average life span for PSP is from four to five years from onset. We still have not had a full report from our doctor but we are, no doubt, well over three years into the process. A natural first response to such news is denial. I was not aware how much of the literature Mother read or understood and was watching to sense her response. On this last trip to Colorado Springs for the missionary furlough seminar, where both Joel and Elin and Uncle Don and Dee were with us, I opened conversations with Mother about where we are. She had not fully understood what the literature was saying but felt sure from the progress of the disease that her time was not long.
>
> It has been releasing to be able to talk openly about the possibility of her soon homegoing. Using the word [possibility] is not denial—remember we have been here twice with my illnesses and God has seen fit to give additional years. We are leaving the door open for Him to make the last move, but we are preparing for death if that is His choice.[4]

For Paul, these were very painful months, but they were not without a silver lining. For the first time in memory, Paul Bubna was the strong one, the one the rest of the family relied upon, especially Jeanie. Despite the heavy load he carried for the seminary and the denomination, Paul took genuine delight in serving his dear wife. He was proud of the way she was facing her death. He told his children:

> You are not surprised, I am sure, to see the strength and pluck that Mother is showing. She continues to walk on with unbelievable patience and balance. It is a joy to serve her and watch God's grace being displayed. Joel and Elin are wonderfully sensitive and helpful. The ATS family is reaching out to us. Our pastor is a source of strength. We are being well cared for.
>
> While there are moments of great pain, on the whole God is enabling us to keep perspective. We are children of the King, destined for eternal glory. The best days are yet ahead. God has privileged us to be His servants and entrusted us with fruitful years of ministry. Our children honor God and are a source of great joy. Our friends are countless and precious. We have no regrets.[5]

The thought of impending tragedy in President Bubna's family had an enormous impact on the seminary community. Jeff Quinn was very close to Paul during that time. His memories are moving:

> As Paul and Jeanie learned more about the nature of Jeanie's deteriorating physical condition, Paul the president had the added burden of coping with each development in the spotlight of his very public position. This proposition was difficult indeed for a man who by nature preferred the privacy of family and supportive friends. Paul understood the demands of his role, however, and placed his trust in God.
>
> In private conversations, Paul spoke both about his growing sense of loss and his thankfulness for the years he and Jeanie had shared. From the days immediately following his first heart attack, Paul had begun to cope with the notion of "till death do us part." He had simply never anticipated that he would be the one to remain behind.
>
> Paul Bubna always believed that a Christian leader has an obligation to model character as part of mentoring those who follow. In no way did Paul's modeling prove more powerful than in the way that he dealt publicly with Jeanie's illness.

As seminary students learned of Jeanie's condition, many asked how they might help. Often they were simply invited to visit with the Bubnas at their home or to go with them for frozen yogurt, a favorite treat for Jeanie. In these visits students saw Paul, tender and attentive, but also positive and even humorous, as he cared for his ailing wife. In these poignant encounters, students couldn't help but be impressed with the joy and peace evident in Paul's life.

Paul was open and honest about Jeanie's condition and realistic about her prognosis, but his words and deeds never centered on himself. On those occasions when Paul did speak publicly about Jeanie, it was almost always to express his gratitude to someone for an act of kindness or to acknowledge God's goodness and mercy in their lives.

More frequently, however, Paul spoke about how their ordeal was giving him fresh sensitivities and new understandings. One chapel sermon addressed his deep new appreciation and need for community. Another devotional talk for faculty and staff related how deeply worship could affect someone in pain. Paul and Jeanie's circumstances were offering painful lessons. Paul Bubna's pastoral heart moved him to share these lessons, authentically, with the seminary community. In many ways Paul's final years with Jeanie were his finest years as a husband and a leader.

When Jeanie, Paul's wife of forty years, died on Mother's Day in 1994, the nearly unthinkable happened: Paul had outlived his wife. For decades the Bubna household had lived with a robust, energetic wife/mother while they painfully watched their husband/father try to keep his heart pumping. Everyone presumed Jeanie would outlive Paul, probably by decades. But it was not to be. For that reason, it was a mercy of God that Jeanie's illness was somewhat prolonged, allowing the family to get used to the idea that she would be departing this earth much earlier than expected.

During those months after Jeanie's death and before moving to Colorado, Paul reached out to a number of friends and family members for special support. Daughter Laurie lived not too far away in New Jersey, and Paul would often drive to Medford to be with her and the Berglund family. That was a great source of comfort to him. On July 7, 1994, he was able to write to the family:

> We have faced death head on and found it to be a defeated foe. The glory of heaven is real and a source of expectancy. The pain of separation is greater than I could have imagined. There are moments when it seems that every cell in my body is screaming for Jeanie. It seems apparent that I have a lot of letting go yet to do. One morning last week I walked up into the cemetery behind the little church near THE FORGE. It occurred to me that each of the graves there represents the same kind of overwhelming grief that I am feeling. I thought of that this evening with the news of the thirteen firefighters killed in Colorado. It is hard to realize that this experience which at this moment seems so much bigger than the whole world, is actually, along with birth, the most common and universal of all experiences. Somehow that is helping a little bit in gaining perspective.[6]

Keenly aware that his own grief had awakened a need in many in the seminary and the Alliance to learn how to respond to grieving people, Paul took the opportunity to write an article in the seminary's quarterly publication, *The Shepherd's Staff.* That material is reprinted in Appendix 2.

Notes

1. Paul F. Bubna, *Second Corinthians* in *The Deeper Life Pulpit Commentary* (Camp Hill, PA: Christian Publications, Inc., 1993), p. 75.
2. Paul F. Bubna, "ATS . . . Looking Ahead" (address given fall 1992 at ATS).
3. Ibid.
4. Paul F. Bubna, letter to his children, August 22, 1993.
5. Ibid.
6. Paul F. Bubna, letter to his family, July 7, 1994.

The Personality and Passion of Paul F. Bubna

Love took us by surprise. Paul and I were astonished by the intensity, the substance of our relationship. Since both of us had dealt with deep losses and formidable challenges in our private lives, we came to one another poised for joy. Paul often expressed the "ease" of our marriage, but in reality, that effortlessness was born out of the grit of frank conversation, expression of needs, vulnerability and willingness to sacrifice for the sake of the other. There was lots of quiet listening and careful attending, a generosity of spirit.

The character traits people admired in public were sincerely lived out in private. Paul was a person of discipline, prayer, wisdom and tenderness. Underneath his soft-spoken demeanor was a steely resolve to do right, to keep the glory of God the "main thing." In addition to family, he loved and prayed daily for each staff member he had ever known. He was slow to acknowledge the weaknesses of others and delayed difficult confrontations. He was quick to acknowledge his own weaknesses and drew people around him to make up the deficit.

Although Paul was clearly a leader—and in the final chapter of his life, a decisive one—he retained a childlike, guileless quality, which attracted people to him. That naïveté also made him amazed at the cost of groceries (his bachelor fare had been cereal and bananas) or a yard of fabric or a new tie.

Early on, we talked about Paul's health. He grieved over the idea that he could leave me—the second time a widow. The poignancy of Jeanie's death heightened his awareness of my potential loss. "I could cause you a lot of pain," he wept. Yet we concluded that we would surely have ten—maybe fifteen—years of happiness together. It seemed well worth the risk. We wondered aloud what the future would look like after his presidency, in two, five, maybe eight years. "I may have another church in me yet," he confided. But mostly, he wanted those after-years to be a reflection of my gifts and urged me to develop them. And so we pledged to cherish each day together.

Paul's prediction came true: He did cause a lot of pain. It has taken many days—years—to reconcile that those few months of exquisite joy outweighed the enormity of his passing. And yet I am so grateful.

It was a remarkable thing to have known the man Paul Bubna. And an honorable thing, indeed, to have been his wife.

—Mrs. Patti Bubna,
wife

Chapter Twelve

President Bubna

I am not asking God to go out in a blaze of glory. I am only longing that my finish will be consistent with the message I have preached and the life I have endeavored to live out. I do not want to get mean and crotchety in my later years. I do not want to lose a singleness of purpose or spend the last years childishly doting upon myself. I do not want to get cynical and critical, or contaminate my environment with a complaining spirit. Lots of people run well in the early part of the race, but do not finish well.[1]

—Paul F. Bubna

To Paul Bubna there was no higher calling in life than to pastor a local congregation. Even when he was running for the presidency of The Christian and Missionary Alliance, Paul's platform was unashamedly based on his being a pastor. The other candidate (certainly not an opponent) presented himself as a change agent, and that was a popularly received idea at the time. Paul gave great consideration as to how he should present himself. He had been vice president of the denomination for many years, served on the Board of Managers, attended dozens of President's Cabinet meetings and given excellent leadership to the denomination's theological seminary. But for Paul Bubna, his prized identity was as a pastor, so the opening words of his campaign speech were, "I am a pastor. This is not just what I do; it is who I am."

He prevailed in the vote by a fairly close margin. Many of those closest to him said later that it seemed he was purposely under-selling himself. The speech was a poor one, not because he presented himself as a pastor, but because he did not speak with the usual passion that people had come to expect. One of his close colleagues mentioned this to him, and Paul responded that he was not running for office and he would have been just as happy if the other candidate had been elected. Furthermore, he did not want anyone to vote for him based on promises, but on character and on the confidence that he was God's man for the job.

President Paul

In 1996 one of the practices of the Nominating Committee for the position of president of The Christian and Missionary Alliance was to have candidates respond to forty-two questions (see Appendix 3) that would elicit profile and perspective information. Reading some of his answers, it is easy to understand why the nominating committee was enthusiastic about presenting Dr. Paul F. Bubna as their nominee for the Alliance presidency.

Paul knew that he was God's man for the job. While he could conceive that God would allow someone else to be elected president of the denomination, Paul had a quiet inner assurance that God had chosen him for the position. In that confidence he walked, not desiring the position, but prepared to take on the challenge. His short tenure in the presidency surprised everyone, but the ongoing influence of the vision he presented has had positive residual effects on the Alliance.

Paul's brother Don recalled some of Paul's convictions and commitments that would influence his presidency:

> He was going to function as a pastor, caring first and fore-most for the people at the National Office and others throughout the denomination.

He had a strong feeling that certain things about Council needed to be changed. He felt that certain business issues had become "the issues" of the annual denominational meeting. The only year he served as president during Council, he preached that great sermon on "The Glory of God—The Issue." He worked many months on this sermon.

He had a great heart for missions and the unreached peoples of the world, including our North American cities.

He had a great passion to help pastors. He stayed after Council for the three days of special training for our "Pastor At Large" couples who were involved in the interventionist work in churches largely through Vision Building Weekends.

He was enthusiastic about changing the context of district workers' meetings at the National Office from a series of lectures to training/mentoring sessions that would demonstrate accountability in the body of Christ in a way that would make the district ministries more pastoral.

In his acceptance speech after the election, he spoke passionately about prayer and missions. He repeatedly said that prayer is our first work. He said that if the percentage of total giving of our churches dropped below ten percent going to the Great Commission Fund, he would move to take the word *Missionary* out of our denominational name.

A Perilous Presidency

As with all of his ministries since his first heart attack in 1968, Paul's presidency of the Alliance carried the threat of an imminent end. Most of the folks at the National Office knew about his health history, but few had known him in his weakened days. They knew him to be at peace with God and himself and that he lived for today with total investment of his energies.

His coworkers could see in President Bubna a serenity that came from being at rest in the freedom of living without anxiety or unwholesome drivenness. Perhaps that was because he had already dealt with the issues of "ownership" and "service" whenever the temptations of self-importance obstructed his vision.

His gift to many other leaders was his ability to live with a sense of "quiet" in the midst of the incessant demands of his work. Once when his administrative vice president Rob McCleland asked him what his top priority was in leading the Alliance, he responded without hesitation, "I think God is most pleased when I keep a quiet inner life before Him. Then I will have the strength and sensitivity to hear God amidst all the noises of life."

Yet in the midst of that rest there also abided a sense of urgency and striving to press on to yet-to-be-revealed blessings of God's future grace. Often he preached on the theme of finishing well. On one occasion he directed that conviction to those in the retirement stage of life:

> Remember, endurance means the ability to use the difficult circumstances of my life to build spiritual disciplines. It appears to me that one of the temptations of old age is to give up, to lose one's endurance, to begin to react to life, to put aside self-control, to enter second childhood and demand one's way. We need to remember that we never retire from our spiritual journey. As long as God gives us life here, His spiritual purposes go on and the witness that God wants to leave to those behind us is often most powerfully demonstrated in living with discipline, love and endurance in our difficult older years.[2]

That conviction was sorely tested when he entered into his own valley of the shadow. Ron and his wife recall one morning when Paul was in their home some months after Jeanie's passing:

> Sitting at our kitchen table he openly wept as he poured out his sorrow and verbalized the loneliness of his journey. It seemed so unnatural and actually quite bleak for this family man to be thrust into the ranks of a "single male," a status for which he was totally unprepared.
>
> But suddenly in the midst of his grief and tears he spoke with great resolve: "If I believe that God is who He says He is, I have to believe that the best part of my life is ahead of me, not behind me." From where did those words originate? He had disciplined himself over many years to trace the good purposes of the "owner," and now in the midst of

his own personal sorrow it was that discipline that brought
him back to God's view of his journey.

As Paul Bubna stepped onto the platform of national leadership in The Christian and Missionary Alliance, he took enormous risks in doing so and was in a sense forfeiting what
retirement he may have hoped one day to enjoy. His motivation to answer that challenge to lead the denomination was
subconsciously spelled out in a sermon he had preached fourteen years earlier. In that message he proclaimed:

> Let me suggest that when the life of the church is at its ebb
> tide, it only takes one individual, one person who both has
> a clear vision of God's design for the church and secondly,
> who has a sense of calling upon his life which gives him au-
> thority. That individual can begin to bring about the
> change that is necessary.[3]

His vision was crystal clear, and the sense of calling upon his
life that gave him authority was unmistakable and, moreover, was
confirmed by his denomination, which invited him to take the
helm at a critical juncture in its history. Knowing the toll it would
take, he unhesitatingly offered to give the last measure of his devotion to the daunting task of steering a missionary movement
out of the harbor of uncertainty and into the open seas—onto a
course chartered to fulfill the Great Commission, powered by the
winds of the Holy Spirit, which were once again filling its sails.
That decision was wholly consistent with his estimation of life, as
summed up in this statement about God's glory:

> The glory of God is seen when we are hard pressed but not
> crushed. The glory of God is best seen not in us never being
> perplexed, but that we are perplexed, and not in despair.
> The glory of God is seen not in that we never suffer, but
> that we suffer and are not abandoned.
>
> We do not like to talk that way in our success-oriented
> society. But the truth of the matter is that the life that most
> profoundly ministers to others is often when the glory of
> God is starkly contrasted with the frailty of our humanness.
> Sometimes by life, and sometimes by death.[4]

Vision-Driven

After his election, Paul gave one of the most stirring speeches ever to resound at Council. He told the large assembly on Sunday morning that the challenge he wanted us to take up with him was to stop the drift toward minimizing our missionary commitment and identity. He presented data that showed that, while the denomination's giving to missions was increasing slowly but steadily, the percentage of total giving of Alliance people for missions was declining rapidly. At that time giving to missions was about eleven percent of total giving, whereas in decades past it was closer to thirty percent. Paul boldly told the Council, "When, God forbid, that percentage gets below a tithe, you can expect me to be back here in front of you, and recommend that we remove our middle name, for we will no longer be a missionary denomination. And I don't want to be part of 'The Christian Alliance.' "[5]

President Bubna then went on to show that if Alliance people would increase their giving to the Great Commission Fund by the price of a cup of coffee a day, we would have $50 million to work with to achieve our vision. People seemed to connect with that idea.

That solemn note sent delegates home ready to challenge their people to give to missions more sacrificially than ever. The rallying phrase was that we wanted to be vision-driven, not budget-driven. And it seemed to be working. For the next few years, Alliance giving actually exceeded budget.

Paul was big on vision. He waited on God for direction for the Alliance and fully expected that God would reveal His heart for the Alliance. Paul wanted to embrace the ideals that had been part of the Alliance's heritage. He resonated with Dr. Simpson's holistic understanding of the gospel. He knew that for many in third-world and developing nations, the gospel was not good news unless it could fill their stomachs as well as their souls.

Mission USA

As he developed the vision he believed God wanted the Alliance to pursue under his leadership, Paul began to see the

United States as a needy mission field. He saw that, apart from the excellent growth being achieved in some of the ethnic districts, the home field's church-planting efforts were barely keeping up with the closing of churches. He began asking himself how the Alliance could reach out to people groups that were unreached and potentially responsive, using the same criteria the International Ministries division had developed.

His answer was fivefold. Paul turned the hearts of Alliance members toward five ethnic groups in America: Jewish people, Native Americans, African Americans, Muslims and Hispanics. He pointed out that a common element with these five groups is that the majority are urban dwellers. "In other parts of the world," he said, "we are targeting key cities as a means of reaching whole nations. It is time to move out of our comfort zones and address the needs of America's cities."[6]

One novel proposal he suggested to move in that direction was to call the division of International Ministries, with its cross-cultural expertise, to work in tandem with the USA-based field force of National Church Ministries. Task forces were chosen and commissioned to develop plans for deploying Alliance personnel and resources toward the mission of reaching these groups. That effort continued after Paul's death and is still being pursued.

Another creative idea was to develop the work of CAMA Services, the international relief arm of the Alliance, to begin work among intercultural peoples in the United States. Paul's hope was to see the Alliance Men organization revitalized to play a key role in that endeavor.

Another part of his vision was to make maximum effective use of the World Wide Web, linking our churches more closely with the work of our missionaries.

And dear to pastor/president Paul's heart was restoring the spirit of unity of Council. Recognizing that in a large and diverse body such as the Alliance there will be many differences of perspective, President Bubna was intent on keeping the Council agenda limited to "the main thing," which meant the fulfillment of the Great Commission. His recommendation for dealing with secondary matters of difference was to create a theological issues commission that would function as a permanent committee to research controversies, such as the "elder authority" issue that seemed to dominate so many Councils.

During the 1997 Council a vote was being taken on whether to permit persons who were divorced or married to a person previously divorced to be ordained. The debate was energetic. Feelings and convictions on both sides of the issue were strongly expressed. Often after a speech from the floor the prevailing delegates would applaud. It was an atmosphere charged with adversarial energy. President Bubna was not the moderator of the business session, but sitting on the platform, he looked disturbed.

When finally the matter came to a vote, Paul asked the moderator for a special privilege to address Council. He said that as he had listened, people he loved and highly respected as biblical scholars had spoken on *both sides* of the issue. He then instructed that after the result of the vote was announced, he did not want people to clap. "This is not about winning," he told the Council. The vote was taken, the result was announced, and you could hear a pin drop in the convention hall. Such was the respect for this leader/president and his moral authority.

A final concern that he expressed came out of his experience as seminary president. Several times each year he and the Alliance college presidents would meet, and Paul was very encouraged by the spirit and enrollment growth of the Alliance undergraduate schools. His concern was expressed this way: "One wonders where they [the new graduates] will fit among us when they enter churches that have no plan for evangelizing their community."[7] His hope was that the young people would bring their zeal and passion for the Lord into the Alliance to renew the denomination rather than drift from it.

When asked where he got so many creative ideas, Paul would always tell about his long walks when he exercised his heart and his spirit. He communed with God during the walks, and he always seemed, like Moses, to come down with a fresh perspective.

His Marriage to Patti

The foothills of the Rocky Mountains in Colorado Springs gave President Bubna great paths on which to keep exercising his heart and his spirit. Besides providing good time for pondering and praying through the cares of the denomination, Paul's walks also gave him time to reflect on his personal life. As suggested earlier, even though Jeanie's illness was protracted, Paul had never considered the possibility that he would one day be a widower. Because he was so committed to Jeanie, at first Paul expected he would remain single. But he did not anticipate how lonely he would become. He prayed for grace to remain single if that was God's will for him, but it was obvious to everyone close to him that he was not coping well with his loneliness.

While reaching out to family members for support was Paul's first instinct, none of them was in Nyack. So Paul drew closer to me (David). As intern at Northbrook in Minneapolis (1968-69), associate pastor at Long Hill Chapel (1978-80), elder at Long Hill Chapel (1982-86) and colleague as president of Nyack College since 1993, I was privileged to have a unique relationship with Paul. So at Paul's request we established weekly accountability meetings. These were times when Paul and I would review how we were handling the essential areas of our lives.

I had suggested that we use the questions on a small card developed by a Christian pastor, so each week we asked each other:

- Have I been with a woman in the past week in a situation that could be viewed as compromising?
- Have all my financial dealings been filled with integrity?
- Have I viewed sexually explicit material?
- Have I spent adequate time in Bible study and prayer?
- Have I spent quality time with and given priority to my family?

- Have I fulfilled the mandates of my calling?
- Have I just lied to you?

These accountability questions have been used by thousands of Christian men, but for Paul Bubna they were about a lot more than accountability; they also gave an opportunity for fellowship and much-needed grief-processing. Paul's honesty in answering those questions each week amazed me. I had assumed wrongly that someone as deeply mature in the Lord as Paul would never be tempted, but Paul knew his vulnerability.

After Jeanie had been gone for quite awhile, Paul began to sense a freedom to take an interest in other women. He really missed having a companion. The worst time of the week would be when he would have to come home to an empty house after being away for a ministry or other kind of trip on behalf of the seminary.

One of his comments to me tells so much about how his heart had been shaped after God's heart. Talking about his desire to remarry, Paul said, "I don't think I need a wife to have somebody love me, but I need someone to love. I long to have someone to make happy by my love."

However, when The Christian and Missionary Alliance chose him to be their president, they elected a widower. As he moved to Colorado Springs, Paul Bubna was a lonely man. So he poured himself into his new job with full devotion. But, if anything, the loneliness increased. Now the closest family member was his son Steve in Colony, Kansas, a day's drive away. And with such a high-profile position and a busy job that took him to so many churches, Paul knew he was more vulnerable than ever. It seems that every pastor and pastor's wife knew the perfect woman for Paul. He actually received letters of inquiry from eligible women. He found this to be rather humorous, but he knew he still wanted a companion. His new accountability partner was Duane Wheeland, who earnestly prayed with Paul for God's perfect choice for him. Even so, Paul continued to be willing to remain single.

One day I received a phone call from Paul, who beat around the bush for a while and then asked, "Dave, do you know Patti Sellers?" I remembered her from working with her at the National Office. "Well, what do you think?" Paul asked.

"What do I think about what?" I responded.

"About Patti?"

"I think she's a wonderful, talented, perky lady, Paul. Why do you ask?"

"Well, I might want to ask her out; what do you think?"

I responded, "Well, I doubt that she will go out with you, but there's a lovely little Italian restaurant up in Palmer Lake that I know she would enjoy."

And thus began Paul's courtship of Patti Sellers. During the next several months a wonderful friendship developed. Patti had been widowed quite early in her marriage after having three daughters—Christina, Mitsi and Melanie. In the early '90s she moved from Nebraska and had served in several demanding jobs in the National Office. With her daughters now in college, Patti lived alone in Colorado Springs.

Where this new friendship was headed was sometimes a mystery to both Paul and Patti, but it was clear that they had come to love each other. The mystery cleared rather decisively and publicly at Council in 1997 in Charlotte. After one of the afternoon business sessions, President Paul Bubna asked the moderator for a special favor. He then stood before the General Council, thanked the people who had prayed for him and told them about God graciously bringing a new friend into his life. Her name was Patti Sellers, and he wanted Council to meet her.

Patti made her way to the platform, where Paul introduced her, and then to the surprise of everyone, especially Patti, he proceeded to ask her to marry him. Patti threw her arms around Paul and whispered, "Yes, you dear, dear man," into his ear. In flashing letters the video screen overhead spelled out the good news: "She said *yes!*" This was greeted by rousing applause by the delegates of Council as dozens of them stormed the stage to congratulate the happy couple.

Patti recalls the moment vividly:

He had asked me in advance if I would mind him introducing me from the platform, so that was not a surprise. What was a surprise was his proposal of marriage. He admitted later that he had been carrying the ring in his pocket all week, just waiting for the opportune moment. In reflection, he said he decided to ask publicly because he felt it was the best way to bestow honor on me and on our relationship.

On August 19, 1997, Patti Sellers became Mrs. Paul Bubna, first lady of The Christian and Missionary Alliance. The wedding was a small affair, attended mostly by family, on a small island in a little lake at the Broadmoor Hotel property in Colorado Springs.

After the wedding, Patti's life went through more upheaval than Paul's, because all her relationships at the National Office were now changed. With great grace Patti accepted the new "behind-the-scenes" role of president's wife. She was fully aware that Paul first "belonged" to The Christian and Missionary Alliance. Patti told me, "In looking back over my journal, I believe we had less than twenty days all alone in our own home. The vast part of our lives was spent ministering to our own families and the larger C&MA family." Christina, Mitsi and Melanie quickly responded to Paul's warmth and took great delight in being with him—being loved by him.

Love and Laughter

Some of Patti's fond memories of her marriage to Paul reveal the humor and tenderness of their relationship:

> One evening soon after we were married, Paul and I were sitting in our home office, my girls lying on the floor. We were absorbed in conversation when the phone rang. It was his brother, Don. They conferred a few moments by themselves, and before long it became apparent the talk had turned to more personal matters. "Yes, yes," we could hear Paul say, "we're having a grand time." The conversation went on a bit, and then Don must have asked a question. "Well," Paul responded, "why don't you ask the lady herself?" Beginning to

hand the phone to me, he quietly shook his head and handed it to one of my daughters instead. For the next five minutes or so, Mitsi carried on as if she were I. "OK, then," she finally concluded. "Bye-bye." She hung up and handed the phone to Paul, whose eyes got very big. Then he chuckled. By now we were all in fits of laughter.

"What?" I gasped. "You're not going to tell him?"

Paul smirked. "Nope. Not telling is half the fun."

Unbeknownst to me, Paul was worried about the first time he would offend me and wondered what it would be.

In private conversation, his voice became soft and low, and with some regularity I could not hear him. Oftentimes I would ask, "What? Say again?" One day, when we were driving from the Miami airport to a dinner appointment with a major donor, Paul got weary of my requests for him to repeat himself. "Why don't you just wait until I get to the end of a thought, and maybe you will be able to figure out most of what I've said?"

"Paul!" I exclaimed, "I don't want to know most of what you've said. I want to know *all* you've said!" It wasn't until later, in the privacy of our room, that I expressed my hurt. "I didn't choose to be hard of hearing."

Paul was distressed. "Oh, I was dreading this day, when I would make you sad. Please forgive me."

In the airport, on his way back from Malaysia just days before our wedding, he stopped at a duty-free perfume shop. Finally, after uneasy moments of trying to understand the clerk, he purchased a bottle that she proclaimed was "new to the market" and "your wife will love." He handed it to me shyly when he got back to Colorado.

"Oh, Paul!" I said. "It's been twenty-five years since anyone's given me perfume!"

"Do you like it?" he asked anxiously.

"Yes!" I responded. "You know just how to please a woman." It wasn't until months after his death, when I went to the store to replace the now-empty bottle, that I noticed the tiny French words *pour homme* printed on the bottle.

Paul, dear, sweet Paul, had given me men's cologne, and I had been happily wearing it for more than a year!

Although theirs would be a short marriage, those eight months were filled with love, laughter, rich conversation and joy for both Paul and Patti. In Patti, Paul got more than his perceived need. He found someone to love *and* someone who loved him—and he *did* need someone to love him. Patti was honored to be that person. Patti's hairdresser, after hearing of Paul's death, said, "Wouldn't it have been *so sad* if someone of Paul's caliber would have died without a wife to love him?"

Back to the Mission

President Paul had enriched his life and was ready to get on with the challenges of rekindling the missionary passion in a great denomination. He cared about all parts of the world, but Africa came to have a special place in his heart. Although he and his family had earlier served in Vietnam, in the latter half of his life Paul gravitated toward Africa. The Alliance had assigned him and Jeanie to bring encouragement and guidance to the African missionary staff, and Paul delighted in those ministries. Scores of African missionaries have testified to the powerful influence his ministry had in their lives.

Even after Jeanie died, Paul continued going to Africa every few years to minister to the Alliance missionaries of the West Africa fields. The presence of Paul's son Joel and his wife Elin, who served in Abidjan, Côte d'Ivoire, heightened his incentive. In fact, just days before his death, Paul and Patti had been ministering to the missionaries in West Africa. Their impact was profound, as reported by Joel shortly after Paul's death (see Appendix 4).

Paul had suggested they spend a few days in France on the way home, but Patti declined, sensing that Paul was quite weary. So they arrived home from Africa on Sunday, and he died on Tuesday. Later Patti reflected, "It was simply God's providence that he didn't die in France."

Paul always welcomed getting back to routines, so on the Tuesday after returning from Africa, he met with his accountability partner Duane Wheeland. As they went through the questions listed previously, Paul joyously went down the list, affirming what was going on in his life. When he got to number six, "Have I fulfilled the mandates of my calling?", he told Duane that never before in his life had he felt so in tune with what God was doing through him. He was excited about achieving a vision he believed God had given him for the Alliance.

But much of his vision and passion would need to be left for his successor. Later that day Paul met Duane and two other friends on the tennis court. From there he entered the heavenly courts.

President Paul has served well. He has put the ball in our court. His large family known as The Christian and Missionary Alliance now has the opportunity to play on his service and win the most important contest of the ages. And, surely, he is among that cloud of witnesses, cheering us on to finish well.

His Estimation of Life

God prepared a man—a man of singlehearted devotion to pursuing the glory of God. A man unusually gifted in communicating the heart of God. A man uniquely inspired with vision to lead a denomination. And a man now re-energized and equipped to get on with that vision. Suddenly, God took that man. Why? Why?

It was a question bouncing throughout the halls of the National Office of The Christian and Missionary Alliance. It was a question leaping across the mountains and plains of the Alliance in the USA. It was being asked in the fifty-five nations of the Alliance World Fellowship. And it was a question that puzzled and even troubled many individuals in the inner sanctuaries of their hearts. Why would God so prematurely take Paul F. Bubna from us, just when the new life we so hungered for as a denomination seemed imminent?

The green recliner chair in my (David's) living room was the setting of hours of such pondering. Tears, anger, confusion, complaints, begrudging submission were some of the emotions borne in that chair. God owed no one, including me, an explanation. But forever I will be grateful that He indulged me. As clear as any voice I have ever heard, the Lord said to my heart, "David, do you really believe that what is going on down on earth is more significant than what is happening here in heaven?" Instantly I imagined Paul prone before the throne of God in abject worship, and instantly the questions of my heart ceased. I put pen to paper to try to convey that insight and comfort to my friends, to Paul's family and also to the larger constituency with whom I frequently communicate:

> My mourning is about over; my grief will take a lot longer. Paul Bubna, my closest friend and mentor, is gone. Probably not news to anyone reading this paper. As David said about a loved one he lost, "I will go to him, but he will not return to me" (2 Samuel 12:23).
>
> I haven't checked the dictionary for the difference between mourning and grieving, but during the first few days of missing Paul I became aware of two distinctly different senses of loss. The mourning was based on an objective sense of loss. The Alliance had lost a great pastor and president, a leader who had inspired a new spirit of hope. I mourned the huge hole in our leadership.
>
> The grief is very personal and subjective. The loss of my friend and "father" will continue to bring pain and sorrow for me as well as for others who were privileged to know Paul Bubna well.
>
> I think the reason the mourning is nearly over is that behind it was the ugly *Why* question. Why would God allow this to happen? Yes, Paul had suffered two heart attacks, one in 1968, the other ten years later. But through his incredibly disciplined lifestyle of strenuous daily exercise and diet, he had become exceptionally healthy and had just received a very encouraging medical report a few months earlier. I had fully expected to see Paul fulfill all three terms as Alliance president. And with the great start we were off to in his first twenty months of leadership, this hope seemed most reasonable. As his wife, Patti, said, "The great vision God had given Paul seemed like life insurance." But God had other plans.

A few years ago I began to ponder the inscrutability of God; we often acknowledge that His ways are not our ways. When we think about God's inscrutability, we include His omniscience and expect that when we review God's mysterious acts, they will make sense, infinitely good sense. But when God acts quite oppositely to what we think makes good sense, we are thrown for a loop and land on the *Why* question. Why would God take Paul Bubna from the Alliance just as we were beginning to get refocused and recommitted to the historic mission of our church? If world missions is so important to God, and if the Alliance is one of His strategic instruments for reaching the lost, why would He take our inspired, anointed leader?

My questions went further than that. If The Christian and Missionary Alliance is not that important to God, then none of its subsets, including Nyack College, are either. So investing all our time and energy in this work suddenly seemed undermined and undervalued by God. Is it worth all the effort and aggravation?

Maybe this kind of thinking seems brazen and impertinent to you, but I am being up front about my thoughts, which I turned into prayers. I guess my prayers were rather confrontational, hopefully not irreverent. I needed to know, so I asked. And I believe God answered, which is why my mourning is about over. The Lord reminded me that Paul had just returned from Africa a few days before he died. I sensed that Paul either learned something important or performed a vital ministry while there, which perfected him. Perfected in the sense of the Greek word *teleos*, meaning completed, or having achieved a goal.

While what God does *through* us on earth is important, what He does *in* us to perfect (complete) us for eternity is more important. I am not implying that Paul or anyone has to do anything to earn heaven or a better status there. The moment we are justified our eternal citizenship is settled. What I mean is akin to Hebrews 5:8-9: "Although he was a son, he learned obedience from what he suffered and, once made perfect, he became the source of eternal salvation for all who obey him."

There will be no C&MAs in heaven, no denominations, no churches, no distinct people groups, not even husbands or wives. So maybe God isn't too concerned about the development of our organizations. What He is doing *in* us is far more important than what He is doing *through* us.[8]

Not Untimely

Paul's ordination mentor, A.W. Tozer, wrote,

The man of true faith may live in the absolute assurance that his steps are ordered by the Lord. For him, misfortune is outside the bounds of possibility. He cannot be torn from this earth one hour ahead of the time which God has appointed, and he cannot be detained on earth one moment after God is done with him here.[9]

President Bubna firmly believed this:

My story of being redeemed by God's grace is not going to be finished until I am part of all things being brought together in Jesus Christ. . . . The story of God's salvation in my life is not just an event. No, the story begins before the world was made. The beginning of the story comes out of the pleasure of God. God's dealings with me have to do with God's pleasure. The end of my story culminates with the praise of God's glory.[10]

Notes

1. Paul F. Bubna, "Living under the Son" (sermon preached June 28, 1987, from Ecclesiastes 5:1-7).
2. Ibid.
3. Paul F. Bubna, "Equipping the Saints to Minister" (sermon preached January 10, 1988, from 2 Corinthians 4:1-12).
4. Paul F. Bubna, "The Glory of God" (sermon preached June 3, 1997, at General Council, Charlotte, NC).
5. Ibid.
6. Ibid.
7. Ibid.
8. David E. Schroeder, *UpFront*, Side 1, May 1998.
9. A.W. Tozer, *We Travel an Appointed Way* (Camp Hill, PA: Christian Publications, Inc., 1988), p. 4.
10. Paul Bubna, "Self Image and Divine Revelation" (sermon preached April 9, 1989, from Ephesians 1:3-14).

Appendix 1

Message for the Memorial of Dr. Paul F. Bubna
2 Corinthians 4
Dr. David Schroeder
April 4, 1998

"My father, my father, the chariot of Israel, and the horse-men thereof." (2 Kings 2:12, KJV)

Well, children, here we are. We have all lost a father. Or at least, I think many of us feel that way. The hole in our souls, which many people have sensed, is sort of shaped like a father figure. For Paul Bubna truly was our patriarch as well as our pastor and our president. The emptiness we all feel, I sensed very soon after I heard Paul had died. First, I had a lot of questions about God's timing, but then I very quickly remembered Paul's own advice: When you are tempted to wonder, it is time to worship. But when I wondered what should I do—go to Colorado immediately? Stay in Nyack?—I realized that I would have called Paul to ask his advice. And I felt empty. I have grieved before, but I think this is the first time I have really mourned.

For Laurie, Steve, Tim, Joel and Gracelyn, our patriarch was also Dad, and to the five of you and your families, our hearts and love just surround you and want to comfort you.

To Patti, few had the opportunity and privilege that I had to stay in your home with Paul and see the beauty of fresh love and joy that God had built into your relationship. Likewise, Patti, we are all your family now in a more profound sense than ever before possible, and we want you to rest in our love.

To Don and Dee, and George, you have lost a brother, and more than a brother, a deeply devoted brother and friend, a colleague and encourager. We feel your loss also.

National Office staff and board of managers, we have lost a shepherd, the one hearing from the Chief Shepherd and leading us into paths of righteousness, hopefulness and vision. As has happened everywhere that I have observed Paul, God had already used him to change his surrounding culture. We sorrow together.

I am grateful to Paul's family for the high honor of bringing this message. I am especially grateful that they did not ask me to sugarcoat the grief in some trumped-up, artificial spin of joy and victory. Not that those things are not real. Of course, there is joy in knowing that Paul went from one thing he loved—tennis—to something he loved even more—worshiping God. And of course there is victory; Paul finished well, and already has heard, "Well done, thou good and faithful servant."

But from an honest human point of view this is a huge loss. Paul certainly would not want us to look at it merely from a human point of view, and that brings me to the two great dangers I face in bringing this message. The first is that in honoring my dearest friend and mentor I will displease him. He wanted only a simple gospel message at his funeral, and I hope to weave gospel into these thoughts, but I cannot detach myself from my love and admiration of Paul to be that objective. The second danger is that I will be too subjective, that I will memorialize, eulogize and canonize Paul out of my own experience, for surely no other person has had the impact on my life that Paul Bubna has had.

I suspect hundreds could say that same thing. Paul's influence in our denomination has been enormous:

- Dozens of missionary couples were greatly blessed by Paul and Jeanie's ministry on the fields;
- Scores of pastors received fresh vision of the holiness of God and the priority of worship as Paul preached at conferences;
- Several hundred seminarians were deeply touched by Paul's personal interest in them while he was at Alliance Theological Seminary;

- Denominational leaders have consistently looked to Paul for godly wisdom and insight;
- And several thousand parishioners in local churches where Paul pastored were taught by pulpit and example the meaning of grace.

I've chosen the fourth chapter of Second Corinthians as the text for this message because it develops three important ideas that were so much a part of Paul's life:

1. Glory, verse 6: God has given us "the light of the knowledge of the glory of God in the face of Christ."
2. Death, verse 11: "We . . . are always being given over to death for Jesus' sake, so that his life may be revealed in our mortal body."
3. Vision, verse 18: "So we fix our eyes not on what is seen, but on what is unseen. For what is seen is temporary, but what is unseen is eternal."

There is another reason I chose Second Corinthians for my text; my favorite preacher wrote a commentary on it, and I want to use some of his words to support these important ideas.

1. Glory

Foremost, as our patriarch Paul Bubna would want us to focus on the glory of God. And now that Paul has a firsthand, primary experience of that glory, he would draw us even more to the God of glory. Many of us here have a vivid memory of one of the greatest sermons we have heard, last year's opening Council message by Paul Bubna on the glory of God, using the book of Ezekiel as the text. Perhaps, like me, your spiritual life took a quantum leap of growth with a fresh, exhilarating vision of the glory of God. He talked about the presence of the glory, the departure of the glory and the return of the glory. He explained that God is jealous for His glory because it is the moral fabric of the universe; it is what gives us a sense of dignity and value; it is both a great weight and a great light. Then Paul referred to this verse: Second Corinthians 4:6, "For God, who said, 'Let light shine out of darkness,' made his light shine in our hearts to give us the light of the knowledge of the glory of God in the face of Christ."[1]

Many of you know that the pastor to whom Paul was accountable during his ordination process was A.W. Tozer. Dr. Tozer once wrote,

> We are witnessing a generation of Christians who have never felt the terror and glory of the vision of the great God of our Fathers. We need a noble conception of the transcendence of God the Father, Son and Holy Spirit. Some say that God is unknowable and unreachable. And it is true that no one can come to God apart from Jesus Christ, because He has honored us by taking human flesh and becoming a bridge, an easy bridge that we can come across to God. Christ lays His hand upon us, taking us in our slimy human sin while touching the eternal Father with His other hand and by suffering in death and resurrection brings us together.[2]

There, that's the simple gospel Paul wanted to have preached at his funeral. And it's the gospel of glory. Tozer went on in the same article to pray:

> O Lord, we pray that Thou will open the eyes of our understanding to see the One walking amidst the golden candlesticks. We're willing to be silent in fear and awe if only we might see Him. We see great men but we don't see Him. Open our eyes that we may see Him whose head is white as snow and whose eyes are like flames of fire and who is girt about with a golden girdle and dressed with a white linen garment, and out of whose mouth comes a two-edged sword, and whose feet are burnished brass.
>
> Help us to see Him. We don't see Him as we should. Take self-centeredness out of us, take the veil away that we may see Him walking in His glory so that we may recapture the wonder, worship, awe and delightful adoration that Thou dost long for the Church of God to have.[3]

I believe if Tozer had been able to observe the inner life of Paul Bubna, he would have been gratified that his prayer was answered, at least in this one man.

In his book on Second Corinthians, Paul Bubna says,

> The Scriptures affirm that we were made for God's glory. Therefore to long for glory, to be driven to obtain it, is . . . the normal pursuit of God-given desire. A.W. Tozer observed that on the whole our problem is not that we desire too much but rather are satisfied with so little. . . . God has created us to taste His glory and infinite joy.[4]

Paul, commenting on 3:18—"And we, who with unveiled faces all reflect the Lord's glory, are being transformed into his likeness with ever-increasing glory"—makes the important point that "the glory that transforms us is not a power that we possess but rather a Person who possesses us." Then he quotes Dr. Simpson's hymn:

> Once it was my working, His it hence shall be;
> Once I tried to use Him, Now He uses me;
> Once the power I wanted, Now the mighty One;
> Once for self I labored, Now for Him alone.
> All in all forever, Jesus will I sing;
> Everything in Jesus, and Jesus everything.[5]

As I pondered the influence of these two great men, A.B. Simpson and A.W. Tozer, on Paul's life, it occurred to me that he really got—and lived—the message of both of them—the majestic glory of the transcendent God celebrated by Tozer, and the all-sufficiency of Jesus Christ witnessed by Simpson.

I think Paul Bubna's eyes had seen the glory of the coming of the Lord. And like his predecessors, his passion for missions was driven by his passion for the return of the Lord.

2. Death

Death was not a strange or uncomfortable topic for Pastor Paul Bubna. Paul's untimely death caught us all by surprise, but I am 100 percent sure that it did not catch him by surprise. Instead, each new day of life on earth was somewhat of a surprise to Paul ever since 1968 when he had his first heart attack. He was a realist.

In 1979, after his second heart attack, as I served with Pastor Paul at Long Hill Chapel, one of the other pastors led a devotional exercise in our weekly staff meeting. He asked us to put a dot on a piece of paper, draw a line and put a dot at the end of the line. Above the first dot we were to write the year of our birth. Above the second dot we were to write the year we expected to die. Although none of us had ever participated in such a morbid exercise, we dutifully followed the instructions. All of us, except Paul, wrote as the year of our death a date well into the future—thirty or forty years away. Paul wrote down 1983.

Although he had recently undergone quadruple bypass surgery, it shocked the rest of us that he would be so pessimistic. His reply, however, was simply that he knew he was living on borrowed time and that, given his condition, statistically he would live less than five years. I think what shocked us even more than the date he wrote was his total peacefulness about that prospect. He understood that he was not indispensable in God's work and that God would take him when his responsibilities were completed; whether that would be four years or forty years seemed almost to matter little to him.

I think 4:11 could have been his theme the past thirty years: "We . . . are always being given over to death for Jesus' sake, so that his life may be revealed in our mortal body." He wrote about this verse in his commentary referring to the Apostle Paul, and since they shared the same name, I don't have to change a thing in applying it to Pastor Paul Bubna:

> Paul was a person who had faced his own mortality. His lifestyle was dangerous by choice. He was never far from death. "For we who are alive are always being given over to death for Jesus' sake, so that his life may be revealed in our mortal body. So then, death is at work in us, but life is at work in you" (4:11-12).

> This preacher did not live with a morbid preoccupation with death, but his value system and priorities took into account that every day might be his last.[6]

And I have written in the margin of my copy, "So true of you, Paul."

Verse 7 of Second Corinthians 4 refers to "earthen vessels" (NASB) or "jars of clay" (NIV). Paul says, "Translate that, 'mud pots.' " And then he writes, "The glory of God is best displayed in mud pots. God is not looking for superstars, just mud pots."

And then follows a section that can speak pastorally to us right now.

> We are hard pressed on every side, pressed down by heavy weights. But not crushed! The glory is not that we escape the crushing pressures that plague the human race, but that by the power of Christ we are not crushed.
>
> We are perplexed. Are Christians bewildered and perplexed at times? Yes, says Paul. The glory is not that believers are never perplexed, but rather that in the bewilderment they do not despair.
>
> We are persecuted. Are believers persecuted? Does God allow that? He does. The glory is not that God's servants are spared persecution, but rather that they are not abandoned. God suffers with them and sustains them.
>
> We are struck down. Are God's people knocked down? They are knocked down but never knocked out! We lose battles but are not defeated in the long run. The glory is not that we always win, but rather that we are not destroyed. God preserves His own.[7]

Pastor Paul has helped countless people deal with grief, and also to learn how to respond to the grieving. In 1995, while president of Alliance Theological Seminary, he wrote the first issue of *The Shepherd's Staff*. Jeanie had just passed away the previous year, and he noticed how so many people had trouble knowing how to express their grief to the family. So, his pastoral heart overruled his breaking heart, and he wrote on the topic "Grief: God Is My Portion." That little booklet has had an amazing ministry and may be needed now more than ever.

3. Vision

Chapter 4, verse 18 brings the two ideas of glory and death together in the idea of vision: "So we fix our eyes not on what is seen, but on what is unseen. For what is seen is temporary, but what is unseen is eternal."

Although President Paul Bubna lived life to the fullest, and his love for his family and his ministry created in him the ambivalence that the Apostle expressed in 5:1-10, I know Paul believed that this mud pot life blocks our vision of the full glory of God. But it didn't block vision altogether for President Paul. Paul had learned to fix his eyes on what is unseen.

Again, in his book he says,

> A pastor friend of mine used to say that there are just three simple things God requires of the Christian:
> - to believe the incredible
> - to see the invisible
> - to do the impossible.

And then he goes on,

> The incontrovertible evidence of inner spiritual life is the ability to see. The true worshiper cultivates the discipline of walking through the moments of the day with God always in view. The ability to see the invisible brings a deepening sense of reality to the pilgrim.[8]

What was unseen until President Bubna unfolded his vision includes:

. . . making prayer the first work;

. . . enabling all Christian and Missionary Alliance churches to become Great Commission churches;

. . . encouraging every Alliance person to become a Great Commission Christian;

. . . becoming vision-driven rather than budget-driven;

. . . reaching the 142 unreached people groups within our reach;

. . . focusing on the great urban areas around the world and in the USA;

. . . reaching out to embrace five minority groups in the

USA: Native Americans, Jewish people, Spanish-speaking Americans, African-Americans and Muslims.[9]

President Bubna's vision of what God wants to do through The Christian and Missionary Alliance has captivated us all. With a renewed sense of God's calling, a renewed faith and courage to be vision-driven to fulfill the Great Commission and a renewed sense of connectedness to the all-sufficient Savior, Sanctifier, Healer and Coming King, we can do nothing better to honor Dr. Paul F. Bubna than obey and follow Jesus Christ as He takes us into the fulfillment of that vision. Dr. Rambo will be reminding us of that vision in a few minutes, and I'm sure we will be called to a fresh, full-hearted commitment to it.

In closing, as we remember and honor our patriarch, our pastor, our president and our friend Paul Bubna, let me quote his final paragraphs from the chapter in his book that I have been using.

> Dr. W.B. Hinson was immersed in fruitful pastoral ministry when he learned that he had cancer. A year later he gave this powerful testimony to his congregation:
>
>> I remember a year ago when a man in this city said, "You have got to go to your death." I walked out to where I live, five miles out of the city, and I looked across at that mountain I love, and I looked at the river in which I rejoice, and I looked at the stately trees that are always God's own poetry to my soul.
>>
>> Then in the evening I looked up into the great sky where God was lighting his lamps, and I said: "I may not see you many more times, but, Mountain, I shall be alive when you are gone; and, River, I shall be alive when you cease running toward the sea; and, Stars, I shall be alive when you have fallen from your sockets in the great pulling-down of the universe!"[10]

That's the glory of the vision of godly mud pots. Amen.

Notes

1. Paul F. Bubna, *Second Corinthians* in *The Deeper Life Pulpit Commentary* (Camp Hill, PA: Christian Publications, Inc., 1993), p. 51.

2. A.W. Tozer, "The Terror and the Glory," *His* magazine, March 1967, pp. 29-30.
3. Ibid., p. 30.
4. Bubna, p. 67.
5. Ibid., p. 46.
6. Ibid., p. 63.
7. Ibid., p. 58.
8. Ibid., pp. 58-9.
9. Ibid., p. 69.
10. Ibid., pp. 70-1.

Appendix 2

Grief: God Is My Portion

Dr. Paul F. Bubna

Printed in *The Shepherd's Staff*, Volume 1, Number 1, a publication of Alliance Theological Seminary

In the newspaper comic strip *Peanuts,* Lucy often says, "Good grief, Charlie Brown, good grief!" The term "good grief" at first seems like an oxymoron. Can there be something good about grief? Most of us think not.

Dr. Paul Brandt, in his book, *Fearfully and Wonderfully Made,* talks about the gift of pain. He illustrates this idea from his experience of working with lepers. While there are destructive elements to the disease itself, Brandt points out that most of the bodily damage that lepers suffer happens because their extremities deaden. With no pain to warn them, lepers unknowingly destroy their fingers and toes with continual burns and bruises. Dr. Brandt points out that pain is a gift from God to bring attention to what needs to be healed.

In much the same way, grief is one of God's gifts to drive us into His arms for healing in our loss. Since death is somewhat of a forbidden subject in the Western world, the gift of grief is often shunned. The result is devastating.

In February of 1993, Jeanie and I made our first trip to the Holy Land. It was an exhilarating experience leaving memories that are still a source of spiritual nurture. For me, the most unforgettable moment was visiting the Wailing Wall in the old city of Jerusalem. Like most of us, I had seen many pictures of devout Jews standing at the massive wall saying prayers and expressing grief. While the wall is not part of the original temple of Solomon, it represents the remains of the ancient temple and is a symbol of the incredible loss that took place in 587 BC when the armies of Nebuchadnezzar overran the Holy City and burned it to the ground. On that day the Jews were driven from the land that Jehovah had promised them; they lost their sovereignty as a nation, they lost the city of David, and they lost the temple where the glory of God had come down to dwell among them. It was an incomparable tragedy. A grief that is still part of what it means to be a Jew.

As I stood there that day at the Wailing Wall, I contrasted this profound grief that yet lingers after 2,500 years with the Western view that expects grief to pass in a few weeks' time. When people tritely comment that "time heals all wounds," I don't think that they have 2,500 years in mind.

Several years ago I preached a series of sermons from the book of Lamentations at Long Hill Chapel and was amazed at the level of interest. It was clear that this series struck a deep chord within people. It seemed that folks not only found help in identifying their own pain and loss, but were encouraged by insights on how to relate to family and friends who are going through grief. Most of us feel awkward about relating to people who have experienced tragic loss.

I remember when our neighbor down the block died suddenly. Ours was a closely knit community but, oddly, few neighbors attended the funeral. I learned later that they cared but were afraid to come because they didn't know how to respond. Believers, because of the hope of eternal life, tend to be there at death, but often feel quite unsure about what to say or do.

The Old Testament Lamentations, attributed to Jeremiah, offer us a place to stand so that we can view the landscape of grief. There are few if any losses in history that compare to what Israel suffered in the exile. Here are things that I am learning from the laments of Jeremiah.

Grief Takes Time to Heal, but Time Itself Does Not Heal

The pain of great loss does not go away with the passing of time. Loss is the kind of pain that, when it is suppressed, wreaks havoc in the inner person. It is not time that heals; rather it is the process of grieving that heals if we allow it to do its work.

Grief Can Be Powerful

The magnitude of grief is measured by the dimension of the loss. Shock, overwhelming emotion, depression, loneliness, physical distress, panic, resentment, guilt, anger, inability to function—these are all expressed in the Lamentations and are common experiences in the face of great loss. Read the Lamentations and identify these responses. It perhaps will help you then to see them in the losses you may be experiencing.

Grief Begins Its Work in Expression

In a sense, grief is a work that one does and it begins by expressing one's feelings. The most helpful thing one can do for a friend in grief is to simply be there and to say little. And then to give them opportunity to tell the story. It was a great release to me as a pastor when I realized that there is little that can be said in the face of great loss and that *it is best to say almost nothing.* I am writing this just nine months into the grief of losing my wife of forty years. My observation is that most people try to say too much and in doing so often end up saying the wrong thing.

The great gift is simply to be there, and perhaps share a brief word of care, a hug or an arm around the shoulder and a sincere question which may open the door to tell the story. Helping people in grief to tell their story is what hastens the grief process and the healing.

The Lamentations are a way that the Jews have been expressing their loss for over two millennia.

Grief Involves Letting Go and Starting Over

Why is grief work such a vital part of life? Part of the answer is that it enables us to let go. When we define our pain, when we express our grief, we are opening our hearts to let go and to accept what is. When that part of the work is done, then the door opens for us to begin anew. My observation as a pastor is that not everyone moves at the same pace. As a person in grief, I am finding that letting go is more difficult than I ever imagined. I appreciate friends who encourage me to get on with life, and I am also grateful for their understanding that it does take time. It takes longer for some of us than others.

I have friends tell me that the pain never goes away. The wound is always there, always tender to the touch. It heals over but never fully disappears. My understanding of the ancient Lamentations, however, leads me to believe that there is a resolution. Let me share with you these convictions from Jeremiah's heart that I have seen displayed in the lives of colleagues who have walked through the valley. They give me hope and a sense of direction as I walk through the pain.

Allowing God to Be God

Everyone in pain asks the "why" question. We make a terrible mistake when we try to answer a hurting person's "why" question with our speculation. Only God can settle that question. Modern people tend to prefer impersonal explanations like fate or chance. Jeremiah was not afraid to name God as the perpetrator of the suffering. Lamentations 3 is a powerful passage to speak one's sorrow to God. The weeping prophet was not afraid to speak of God's anger because he knew that mercy was ahead. This is not to suggest that God's anger is the cause of all of our losses, but it is important to see that God is present in the circumstances. "Because of the LORD's great love we are not consumed,/ for his compassions never fail./ They are new every morning;/ great is your faithfulness" (Lamentations 3:22-23).

I have wrestled with the "why" question. I don't expect to have it answered on this side of glory. I do understand that I have already received more grace than I could ever deserve. *My grief is bringing me to the place of allowing God to be God.*

Acknowledging God's Goodness

I can understand that if God had not kept His word to Israel, and had not driven them out of the land as He told them He would, they probably never would have left their idolatry behind.

I can see His goodness in the tragedy of the exile. Three times Jeremiah spoke of goodness in regard to the pain of Israel:

> The LORD is good to those whose hope is in him. . . .
> It is good to wait quietly
>   for the salvation of the LORD.
> It is good for a man to bear the yoke
>   while he is young. (Lamentations 3:25-27)

Tragic loss is never good in the short run, but because God is God, it can be good in the long run:

> For men are not cast off
>   by the Lord forever.
> Though he brings grief, he will show compassion,
>   so great is his unfailing love.
> For he does not willingly bring affliction
>   or grief to the children of men. (3:31-33)

My theology tells me that God's choice to take Jeanie was good. Someday when I see the whole picture as He does, it will be clear. But it will be a while before my feelings will be in line with my belief. Meanwhile, I choose to believe. That is where my grief needs to lead me.

Appropriating God's Fullness

A key phrase in the Lamentations is "I say to myself, 'The LORD is my portion;/ therefore I will wait for him' " (3:24).

When the Israelites entered the Promised Land, every tribe received a portion of the land, and every family a piece of land as their inheritance. The tribe of Levi, however, received no inheritance. They were assigned to care for the tabernacle where Israel worshiped God and where He came to dwell among them. On a number of occasions God said of the Levites, "I will be their portion."

Friends of mine who have suffered profound losses tell me that in their pain they have experienced depths of God's love that they could not have known otherwise. That gives me hope.

I don't expect the pain of grief to ever be totally gone. I do see that as I allow grief to do its work and drive me into the arms of God, that this pain will become part of God's grace in my life. Someday it will be a friend instead of an enemy. I want to be able to affirm with Jeremiah, "God is my portion."

Due to the loss of Jeanie, his wife, in 1994, Dr. Bubna personally knows the pain of grief. He experiences daily the comforting presence of the Holy Spirit. Dr. Bubna's five children are actively serving the Lord in the United States and overseas.

For Further Reading

A Grief Observed. C.S. Lewis. Bantam Books, 1976.

Good Grief. Granger B. Westberg. Fortress Press, 1971.

The Many Faces of Grief. Edgar Newman Jackson. Abingdon Press, 1977.

The View from a Hearse. Joseph Bayly. David C. Cook Publishing Co., 1969.

Appendix 3

Candidate Questionnaire for
The C&MA Presidency (excerpted)

Service record

Kincaid Methodist Church, Kincaid, KS (1954-1956)
C&MA church, Boone, IA (1957-1961)
Northbrook Alliance Church, Minneapolis, MN (1961-1969)
International Protestant Church, Saigon, Vietnam (1970-1972)
Northbrook Alliance Church, Minneapolis, MN (1972-1977)
Long Hill Chapel, Chatham, NJ (1977-1991)
Alliance Theological Seminary, Nyack, NY (1991-present)

Spiritual journey

My parents, raised in unbelieving homes, were led to Christ by Alliance laypersons. I grew up in a Christian home, attending the Alliance church in St. Louis, Missouri. I gave my heart to Christ when nine years old and sensed a call to ministry as early as I can remember. During my second year in college, I came to the end of my self-efforts and completely surrendered to the indwelling Christ. Developing an inner walk with Christ has been the central passion of my life for over forty years. Being a man of integrity and finishing my spiritual journey well are of first importance to me.

Vision for the future of The C&MA

The Christian and Missionary Alliance has been one of the most powerful missionary movements of the twentieth century. The revised mission statement being proposed at this Council seeks to clarify this calling, recognizing that the Great Commission encompasses world evangelization and church planting beginning in our communities and reaching to the ends of the earth.

The challenge facing us is that in functioning as a denomination we retain this global vision of the Great Commission. *I see that nurturing the spirit of a missionary movement at the heart of our denomination can be a powerful and growing dynamism motivating us to reach the whole world with the gospel.*

Philosophy and practice of leadership

I like Max DuPree's comment that the first task of the leader is to define reality for the organization—and then in the end to say, "Thank you." The leader's role is to keep people in the denomination thinking about:

- Who God is and what He is doing in the world;
- Who we are and what our part is in what He is doing;
- What the facts are about the context in which we are called to work, and how we can go about doing what we are called to do.

The leader is a visionary who calls the denomination to a higher level of character and endeavor, but is also a truth-teller, one who calls the denomination to face what is.

To implement this philosophy, I am committed to a collegial style of leadership. I want to be a person who clearly points the way and becomes a servant in creating an atmosphere where people can grow and be effective in contributing to the overall good of the denomination and its objectives.

Strengths and weaknesses in ministry

I think my *strength* as a leader is the ability to attract a group of strong leaders around me and enable them to be effective in their roles. My ministry gifts are preaching and pastoring. My motivational gift is showing mercy, in the spirit of the Apostle Paul's words, "If [a man's gift] is showing mercy, let him do it cheerfully" (Romans 12:8). I think that I have been able to create an atmosphere of caring and healing among the people where I have served.

One of my strongest motivations as a pastor also makes for *a weakness*. Having the gift of mercy, I tend to identify strongly with hurting people. I am tempted to become absorbed in wanting to bring healing to individuals and can be distracted from the larger goal. I try to balance this by having strong leaders around me who have other gifts and are willing to be open with me about focusing on the big picture.

What would I do as president?

If I had time, money and staff; if God gave me the green light; and if knowing I could succeed, I would lead efforts to restructure The C&MA in ways to maximize its resources—people, institutions, finances—to fulfill its mission of exalting Jesus Christ, establishing outward-focused churches in our nation and planting missionary churches among both unreached and responsive peoples.

What would be priorities held and changes made in the Alliance?

Among my *priorities* as leader would be:

- To challenge pastors and leaders to be committed fully to the mission of The C&MA and its vision to see the Church among every people of Planet Earth. This would be the first step in addressing our funding issue.

- To mentor a number of younger leaders in preparation for national leadership.

- To exercise a pastoral role before the denomination to enable us to discuss difficult issues in a godly manner.

- To work closely with district leaders in developing more help and encouragement for pastors.

- To encourage a larger role for laymen and laywomen.

My life/ministry purpose and related objectives

I have been a Great Commission person from childhood. Looking back over the years, this clearly has been the overriding drive of my life. It continues to be so. Objectives that have flowed from this purpose and contributed to it are the pastoring of Great Commission churches and the building of a godly marriage and family.

Guiding principles of my life

The three principles that have more impact on my life than any others are:

1. Seek first the kingdom of God—all else will be added.
2. God's first concern is people—relationships are more important than things or success; therefore keep short accounts on whatever could cloud or obstruct positive relationships.
3. Maintain a clean conscience—by cultivating a moment-by-moment awareness of His presence.

Most significant milestones in my life and ministry

To this point in my life, these are the most significant among many:

- Believing in Christ at the age of nine.
- Being broken before the Lord at age nineteen and receiving the fullness of the Holy Spirit.
- Marrying Jeanie at age twenty-one and establishing a Christian home.
- Having a coronary at age thirty-five, then heart surgery and learning to live a day at a time.
- Pastoring the International Protestant Church in Saigon and becoming a world citizen.

Most desired area of growth in my life this year

To let go of personal needs, including my lack of a partner and desire for a predictable future, and trust in God's sufficiency one day at a time.

My personal time alone with God

I take long walks every morning, often at night as well, and talk with God. Sometimes there are moments of worship and wonder as I speak with the infinite Creator who dwells in unapproachable light. Sometimes I speak with God as my Father, and these are moments of intimacy and learning as I tell Him my heart's deepest needs. I read though the whole Bible each year and use a daily prayer diary as well.

Top items of prayer

Over the past month, these are the three matters I have been praying about most:

- holiness in my daily life;
- unreached peoples of Planet Earth;
- personnel and financial needs of the seminary.

My current relationship with God

He has never seemed greater to me than at this point in my life. His choices for me have made me deeply aware that He is the sovereign Lord and that His ways are far beyond my wildest imagination. I stand in awe of who He is. And yet I am driven into His arms to experience His father-love to a degree I have not known before. Knowing His presence is as necessary as air or water to my life.

The most meaningful spiritual highlight that took place recently was in an ATS chapel service in November. I had been traveling a great deal and came home feeling the need for a fresh touch from God. The meeting was a time of praise and prayer led by Chinese students. God's presence so filled the place that my soul was filled to overflowing. When chapel ended, no one wanted to leave. There seemed almost a fragrance in the room.

My personal approach to soul-winning

I believe the gospel is best communicated through relationships of integrity, as Paul says in First Thessalonians 1:6, "You became imitators of me and of Christ" [author's paraphrase]. My focus has been on establishing authentic relationships with people as a means of earning the right to speak of the hope within me.

Evangelism Explosion was very helpful in releasing me to be able to share my faith in a natural way.

Major sources of frustration, tension and pressure

Frustration is not a major issue at this stage of my life. God has broken me through a series of events so that not very many things are of importance personally. That which brings the most pain and tension is being forced into relationships where mutual trust seems impossible.

Major sources of joy and fun

Joy in life flows out of knowing that God finds pleasure in me. The greatest personal joy flows from knowing that God is using my life to affect other people toward maturity and godliness. Fun means to be relaxing with my children and grandchildren—and playing tennis.

My marriage and family relationships

Jeanie and I decided early on that our first focus in ministry was to one another and to our children. My children and grandchildren are not the major time commitment in my life, but next to my relationship with God they are my first priority. Being a mentor and model for them is of first importance.

Skeletons in my closet

I believe that all my dealings with God and with people are where they ought to be, and that all my relationships are open to scrutiny without fear of reproach.

Why I am open to serving as president

My calling is to be a Great Commission person. At this point I know of no better place to make an impact for the kingdom of God than in The C&MA. Years ago I made a commitment to serve God by being a servant of The C&MA. Knowing something of the pressures and responsibilities of the presidency, I would not be inclined to seek it, but I must do what I believe God asks of me. A person can never be quite sure of his own heart motives, and this is why long-term commitments are so important.

The most personal fulfillment in my work

Enabling people to grow and become what God intends them to be is the most rewarding thing imaginable to me. I see this as the most basic pastoral calling. At the seminary, I view my role as creating an atmosphere in which people can grow.

My understanding of leadership and how I fit the description

In simplest terms, a leader is one who sees the goal and is committed to it, and who helps others see the goal so that they too commit to it and work together to fulfill it. I also like Peter Drucker's comment that the first task of the CEO is to be the keeper of the values. The work of the leader is to guard and model the core values held by the organization.

I see myself as a big-picture person. In most situations I find it natural to involve myself in helping the group see the goal and defining the things that are important.

Role of The C&MA president

He needs first to be a visionary. His task is to discern the role that God intends this denomination to play in the completion of His redeeming purpose in history. He is to lead by articulating that vision and calling the constituency to commit their lives and resources to it.

Appendix 4

"And It All Happened in Africa"!
Rev. Joel Bubna

Flying back across the Atlantic Ocean, having been at my dad's funeral, I was visiting with my dear friend, Isaac Keita (dean of the West Africa Alliance Seminary and representative to Alliance World Fellowship for the Africa region). It was beautiful to hear his interpretation of the last week of Dad's life. As many of you know, Dad was here in Africa speaking to the leaders of the mission and Church. Isaac said that he had gone over the week numerous times in his mind and God's careful hand was evident in each event. We, as Westerners, have a tendency to see events as unrelated or coincidental. However, in people's minds here, nothing "just happens."

Isaac started out by explaining the reception that our Sunday evening church group had had in honor of Dad when he and Patti first arrived. The group really did it up big. The dinner was done out on our front lawn under a canopy and catered by a hotel. Before dinner we had a time of worship and Dad spoke for a few minutes. When I introduced Dad that night, I gave a speech about what a great man my dad was and how he was not only my father but also my dear friend. Isaac said that in looking back it was as though I was saying good-bye to my father.

During Dad's talk it started to rain and actually poured for fifteen minutes. For me that was like a curse, but here, rain is seen as a sign of blessing. Though the rain held things up a bit, we were able to get new tablecloths on the tables and things back in place so that the dinner could go ahead. Isaac went on to explain that with the lamb that had been roasted and the festive atmosphere, it was like a banquet for a king. At the end of the evening the group gave Dad and Patti a gift, which they opened. In expressing their gratitude, Dad said, "You did not need to get us this gift to remember you by, because even without the gift I will never forget this night and how you have received us as long as I live." He used those same words another time that evening.

Isaac went on to talk about the significance of Dad's messages. Dad had been invited by Alliance World Fellowship to give a series of messages on the fourfold gospel and its implication in the life of a leader. He had the privilege of preaching to the leaders of the church in Africa, the first place that Alliance missionaries were ever sent, about the central message of the Alliance. Isaac went through each message and highlighted different things Dad had said, especially in the last two messages.

In his message on Thursday evening, Dad had talked about Christ our Healer. He said that the important thing is not the healing, but the Christ. He talked from his own life, about how over the last thirty years he had lived with a heart condition. Though God never chose to heal his heart, he learned to accept the life of Christ as his portion for every day. The last message, of course, was about Christ, our Coming King. The point of the message was that all of us as believers need something that can motivate us to reach the end of the race. The motivation that the Scriptures give us is the return of our Lord. In it Dad used Cliff Westergren as an example. He asked, "Why did Cliff do all the things he did: going to Cambodia, to Hong Kong, risking his life? It certainly was not to prepare himself for retirement; it was for *that day!*"

He closed with an illustration about his own father. Dad talked about the fact that though he knew his father loved him, his father had rarely expressed those kinds of things. The day that Grandpa went into heart surgery, he called his sons to his side. He took their hands and said, "Today I am going to win. If I go home I win; if God gives me more time to serve Him here, I win! However, if I die, I will die a very rich man. I am leaving behind sons that love the Lord and who preach the gospel!" Dad talked about the influence those words from his father had

had on his life. If those simple words from his earthly father had had such an impact, how much more should we be motivated to hear those words one day: "Well done, my good and faithful servant! Enter into My joy!"

The last day of the conference there was a closing ceremony. The district choir began the meeting with the "Hallelujah Chorus," and when I looked over, Dad was already on his feet. He was one of the first, if not the first, to stand, and the whole place rose to its feet.

The last thing on the program that day was a gift for Dad. Isaac said that the significance of this was just too much. The gift was rich Baoulé cloths. The men have a certain way of wearing these cloths draped over the shoulder. They are worn around the house or when there are important ceremonies. Patti was not there that day (she had stayed home to spend time with Josiah [Paul's grandson], something Josiah will never forget), and so Dad was standing up there alone. When they gave him the gift there were about three or four men gathered around him draping these cloths over his shoulders. Everyone clapped and they were taking pictures. Isaac said it was as though Dad was being prepared for a coronation.

Then the president of the church in the Republic of Congo asked to say something, even though he was not on the program. He got up and said that when he had come into the church he had noticed three pots of flowers on the stage. He said the last time he had seen this was about a year ago at his daughters' funeral. He explained that while he and his wife were away on an evangelistic trip in the village, his three daughters were home. One of them had mistaken some poisonous powder for salt and mixed it into the sauce. As a result all three daughters died. He just wanted to give testimony that even in this tragedy God's glory could not be denied. Isaac said when he was talking he kept thinking, *Why is he talking about death? This week together has been about life—what is the relationship between what went on this week and death?*

Isaac's last comment was, "God was preparing Papa for glory and none of us knew. And it all happened in Africa."